"To Granny"
may I always
prove ever
your friend
Since
Lou Ge

This **M**emorial **E**dition
copy of the first printing of

GRANTLAND RICE'S
AUTOBIOGRAPHY

is for the personal library of

Presented by

The Tumult and the Shouting

The Tumult
and the Shouting

My Life in Sport

by Grantland Rice

MEMORIAL EDITION

A. S. BARNES & COMPANY, NEW YORK

Published on the same day in the Dominion of Canada by The Copp Clark Company, Ltd., Toronto.

Library of Congress Catalog Card Number: 54-9173

To Katherine Hollis Rice,
who has been of incredible
help in every way along
the long highway.

Acknowledgment

I want to extend deepest thanks and appreciation to Dave Camerer, former Dartmouth football tackle, and sportswriter, for the fine work he contributed in routing out old and sometimes fading memories from over fifty years ago. His assistance was invaluable.

I also wish to thank "the many" who helped in the preparation of this book by rekindling with me so many experiences along the way . . . and to those who so graciously made available many of the pictures chosen—my sincere appreciation.

Grantland Rice
East Hampton, L.I.
July 1, 1954

The Hat

Much of our gold is hidden at Fort Knox, but the greater part of it lies buried at Woodlawn under a stone marked "Grantland Rice." He was twenty-four carat, our fellow, and some of the Rice gold rubbed off on everyone he met, especially on young newspapermen, when the going got rough on Park Row.

Granny Rice never knew it, but he wore a halo under his hat. That beaten-up fedora would have made anyone, other than the handsome Granny, look like a Mulberry Bend bum. It was Confederate gray, of course, and could be seen in any breed of weather at the tracks, where Dean Rice tried for years on end to win the daily double.

Just where he got the hat, Granny never would say, but Rube Goldberg believed it had been rejected by both the Salvation Army and the Volunteers of America. Snow fell on the Rice hat at the Yale Bowl; sleet at Soldiers Field; rain made gutters of its brim at Pimlico; lightning singed it at the Polo Grounds. Beer splotched it at Toots Shor's; and Jack Dempsey sat on it, perhaps deliberately, at the Garden. Nothing fazed that fez, nor would its loyal owner accept a new one from the embarrassed stylists of Danbury. But even the vintage hat could not spoil the good looks of the Dean. More and more, as he graced the years, he took on the appearance of the noblest Roman ever embossed on an ancient coin. Everyone knew the man and the hat. Everyone but Granny knew there was a halo under it.

One of the Dean's oldest pals was George Ade's Negro caddie, Jessie. That six-foot-four golfball-shagger liked a drink once in a while, or perhaps twice. When Rice asked him what his favorite drink was, Jessie replied, "Gin and honey."

"Gin and honey?" asked Rice. "Is that a good drink?"

"Is that a good drink?" Jessie said. "That's what they drink in Heaven!"

Something that Rice said when George Ade died might appropriately be spoken of our Dean: "He was not one of the expendables, but one of the irreplaceables."

Granny Rice left the old hat behind him, but he took the halo along; and, as always, wears its modestly. Indeed, he probably still does not know that he has it on, as he tries out some of that gin-and-honey.

Gene Fowler

Contents

Grantland Rice

Grant came into the world at a fortunate time for us all. The country was changing. The conquest of the frontier had been concluded. The harsh rule of the Puritan tradition had begun to be relaxed. Yet some vestige of that rigid, fun-denying code of our ancestors remained. Life still meant, to the great majority of Americans, only work—hard work, long hours—the harder and longer the more commendable. Play was for boys and for fools. It was the function and duty of men to work.

This austere tradition Grant helped mightily to break down. He was the evangelist of fun, the bringer of good news about games. He was forever seeking out young men of athletic talent, lending them a hand and building them up, and sharing them with the rest of us as our heroes. He made the playing fields respectable. Never by preaching or propaganda, but by the sheer contagion of his joy in living, he made us want to play. And in so doing he made us a people of better health and happiness in peace: of greater strength in adversity. This was his gift to his country; few men have made a greater.

In his life among men he might well have been named America's foremost gentleman. It was not merely that he was courtly, gracious, well-mannered. He was all these, of course, but also something much deeper, far rarer—the something from which all these spring if they are genuine. He had *pure courtesy*. He was the most courteous man I ever knew.

Courtesy is no easy virtue. It means, first of all, being instinctively and sincerely aware of the other person, with spontaneous respect and consideration for his feelings, and the instinct to react always appropriately.

Grant was most sensitively aware, most quick to respond and respect, most unerringly appropriate. Once aware of the feeling of fear or timidity in another, he became instantly the staunch encourager and ally. Aware of worry in another, he beamed sympathy and solace and hope. Aware of financial need, he would, if necessary, lend his last dollar.

Finally—and this is in a way the greatest test of courtesy— aware of merit in another, he gave prompt and unstinted praise. Aware of good fortune, he was the first to rejoice, the last celebrant to leave.

People felt better in his presence. He made us all feel better —made us feel that somehow we could do more, be more. This was his gift to his friends.

In the first poem in his last book, he wrote:

> Only the brave know what the hunted are—
> The battered—and the shattered—and the lost—
> Who know the meaning of each deep, red scar,
> For which they paid the heartache and the cost.
> Who've left the depths against unmeasured odds
> To ask no quarter from the ruling gods.
>
> Born—live—and die—cradle along to the grave.
> The march is on—by bugle and by drum—
> Where only those who beat life are the brave—
> Who laugh at fate and face what is to come,
> Knowing how swiftly all the years go by,
> Where dawn and sunset blend in one brief sky.

This was a familiar theme of his; he returned to it again and again—that courage is the major virtue; that all things work together for good to him who is unafraid.

And the God of the courageous heard him, and gave him the last great reward that life can bestow—a sudden and painless and unexpected death.

To believe that such a life is ended is to say that human life itself is meaningless and the universe a ghastly joke. No one of us believes that. Grant is not lost to us.

Gainsborough, the artist, cried exultantly: "We are all going to Heaven, and Vandyke is of the company."

We are all going to Heaven, and Grant is there already— telling his stories, talking his wisdom, cracking his jokes, and, we may be sure, encouraging play. Already they have learned to love him. And he is waiting for us—still with his joy in living and his eternal courtesy.

Grantland Rice passed away on July 13, 1954, while working at his type-writer. He would have reached his 74th birthday on the following November 1st. These words were expressed by Bruce Barton, long time friend of Mr. Rice, at the funeral on July 16th at the Brick Presbyterian Church in New York City..

Prologue

Why This Book?

It seems to me that I have already written too many words. I know, better than anyone else, that I should have ceased firing years ago. Well, work, above everything else, is habit-forming. From 1901 through the better part of 1954, I have written over 67,000,000 words, including more than 22,000 columns, 7,000 sets of verse, over 1,000 magazine articles—plus radio outbursts for 32 seasons, starting with the Giants-Yankee World Series in 1922, when earphones were the rage. And I'm still turning out a column six days a week for some 80 newspapers throughout the country.

However, this book is no rehash of my columns. In a sense, it is a "summing up"—the story of my life and of the great men of sport who helped to make it an exciting and rich history.

I owe sport a great deal. Not only has it enabled me to earn a comfortable living; it helped me to grow up. I wasn't privileged to be an athlete. Sure, I played football and baseball when I was a kid, and was keen about track and field. But I was raised in a neighborhood where most of the kids were better than I.

From the start, however, I learned a lot more from defeat than I ever learned from winning—something that has held true for the best part of 75 years. I remember very little about the games I won or lost, but I always had a deep feeling of enthusiasm for the *contest itself*.

I have always been a great believer in keeping fit. When I graduated from Vanderbilt University, I hadn't broken training in four years—hadn't smoked a cigarette or taken a glass of beer. I simply figured I had too little to give, physically, not to give my limited equipment a fair chance.

From sport and chores on the family farm I got used to hard work and long hours—a 12-hour day was practically a holiday. I came up that way. I was lucky enough to love work. I don't mean always—many and many a time I've circled a typewriter as though it were a king cobra on the desk. But force of early habit somehow overcame the lethargy.

You'll learn most about Grantland Rice by the memories that I will fetch back about the champions I have known. Since I describe one champion at a time, unlike most autobiographies, this book doesn't follow strict chronology. Almost every one of these heroes of sport taught me something, gave me some insight into how to live and added to my philosophy of life. And, I think these champions and the way that they lived have something to say to all of us, especially in these uncertain times, which the editorial writers call "The Age of Anxiety." To reach the top in any sport—or in life—you need confidence and belief in yourself. Can you imagine Babe Ruth ever considering the possibility of failure? Many years ago, Babe told me, "Once my swing starts, I can't change it or pull up. It's all or nothing at all."

The qualities of self-confidence and belief in oneself seem to me to be relatively rare today. They are sometimes even openly ridiculed as naïve or worse.

But enough of the preaching. Let's get on with it. . . .

I

Yesterday Is Gone

THE START

The dawn is breaking, crimson white,
The sun is up in flaming spread.
The road is dim, beyond all sight,
Where none can see the way ahead.
Through blackest night, or dawn's red glow,
Where will it end? I do not know.

Through mist and fog—through storm and sun,
Through pain and sorrow—love and care,
Through cheering millions—lost or won,
How will the new born marcher fare?
Who knows? Amid world beating hearts
The Tumult and the Shouting starts.

CHAPTER ONE

Beginning at the Beginning

The beginning of life really dates back to your first memories. However, for the record, I was born at Murfreesboro, Tennessee, 30 miles from Nashville on November 1, 1880. Christened Henry Grantland, I was the eldest of three sons, my brothers John and Bolling following me by several years. My father and mother were Mr. and Mrs. Bolling Hendon Rice, two very gentle people from a state that gave the nation Andrew Jackson, Davey Crockett, Nathan Bedford Forrest, John B. Morgan and "Little Giffen" —a flaming banner of youthful courage.

> Smitten with grapeshot and gangrene,
> Eighteenth battle and he fourteen . . .

Immortalized in Ticknor's verse, Little Giffen's uniform happened to be Confederate gray.

The first evidence of life that I remember was a big Newfoundland dog that I loved as any kid loves his dog. I was only

four years old at the time. Even now I find that three of my favorite "people" are Czar, Chiota and Gay, Siberian huskies that
belong to my daughter Florence and her husband Fred Butler
of Venice, California.

The central figure in our family was my grandfather, Major
Henry Grantland, for whom I was named. He died, grudgingly,
in 1926 when he was 95, following a bad fall. When I was four,
the Rices moved from Murfreesboro to Nashville—into a large,
high ceiling'd house on Woodland Street that belonged to
grandfather. A cotton farmer, Grandfather Grantland, 100-proof
individualist, originally came over from England in 1835. He
settled in Fairfax County, Virginia, and later worked south
through Alabama and up into Tennessee. Quite a roamer, when
the wanderlust seized my grandfather he would take off for
Pittsburgh, Pennsylvania, "to buy tools for the farm." The trip
consumed between five and six weeks, being made by boat, train
and horse and wagon.

I recall vividly his stories about the Civil War. In 1861
he was working his plantation at Triana, Alabama, on the banks
of the Tennessee River by the Big Bend. Invaded by a Federal
gunboat at the war's outbreak, my grandfather assembled his
help, and armed with rakes, spades and one new shotgun, they
headed for the river. The gunboat won that one.

En route to his rendezvous with war, my grandfather carted
off six bales of cotton—500 pound bales—and hid them in a cave.
I always got a kick out of his recitation of what became of those
bales . . . after the war. I'd make a point to ask him about
them.

"Well," he'd say, "when the war was over, I threw down my
musket, grabbed my horse and galloped back to the farm. I didn't
forget those bales. There they'd been—for almost four years—in
a damp, dripping cave . . . known only to God and me. The
selling price in 1864 was one dollar a pound, but all the water

had swollen those rotting old bales till they weighed about a half ton—one thousand pounds apiece! When the Yankee carpet-bagger, Butler the Buyer, came through, he paid me a thousand dollars for each waterlogged bale."

With that fresh start Grandfather Grantland proceeded to run up a fortune in a world starving for cotton. As a soldier, incidentally, he was a Major under General Braxton Bragg, whom he never respected. His hero was Nathan Bedford Forrest, one of the great cavalry men. Forrest, individually, killed 30 men in the war and had 15 horses shot from under him. He enlisted as a private and, a few months later, was a lieutenant general. He never lost a battle. General Lee called him "my finest general."

When I was seven or eight we moved from my grand-father's place to a home on Vaughan Pike, out in the country. With my two younger brothers, John and Bolling, I had trees to climb and room to roam. It was my first Christmas on Vaughan Pike when a football, a baseball and a bat landed under the tree—for me. No glove. My hands have been calloused ever since.

Those three presents were the sounding instruments that directed my life. I can still hear the echoes from far away and long ago. They were the Pied Piper in my march through life.

During those summers on Vaughan Pike, my father put me "in charge" of several acres of good farming soil with the general idea that I was supposed to make the land yield a profit. With the help of Horace, our gentle Negro hired man, plus my two brothers, we grew tomatoes, potatoes, beans, asparagus, onions, beets, peas, cabbage, lettuce and practically everything else that grows including all kissin' kin of the worm and grub family.

Once the crops started coming in, my day began at 3:00 in the morning, when, with a wagon loaded with greens, I'd drive in to market. Disposing of my wares around 5:30 or 6:00

in the morning, I'd then drive back home and work. I recall the thrill I got at selling the first crates of tomatoes at four dollars a crate . . . a price that later fell off to 10 and 20 cents a crate. I usually worked until 7:00 in the evening, which made a working day of nearly 16 hours.

Yes, I knew work, hard work, at 12. After this type of training, no amount of toil seemed hard or long. But I must admit that I liked plowing better than any other form of farm work, probably because the horse was pulling the bulk of the load.

I was 13 when the Crash of 1893, a world-wide affair, hit. That crash took more than a million dollars from my grandfather. England could no longer handle her cotton assignments; the break followed. The Grantland Cotton Company was stocked with cotton but the selling price tumbled to five cents a pound. I still wonder how my grandmother and mother were able to serve meals that I couldn't buy today for 20 dollars. There were hog brains—the most magnificent of dishes—hominy grits, ham and ham gravy, waffles, fried sliced apples, corn pone, fried and scrambled eggs—food I've dreamed of but have seldom seen for half a century, at least in such profusion.

While living on the Vaughan Pike, I attended two military schools, Tennessee Military Institute and the Nashville Military Institute. I was then around 14 or 15 and weighed about 120 pounds. I was nearly six feet tall, so you can figure out the string-bean aspect.

It was at these two schools that I learned a lot of football and eventually got my biggest thrill out of a game for which I was totally unfitted, physically. Our fullback, named Percy Tabler, was 6 feet 1 and weighed 195. I was one halfback but our real halfback was my old friend, Charlie Moran, of Horse Cave, Kentucky. Charlie weighed about 185. You can see I had protection. Tabler later starred in the flickers as one of the famous "Tarzans." Moran went from our school to Tennessee and from there to the Massillon Tigers, where he ran one of the first professional football clubs from quarterback. Later he coached the famed Centre College Praying Colonels of the Bo McMillan era around 1920. Moran was also one of the top umpires of the National League for more than 20 years.

The Rices finally moved back to Nashville where I was enrolled at the Wallace University School. After one year there, I entered Vanderbilt University in the fall of 1897 and pledged Phi Delta Theta. I managed to do well in my studies, majoring in Greek and Latin. I graduated Phi Beta Kappa with a BA degree with the Class of '01. As a football star, although lettering my junior year, I would not have scared "Doc" Blanchard, Army's dreadnaught fullback during World War II. In my freshman year, I broke a big bone in my foot trying to throw a 16-pound hammer. My top weight through four years at Vanderbilt was 134 pounds.

Reflecting on those four years, I am eternally grateful to my old prep-school master, Dr. C. B. Wallace, and the Latin and Greek background he pumped into my head. I enjoyed my induction into both tongues and so it was natural that these two subjects became the foundation stones for my college majors. As for English, I honestly can't recall having studied it.

With a real affection for football, I tried for three years but only succeeded in accumulating a broken arm, four ribs torn from my spinal column, a broken collar bone and a broken shoulder blade. The latter injury kept me from trying professional baseball at shortstop, as I had to throw underhanded my last year. However, in four years as an undergraduate I never missed a practice baseball session and after the first year never missed a game.

The best game I ever played was against Tennessee in

Knoxville. I had 15 assists, no errors, plus a home run and a double. Vanderbilt won 4–3. Baseball was much more fun for me to play since it lacked the body contact which too often left me crippled or headed for a hospital visit.

In the summer of 1901, I barnstormed for several weeks through Tennessee with a semi-pro team. We were playing the Memphis Chickasaws when I received a wire from my dad suggesting that I "come home to Nashville." Vanderbilt had won the Southern Conference baseball title that spring, and, with several of my teammates, I was riding pretty high—both at bat and in the field—when the summons arrived. I didn't question the order and, taking a long last glance over my shoulder, packed my glove and spikes and returned to Nashville.

Wandering into the J. S. Reeves store, a wholesale drygoods concern, I landed a job as stock boy in the notions department at five dollars a week. I didn't pick up my first paycheck.

It was July, 1901, and the *Nashville Daily News* had just got going. My dad figured that inasmuch as I hadn't gone in for engineering, law or medicine at college—but had done creditably well in the arts—I might try my hand at journalism. I went down to the *News* and applied for the job as sports editor—and lo and behold—got it! However, reflecting on that baptism of fire, I think Edward Martin, the managing editor, figured that writing sports was akin to playing in the back-yard sand pile. Martin gave me the "added" jobs of covering Capitol Hill, the produce market and the customs house—for five dollars a week.

There were no Grantland Rice bylines in those first few issues. Then one day Martin commented on an unsigned story he had stuck on the front page.

"You write rhythmic heads for your leads," Martin said. "Keep it up. Perhaps one day you'll make a good inside man on the desk."

Heaven forbid! I tore out that column . . . still have it,

on faded newsprint that crumbles like an ancient tobacco leaf.
From that August 13, 1901 paper:

> *Baker Was An Easy Mark*
> *Pounded Hard Over Park*
>
> *Selma's Infield Is a Peach*
> *But Nashville Now Is Out of Reach*
>
> *All of the Boys Go Out to Dine*
> *And Some of Them Get Full of Wine*

> *After their long, successful trip the locals opened up against Selma yesterday afternoon at Athletic Park, and when the shades of night had settled on the land the difference that separated the two teams had been increased by some dozen points.*
>
> *Throughout the whole morning a dark, lead-colored sky overhung the city, and a steady rain dripped and drizzled, only stopping in time to play the game, but leaving the field soft and slow . . .*

—I wonder what the score was!

How or why I ever fell into the habit of breaking up my columns with verse I don't know, but rhythm and rhyme seemed to come naturally, perhaps as a reflection of the meter I had enjoyed scanning in Latin poets.

One afternoon, editor Martin called me in and assigned me to cover a big society ball that night.

"But I can't write society news," I protested. "I know nothing about names and fashions. That's a woman's beat."

"We're all out of society writers," replied Martin. "Tonight you're it!"

I went back to the morgue, found an old copy of the Sunday *New York Tribune* and turned to the society section. I found a description of a big event at the old Waldorf and copied out practically everything but the names. The next day's paper ran a solid column. Armed with the patron's list and the cream of the guest list, I had attributed all the current New York styles and descriptions of the fashionable gowns worn at that New York dance to the madames and belles of Nashville's upper crust. All seemed happy with that column because Martin received nary a kick and congratulated me on a job well covered. I never have divulged how I covered that soiree until right now.

During that same year, 1901, Herman Suter, Sewanee's coach from 1899 through 1901, edited a publication called *Forester Magazine.* I didn't know a Christmas tree from a Northern Blue Horned Spruce; I don't today. But when the call came from Suter, I joined him.

Financed by one of the Pinchot boys, Suter's magazine was being turned out in Washington, D. C., pretty far north for a Rebel, but I was all eyes to see the sights. However, I had no sooner planted my pigeon-toed feet before the Capitol when I was stricken with appendicitis. I spent five weeks in the hospital and was a pretty sick pup when my mother arrived and carted me home to Nashville.

I had tried my journalistic wings up North, only to be flattened with a blow to the lower solar plexus. (This was a term that came into vogue when Bob Fitzsimmons knocked out Jim Corbett on March 17, 1897, in the 14th round of their championship fight with a terrible left hook to the stomach.) So I set my sights to the South—Atlanta, Georgia. From 1902 through the World Series of 1905 between the Giants and Philadelphia, I wrote for the *Atlanta Journal.* Starting under its erstwhile editor, John S. Cohen, at $12.50 a week, my job was to write the entire sports page.

I well recall a cityside assignment I drew—to cover the funeral of Lieutenant General John B. Gordon, the great Confederate General. How the multitude wept, including reporter Henry Grantland Rice, grandson of Henry Grantland, a true soldier of the old Confederacy. During those days, the great from New York's Broadway would make one-night stands throughout the cities of the South, with such marquee'd names as John Drew, Richard Mansfield, the Barrymores et al., all putting in their licks for the culture of the Confederacy. The theatre beat was handed to me. I can't tell you how many nights a young writer from Indiana—a squat, heavy-set ex-athlete from De-Pauw University named Don Marquis—and I had two-on-the-aisle as theatre critics for the old *Journal.* This was the same Don Marquis who later went to New York to make his fame with the *Sun* and the *Tribune,* writing a breed of prose, verse and philosophical humor that, in my opinion, has never been equalled. He was a firebrand and a genius. In those days we shared a room and once tried living on ten cents a day—the cost of a huge mince pie for breakfast, guaranteed to induce acute 24-hour indigestion for two. I bequeath this gem to Gaye-lord Hauser as my contribution towards the American diet.

This was the same Don Marquis who later would tickle the world with such stories as "The Old Soak" . . . "Captain Peter Fitzruse" . . . "Mehitabel" and "Archie the Cockroach." Born in 1878 at Walnut, Illinois, Don had gone to work on a small weekly paper, where he broke pens, typewriters and presses in his journalistic efforts to carve a place for himself in midwestern journalism. His break came when a state senator, running for re-election, was stumping a campaign loaded with generalities. He was a shoo-in—until Don, tracking down his record, asked in print just how this particular Senator worthied himself for re-election with a record in Washington that apparently equalled that of the little man who wasn't there. Don did such a job of rock throwing that the senator contacted him and asked if he'd like to go to Washington. Answering "yes," Marquis landed on

the *Washington Times*. Don attended art school, worked in the
Census Bureau and then hopped to the editorial page of the
Atlanta Journal—which is where our paths crossed. The senator,
incidentally, was re-elected.

As two demon reporters, we shared a flat for three dollars a
week. It was Christmas Eve of 1902 that I wandered in about
midnight and found Don high as two kites and lathered with
red ink and oil from a battered old hand letter press.

"Grant," he roared, "I'm putting out Page One of my
Christmas issue—the way Hearst would do it!" Screaming across
the top half of his front page, in red, 40-point letters was
"CHRIST IS BORN!" By the time I'd added my four cents, we
were both loaded on Georgia corn likker. We finally crawled into
bed, smug in the feeling that we had indeed saluted the Lord.

How Marquis could write! An unaffected genius, at times
he was a black brooder, but his physical and mental courage
were magnificent.

> . . . There I stood at the gate of God,
> Drunk but unafraid.

That closing line of one of his verses mirrored Don's scorn
for any human soul lacking the courage of its convictions.

Don and I used to spend a few afternoons each fall helping
with the coaching at Georgia Military Academy, some 20 miles
from Atlanta. I recall one afternoon I was particularly impressed
with one youngster. A back, he moved well. After practice I remarked to the coach, "That kid I was working with this afternoon . . . he's a good boy with that ball . . . but he needs
more scrap . . . ought to be more aggressive."

The boy was Stonewall Jackson Christian, grandson of
probably the youngest lieutenant general in the Civil War. It
was around 1920 that I renewed my acquaintance with Christian, then an instructor in mathematics at West Point.

One evening, in 1903, while putting the sports pages to bed, I happened across a story from Shreveport, Louisiana, about a pitching freak who had made a bet that he could drink two bottles of bourbon, bolt down a whole turkey and win a double header. His name was "Bugs" Raymond. As an unofficial scout for the Atlanta club, I told Abner Powell, the owner, about Raymond and persuaded Ab to buy him.

He reported next spring. I happened, by rare chance, to be standing at a bar having a free lunch before starting for the ball park. Someone slapped me on the back and said, "What about a drink, pal?"

I recognized Raymond, then 22 years old. I bought him a drink. He asked for another. "I thought you were going to pitch today," I suggested. "I am," retorted Raymond. "What of it?"

"Do you know what team you are pitching against?" I asked.

"No," he replied, "and I don't care."

"It's only Boston of the American League," I said. "Champions of the world. You recall, perhaps, they beat Pittsburgh last fall. It's an important exhibition game—for Atlanta."

Bugs wasn't interested but wanted to know how to get to the park. "I'm walking," I said. "It's only two miles."

Raymond didn't have a nickel, either, for fare. All the way out to the park he threw stones at pigeons, stray dogs and telegraph poles. He must have pitched a complete game before we got there.

Then, given a uniform, Bugs appeared and started insulting and kidding Boston's star third baseman and manager, Jimmy Collins. He would walk from the box and bawl out the World Champs. By the third inning, he had them all raving. As a net result, using that famous spitter with what John McGraw later called, "the finest pitching motion in baseball," Raymond struck out 12 men and won 3–0, with three scattered hits.

Another Atlanta friend was Joel Chandler Harris, renowned for his Uncle Remus (Brer Rabbit and Brer Fox) series —books that had tremendous appeal in the early 1900's and are still selling because, thank God, kids will always be kids. Perhaps the un-stuffiest man I ever knew, Chandler often picked up his mail by asking, "Anything for Uncle Remus?" I recall that after Stanley "discovered" Doctor Livingston in darkest Africa, he toured the country for many years and one of his stops was Atlanta. He wanted to meet Chandler who refused to meet him because, "He wears a beard . . . and I don't like beards . . . whiskers . . . or goatees. They're counterfeit. Besides, Stanley's older than I am. I like youngsters. They're more my kind."

Marquis and I also revered one of America's great poets and song writers, Frank L. Stanton, who for many years wrote a column in the *Atlanta Constitution*. Perhaps you never heard of Stanton; but if your mother has ever serenaded you, her baby, with "Mighty Lak a Rose," she was singing Stanton. "Just a Wearying for You" is another of many. He fought many a losing fight with liquor but the inbred sweetness of the man never deserted him. After a rough night, Stanton might wander into the old Aragon Hotel and offer to "write a poem for thee" in exchange for three fingers. He turned out more classic lines for bartenders than most mortals have composed for publishers. A sheet of wrapping paper, butcher's paper . . . anything that could hold a line served his mood.

Years later, in New York, Don and I were having dinner at The Players at 16 Gramercy Park, something of a convivial eating and drinking shrine to Edwin Booth, its founder back in '88. We were reflecting on the old days . . . and Frank Stanton.

"We loved him, Grant," said Don. He drew a sheet of typewritten paper from his inside pocket.

"Here's a piece of verse I just wrote. I think Stanton would have liked it. I want you to have it."

Here it is, in print for the first time.

Haunted!
The Ghost Speaks

Do ye whiten with fear at the whine of the wind?
  Was it fancy that mingled a moan therein?
Did ye dream? . . . did ye wake? . . . when ye saw my face?
  Are ye feared of a dead man's face, Barr Wynee?

Barr Wynee, are ye there? . . . are ye there, Barr Wynee?
  Brooding and thinking of me and your sin,
Are ye there . . . do ye hear, Barr Wynee, Barr Wynee?

A ghost is the whim of a sick man's brain?
  Then why do ye start and shiver so?
That's the sob and drip of a leaky drain?
  But it sounds like another noise we know!

We know, Barr Wynee . . . and so did Cain!
  How the heavy drops drummed red and slow . . .
We know, we know, we know, Barr Wynee!

Souls there be that have passed in peace,
  But I went forth in a whorl of hate;
There's a whisper would draw me hence did I heed;
  But heaven must wait, and Hell must wait,
Till I get my grip on your naked soul
  And drag you along, Barr Wynee, to the gate!
Bar Wynee, do ye hear? . . . it is I, Barr Wynee.

That's naught but a trick of the light on the fog?
  Then why should ye see my face therein?
There's naught to fear from a dead man's hand?
  Then why do ye shrink from my touch, Barr Wynee?
The hour that I meet ye ghost to ghost,
  Stripped of the flesh that ye skulk within,
Ye shall learn whether dead men hate, Barr Wynee!

—Don Marquis '16

CHAPTER TWO

My First Big Story, Ty Cobb

Those two writers, Ty Cobb and Ted Williams, recently have been waging a public vendetta. You may recall that Cobb said that the old timers were much better ball players. Ted countered by saying the moderns outranked the former stars and that he could name many men better than the players of Cobb's day. "All except Cobb and Ruth," wrote Williams. "They stand alone."

I have no particular argument about all this except that John McGraw and Ed Barrow, with the angels after devoting their entire lives to baseball, picked Honus Wagner as the greatest "all around" player. From that "all around" stand, they could be right. Wagner could play more positions better than either Cobb or Ruth.

It was in 1895 that I saw my first professional ball game at Nashville. George Stallings brought his black-uniformed Augusta team to town. That was 60 years ago. Since then I've seen the entire parade go by.

I've occasionally compared the youngsters with the old-

sters—for what it's worth, which isn't much. Any more than
Cobb's and Williams' appraisals are worth much—except as a
bit of synthetic excitement.

Connie Mack, years ago, told me, "Grantland, you can't
judge or measure the ball players of one era by those of another.
From 1900 to 1920, baseball was an entirely different game
from the game we now know. Until 1920, it was Ty Cobb's type
of game—belonging more to speed, skill and agility than to
power. They played with a dead ball, so it was a day of base
running. Came the Golden Twenties and we had Ruth, the
livelier ball and we watched speed give way to power. You
simply can't match two entirely different games which call
for dissimilar skills. An outfield composed of Cobb, Speaker
and Ruth, even with Ruth, lacks the combined power of Di-
Maggio, Musial and Williams."

So it is quite possible that Williams' modern outfield is
more useful in today's game than the old trio, as great as they
were. Incidentally, I agree with Ted that Cobb was wrong in
his estimate of the moderns. Any era that gives us DiMaggio,
Williams, Musial, Slaughter, Rosen, Kell, Campanella, Robinson,
Rizzuto, Berra, Roberts, Reynolds, Lopat, Gordon, Doerr,
Schoendienst, Feller, Kiner, Mantle, Greenberg, Dickey, Cochrane, Gehringer, Raschi, Rolfe, Reese, Hodges—we can go on
and on—is right up there with the all-time best. Defensively,
Musial and DiMaggio were better outfielders than Cobb or Ruth;
neither was the defensive equal of Tris Speaker. Williams
doesn't rank too high on the defensive side. You might call him
adequate, but he is no Jim Piersall, Willie Mays or Duke Snider,
currently climbing fences for the Red Sox, Giants and Dodgers.
Few are or have been.

—Which brings me to Cobb, a man apart. The shrewdest
athlete, and perhaps the shrewdest man, I ever knew, Ty played
a trick on me that stood up for more than 40 years.

It was a late afternoon in February, 1904. The paper had just been sent to press and, as a "veteran" reporter of 24, I was involved in a poker game in the *Atlanta Journal* office.

A messenger boy came in with a telegram from a news tipster. I took the message and read the following, fresh from Royston, a town in Georgia—

"Tyrus Raymond Cobb, the dashing young star from Royston, has just started spring training with Anniston. He is a terrific hitter and faster than a deer. At the age of 18 he is undoubtedly a phenom."

I tore up the wire, returned to the poker game and later sent the following to Royston—

"After this, the mails are fast enough for Cobb."

It was a sad mistake. I should have asked the *Journal* to get out an extra. For this same Tyrus Raymond Cobb was on his way . . . on his way to make more than 4,100 big league base hits . . . to steal nearly 900 bases . . . to break almost every record in the books except the home-run mark.

It might be recalled that today good ball players are justly proud of the fact they have made 2,000 base hits . . . like such great hitters as Enos (Country) Slaughter and Johnny Mize. Think what it took to run up more than twice that number and move into the 4,000-hit territory!

In addition to being the greatest competitor I've ever known, Cobb was the most ambitious kid that ever entered sport. And he appeared to have a lot of fans who believed in him. During that 1904 season Cobb played with both Anniston (Alabama) and Augusta (Georgia) in the Southeastern and South Atlantic Leagues. That spring I was deluged with letters and postcards from wherever Cobb was playing. The messages were meaty.

"Keep your eye on Ty Cobb. He is one of the finest hitters

I have ever seen." . . . "Watch Cobb of Anniston. He is sure to
be a sensation." . . . "Have you seen Ty Cobb play ball yet?
He is the fastest mover I've seen in baseball . . ." These and
dozens like them were signed Brown, Smith, Jackson, Holmes
. . . and they showered in from all points of both circuits.

Under pressure I finally wrote a column that a new wonder
had arrived, "the darling of the fans"—my first big story but I
didn't realize it at the time. A few days later I journeyed to
Augusta's ball park to see my discovery. At 18, Cobb was something to look at. He was around 5 feet 11, weighed 155 and had
the legs of a deer—legs destined to carry him for 24 years of hard
campaigning.

I went down to the dugout and talked to the lad, six years
younger than I, before the game.

"I've been hearing about you," I said. "My name is Rice. I
write baseball for the *Journal.*"

"Is that so?" he replied. "I've heard of you too."

During those early years, I found Cobb to be an extremely
peculiar soul—brooding and bubbling with violence, combative all the way, a streak, incidentally, he never lost. Although
our greatest American essayist, Ralph Waldo Emerson, may not
have known it, he was writing to a vision of Cobb when he
penned his immortal challenge on Self-Reliance. Always the
non-conformist, except when it involved team play on the diamond, Cobb's frequent and violent explosions with his teammates as well as the enemy were the rule. From the first, Cobb's
life was a constant war, and Ty lived in a hostile camp.

Cobb moved to Detroit in 1905. A year or so later, when
pitcher Bob Willett moved in with him, his Detroit teammates
ordered Willett to move out.

"Having to live alone," Cobb told me, "I spent all my time
thinking baseball—of plays I could make . . . of tricks I could
try. Baseball was one hundred per cent of my life."

From the start, Cobb never lost an opportunity to study his craft. I recall that in 1904, working on a tip, I got Ab Powell, Atlanta's manager, to sign a long, loose-jointed fireballer known as Happy Harry Hale, from Happy Hollow, Tennessee.

Cobb was then with Augusta. I made considerable copy of Happy Harry's debut. On the day he was to pitch, Cobb got permission to come to Atlanta to study the unveiling of the young phenom.

Built like a tuning fork, Harry Hale was 6 feet 6—and all up. He couldn't have weighed more than 140, soaking wet. For four innings that day, with his long, lean arm and his tall, lean body, Hale's fast ball moved 'em down. At the end of the fourth he was breezing along with a potential no-hitter.

Then in the fifth some dastard in human form bunted. Happy Harry had never seen a bunt. By the time he'd unraveled his frame, the runner was on first. Another safe bunt! When the third man bunted, Hale crashed in, arms and legs akimbo, tried to scoop up the ball and spiked his own hand. That was the finish of Happy Harry Hale and sportswriter Rice's discovery.

Three years later, in 1907, in Washington, a country pitcher from Weiser, Idaho, was mowing down Detroit—along with Cobb. For three innings they couldn't dent him. Cobb remembered the episode of Harry Hale. He told his manager, Hughie Jennings. The Tigers started bunting on the young smokeballer named Walter Johnson, who, like Hale, couldn't field bunts at the time. That was also Johnson's end—that day. But it never worked again.

"I'd sometimes figure out a play—or a weakness—and then have to wait a month or a year before the chance came to use it," reflected Cobb.

Incidentally, while returning on the train next morning to Augusta following Harry Hale's losing battle to the bunt, young Cobb fell into conversation with a large fat boy from Milledge-

ville, Georgia. His name was Babe Hardy, later famous as a
member of the comedy team, Laurel and Hardy. Cobb told
Hardy he was with the Augusta team.

"Are you the bat boy?" Hardy asked.

"Bat boy?" blurted Cobb. "You come to the game today;
I'll show you."

Babe took in the game. "It was something at that," reflected Hardy one day 40 years later on the Hal Roach lot. "Cobb
hammered a single, two doubles, a triple and a home run—and
stole two bases."

"You're not the only one he fooled," I replied, mentioning
the telegram from Royston, Georgia, I'd snubbed back in 1904.
It had hardly occurred to me then that in addition to his 4,191
hits and 892 stolen bases—including 96 during the 1915 season—
Cobb would also lead the American League for 12 out of 13
consecutive years and average a .367 mark for 24 seasons.
During those years Cobb outshone the likes of Joe Jackson,
Napoleon Lajoie, Sam Crawford, Tris Speaker, Elmer Flick,
Eddie Collins—fellows who lived to hit. There was also a
young fellow named George Sisler, who hit .420 in 1922. In
those days they threw the .350 hitters back.

Almost from the start, Cobb figured out every baseball
record that he might break. During those evenings alone he
studied the record book. Home runs were fated to be Ruth's
domain, but Cobb trampled most of the others. He scored 2,244
runs. Lord, how he concentrated on runs! He scored more than
once from first on a single.

Durability? In 1922, 18 years after he broke in at the age of
19, Cobb batted .401. That, to me, is the most incredible mark
of the list—surpassing even the .323 he hit in his 24th and final
year. He batted over .300 for 23 consecutive years, his first year,
1905, being the lone season he failed.

I doubt that many minutes passed during Cobb's entire

major-league span when he wasn't ready to take full advantage of any chance that might develop . . . including the psychological.

An example of Cobb, the psychological tail-twister, involved Shoeless Joe Jackson of the old Chicago Black Sox. Jackson got the Shoeless Joe tag when he played with some little, dinky league in East Tennessee before joining Connie Mack's Athletics in 1908. A farm boy from South Carolina with no spikes of his own when he first joined the club, Jackson played the outfield barefooted. The field, a former dump, was cluttered with sharp stones and broken glass. After the fourth inning of a particular game, Jackson came in shaking his head, slammed down his glove and blurted, "I quit."

"What's the matter, Joe?" asked his manager. "That outfield too tough on your feet?"

"It ain't the feet," complained Jackson. "It's just that all that busted glass is fuzzin' up the ball so's I can't peg it good."

The rhythmed beauty of Jackson's black bat was hitting over .400 down the home stretch of the 1911 season. Joe was leading Cobb by several fat percentage points. Detroit was playing Cleveland. During batting practice the always amiable Jackson greeted Cobb.

"Hello, Ty," said Jackson.

"Get away from me!" blurted Cobb.

"Why, what's eatin' on you? . . ." replied Jackson, hurt and wide-eyed.

"Stay away from me," hissed Cobb.

A brooding Jackson went hitless during those first three games while Cobb fattened his average. On the last of the four-day series, Cobb, seeing Jackson in batting drill, was peaches and cream.

"Why, hello Joe . . . and how's everything?" beamed Ty.

Jackson never did know quite how or why Cobb pulled the

rug from under him. Cobb did. He would have given his own grandmother the "treatment" if she had been leading him. Cobb finished the season with a .420 BA; Jackson with a .408.

On August 16, 1920, when Yankee pitcher Carl Mays killed Cleveland's brilliant infielder, Ray Chapman, with a pitched ball, Cobb was drawn into the headlines. The accident occurred in the fifth inning, with bases empty, when Mays let a fast ball get away from him. The ball struck the plate—crowding Chapman so squarely over the left temple that it dribbled down the third base line where Aaron Ward, thinking it a bunt, pounced on it and rifled to first baseman Wally Pipp. Standing motionless an instant, Chapman then collapsed. He regained consciousness in the clubhouse long enough to say, "Tell Mays not to worry," then died during the night.

Detroit, meanwhile, was playing in Boston. The morning papers featured Cobb's "statement" that Mays had beaned Chapman on purpose. The Detroit team arrived in New York on Friday, an off day, prior to a week end series with the Yanks. That morning Ty called me at home and asked me to come down to the Commodore Hotel.

I found Cobb in bed with a temperature of 102. Both thighs were a mass of adhesive and torn flesh, testimony to some rough base stealing. He was up to his chin in morning papers—all blasting him for that interview back in Boston.

"The first thing you need is a doctor," I said.

"Never mind the doctor," Ty replied. "I've got to be at that game tomorrow and face the wolves. Your New York papers are sure steaming things up. But this, Grant, I want you to know! I never gave out any interview! I knew nothing of what happened until long after that game."

On Saturday, 33,000 stormed the Polo Grounds—the Stadium wasn't completed until 1923. Cobb didn't take batting practice, in fact didn't appear on the field until ten minutes before the game. When he did show, the crowd stood up and booed. Making the long walk from the center-field clubhouse, Cobb stopped near home plate, stared at the crowd and bowed towards the press box, then situated himself behind home plate in the lower grandstand. In effect, he was saying, "There's your story, gentlemen. They are responsible for it."

Detroit won that game, Cobb getting one single, stealing one base and scoring one run—the difference. My interview with Cobb stating he had not blamed Mays was put on the wires. Sunday's fans gave Ty a warm ovation. He replied by getting five hits in six times at bat—including four singles and a double as the Tigers cakewalked.

With nearly a quarter of a million balls being pitched during a big league season alone, helmets or no, the miracle remains that there are not more killings, especially with night baseball in such vogue.

One day in 1928 I sat in Philadelphia's dugout at the Yankee Stadium talking with Cobb. He had come to Connie Mack from Detroit after putting in 22 years with the Tigers. Now, in his last year, at the age of 42, Ty was in a reflective mood. Vain of his skills to the very end, Cobb was slowing up . . . and he knew it.

"Speed is a great asset; but it's greater when it's combined with quickness—and there's a big difference," he said. "I'm about as fast as ever—once I get in motion. But my 'flexes are fading. I'm starting much slower. I don't get the jump any more. I can see the ball as good as ever, but I don't get that quick start from the plate like I used to. If I could, I'd be a .350 hitter right to the end!"

Cobb played in 95 games that year. He hit .323.

One night—it must have been in 1935, a half dozen years after Cobb had quit baseball—we were together in the Detroit Athletic Club. "Nig" Clarke, the old Cleveland catcher, came by. We were jabbering about the old days when I happened to mention Clarke's rapid tag and immediate throwing of his glove aside, signifying the third out.

Clarke laughed. "I missed many a runner who was called out," he said. "I missed you at least ten times at the plate, Ty— times when you were called out . . ."

Cobb was on Nig with one wild charge. "You cost me ten runs . . . Runs I earned!" roared Ty. It was all I could do to pull him off and calm him down. Clarke left. Ty was still burning a half hour later.

The first player I can recall who sensed the great change that hit baseball in 1920 was Cobb and he was blunt about it.

"Well, the old game is gone," he said one day in 1924 as we watched Babe Ruth rocket batting-practice pitches into the new Yankee Stadium bleachers. "We have another game, a newer game now. In this game, power has replaced speed and skill. Base running is about dead. They've all just about quit stealing . . . now they wait for somebody to drive 'em home."

Cobb pointed to Ruth, who was being watched by the players from both clubs.

"Babe Ruth has changed baseball," he continued. "I guess more people would rather see Babe hit one over the fence than see me steal second. I feel bad about it for it isn't the game I like to see or play. The old game was one of skill—skill and speed. And quick thinking. This game is all power. But there'll never be another power-man like this fellow.

"The Babe was a really fine pitcher . . . with control, speed, a hook and the guts up there," continued Cobb. "But he can blast that ball harder than anyone who ever lived. Just watch the ball next year . . . they'll start juicing it up like a tennis ball because Ruth has made the home run fashionable.

"But they'll ruin more sluggers than they'll make. A lot of these kids, in place of learning the true science of hitting or baserunning, are trying to knock every pitch over the fence."

Ty reflected for a moment. "There'll be a few of these youngsters who'll make good with the big blast. But most of 'em won't."

Cobb was right. Just as Connie Mack was right! Ty might have considered the change when he authored that magazine blast against the modern players.

Cobb always resented the idea that he was a rough, or spiking, base runner. I won't forget the day that Hal Sims, the bridge expert—and a sharper mind never cogged—tried to nettle Cobb about his base running.

It was in 1939—during the winter. I was taking my annual sojourn in California which, for years, has been an excuse for a wonderful reunion for Kit and me with our daughter Florence. Cobb was living out there and I arranged a friendly foursome at Pebble Beach with Cobb, Sims, Mysterious Montague, the fellow who shoots par with a rake and a shovel, and me. It was a four-ball match, with Cobb and me playing Sims and Montague, perhaps the strongest fellow I ever knew.

Sims was in good form . . . and when he was in good form, there was no better, or worse, needler. At breakfast, before teeing off that foggy morning, Sims settled his bulk over a third cup of black coffee, looked at Cobb and said, "Ty, I've always admired you. As a ball player you were in a world apart. But tell me this if you will. Why did you have to spike so many men?"

Cobb colored up like an old gobbler, the cords jumping up the back of his neck. He was furious, but managed to contain himself.

We teed off. Normally a pretty fair player, Cobb, still writhing, lunged at the ball as if to kill it. We lost the first seven holes.

Sims, as happy as he was tremendous, was playing lovely

golf. Montague, of course, could spot us all ten strokes each and murder us; but awaiting the explosion, his mind wasn't on the game. I, meanwhile, was trying to soothe Cobb. It was like throwing water on burning oil.

On the eighth tee, Cobb pushed his drive almost out of bounds and hit a provisional. However, both balls had landed in a bunker, so naturally Ty played his first ball. He came out all right and managed a bogie 5. Sims was keeping the card.

"What did you have, Ty?" asked Hal, as we headed for the ninth.

"A five," said Cobb.

"A five?" questioned Hal.

Cobb exploded. Grabbing Sims' arm in his vise-like grip, he snarled, "Listen, no one questions my word or score!"

Montague shot between the two over-age destroyers. Holding each at arm's length, Monty advised both to act their age or he'd bash their heads together.

Hal was visibly upset by Cobb's charge. Cobb, however, settled down and from that moment shot fine golf coming in. Sims couldn't hit a shot.

That evening, Cobb returned to Sims' insinuation that he, Cobb, had been a dirty base runner.

"I only recall intentionally spiking one man in twenty-four years," he told me during dinner. "He was Frank Baker, who was squarely in the path in a Philadelphia game—in 1913 it was. There was no other way to reach the base. From the start, I concentrated on a new form of sliding. This was to send my toe for the bag. I only gave them my toe to tag! It was exactly the opposite of crashing in, hurling spikes or body at the baseman. I don't know how many hours I worked on my type of sliding—a slide that avoided the tagger. Why, I couldn't have been a rough base runner under my system even if I'd wanted to.

"I'll admit I used to run wild, but I did it for a purpose," he
continued. "I wanted the other team to think I was a crazy base
runner . . . to establish mental hazards . . . one way to keep
up the tension. But I actually didn't do much crazy, more particularly, dirty base running!"

As great as any of Cobb's features was his stamina. He had
that at 18—he still had it at 58. As a youngster and as a veteran
ball player, Cobb hunted all winter and played ball all spring,
summer and fall. He actually lived on his legs practically 12
months a year. As a result, he was able to play 3,033 big-league
games and appear at bat 11,429 times.

I recall one spring, I'm sure it was 1911, the year after I'd
left Nashville to come to New York, that Cobb was a holdout.
He'd been with Detroit five years—a veteran. The stories drifting back from spring camp questioned Cobb's fitness, when and
if he decided to report. I didn't hold much stock in them. Cobb
never had to work into condition . . . he was always in condition. Knowing he was ready, he merely didn't care to report
so soon. He got his raise and reported one week before the
season opened. That was the year Cobb rapped out 248 base
hits for an average of .420 while stealing 83 bases. His legs
must have been the most remarkable pair ever known to man—
even Paavo Nurmi.

The annals of sport don't record Cobb the polo player, but
he did take a crack at that sport too. It was during the early
1930's; he was out of baseball but the old competitive fires were
still burning.

One day, at Aiken, South Carolina, Cobb watched a polo
game. Something about the speed and fury of men on horseback
galloping down each other's throats appealed to him. In short
order he was riding, and pretty well, but after he'd got in a few
licks of polo he wanted to change the rules. Instead of three men

to a side he wanted to play it one against one! Nobody wanted any part of him—including the ponies.

"That Mistah Cobb's a madman on a horse," an old colored groom told me one day. "He don't ride *over* you! . . . He rides *through* you!"

That short interim with the horses marked Cobb's entrance and exit from polo.

Cobb never played football. At 17 he was in baseball to stay. But many times I sat with Zuppke, Warner, Jock Sutherland or Rockne and watched them marvel at Cobb. To a man they thought he would have made a great end . . . with his speed, size, hands and overpowering will to win, he would have been a tartar.

Those who claim to know Cobb insist he's one of the coldest men ever. Flint hard, perhaps, but not so cold—at least in my book. One spring day in 1947, Ty and I were motoring north from Augusta where we'd taken in the Masters Golf tournament. As we drove into Greenville, South Carolina, Ty said, "Grant, I've got an old friend in this town. Let's find him."

Driving up to the next cop he asked where he might find Joe Jackson. Informed he worked in a small liquor store on such and such street, we found it and went in. Behind the counter was Jackson. Waiting his turn, Ty stepped up, looked the old boy in the eye and said, "How's business?"

"Just fine, sir," replied Jackson, turning his back to rearrange a shelf.

"Don't you know me, you old buzzard?" said Cobb.

Jackson wheeled around. "Christ, yes I know you!" grinned Joe. "I just didn't think you knew me after all these years. I didn't want to embarrass you or nothin'."

It was a nice reunion—with three old gaffers fanning about the days that used to be. Jackson died four years later, in De-

cember 1951. Cobb's paying Jackson a visit must have been the
high point in the waning limbo years of one of baseball's natural
"greats" . . . a "fall guy" in that 1919 Black Sox scandal.

Not long ago, Gene Fowler, Henry McLemore and I were
being driven by Cobb from the San Francisco airport to his home
at Menlo Park. Gene and I were in the back seat, Henry up
front with Cobb. Ty handles a car like he ran the base paths . . .
full steam ahead. Also, he has a way of turning his head to
talk to you while driving that makes me uncomfortable.

"Grant," he said, suddenly stopping near the end of the
runway while a giant transport buzzed us, "do you remember
the wire you received back in 1904 . . . about the phenom from
Royston?"

"I sure do, Ty," I replied.

"And do you remember a flock of postcards from all over
Alabama and Georgia, telling you what a hot shot I was . . .
all signed with different names?"

"I certainly do . . . why?"

"I sent you the wire and all those notices," chuckled Cobb.

"It's taken you a few years to get around to telling me,"
I said. "Why did you do it?"

"Because I was in a hurry," replied Cobb. "We were both
youngsters on the way up. I didn't know it then but I was trying
to put you onto your first big scoop!"

Self-confidence is the hallmark of a champion . . . any
champion. Not only had Cobb had that amazing cheek and
flare at 18—more important, he knew how to use it, something
few can handle at any stage of life.

Babe Ruth's record of 60 home runs in one year may be
broken, although personally I hope it stands for eternity. It
has almost been equalled twice.

But it is a sure thing that Cobb's mark of 4,191 base hits
will never be approached. And it's just as certain that no ball

player during our sojourn on earth will bat over .300 for 23 consecutive big-league years!

Cobb had too much of the physical and mental strung together, too much of the eternal will to win plus the physical sinews to carry him along. He had too much co-ordination, too many perfect reflexes ever to be equalled on a ball field.

Ty Cobb, the Georgia Peach, had too much of everything.

CHAPTER THREE

The Big Step

During the baseball season of '03 I became official scorer for the Atlanta Club of the Southern League. Atlanta was used by the old Cleveland Indians as spring-training quarters. Their star, Napoleon (Larry) Lajoie, and I became friends.

Philadelphia and the Giants clashed in the '05 World Series and I was sent North to cover the games. McGraw's Giants won as Christy Mathewson pitched three shutouts! I marvelled at the handsome righthander and wrote as much. Returning home, I found a letter from the *Cleveland News* offering me 50 dollars a week to handle their sports page. It took me less than a minute to accept. That was real money and for a fellow with marriage on his mind—money never hurt. I'd been going with a girl named Katherine Hollis from Americus, Georgia, long enough to realize she was to be the one. I invaded Cleveland only to walk into a fight. Half the *News* people, apparently, wanted a midwest writer named Bill Phelon for the job. Phelon and I found ourselves fighting for the same bone. A few years later

I was to discover what a tremendously gifted writer and magnificent screwball Phelon was, but at this particular time we must have had little use for each other. Phelon moved on to Chicago; I moved into Cleveland. The paychecks started rolling in and I told Kit to set our wedding date.

Right here I think my bride should be allowed to describe her own wedding. Kit, will you take over?

"Well, you may wonder how Granny and I met in the first place. I'd gone up to Atlanta from my home, Americus, to visit a girl friend. It was Saturday and we were taken to an amusement park by her brother and a friend. I was riding the merry-go-round—sidesaddle—and having a gay time when I noticed a tall, blond young fellow standing to one side watching me. He was smiling and he looked awfully nice.

"The next day Granny Rice came to call and we took a walk out into the country. I remarked on the fine-looking overcoat he was wearing. 'It's not mine,' he said. 'It belongs to my pal, Bill Newman.'

"A few days later, he came calling for me again—this time with a rented horse and buggy—and took me for a ride. I recall he wasn't very sure of himself . . . or the horse. It started to rain. There was a clap of thunder and the horse bolted and started running————away! Granny couldn't stop him, and the next thing both of us were pitched out of the cart. The horse galloped clear out of sight. We 'hitched' a ride back to Atlanta on a milk wagon.

"After that we began to see more and more of each other. . . . and when he finally visited me at Americus and proposed, perhaps I wasn't quite as surprised as I should have been. But I was awfully proud—and happy.

"The date was set for April 11, 1906, and we were to be married in Americus at the Methodist Church. Granny was off at spring training with the ball team but got a short leave of absence. His younger brother John was the best man. John was to arrive on the wedding morn from Nashville. When the great day arrived, Kate Hollis, one of eight Hollis children, was ready.

"It was an evening affair. As the strains of 'Here Comes the Bride' pealed from the old church organ, I took my brother-in-law's arm (my father had died when I was a baby) and proceeded down the aisle, cloud walking. As I approached the little side door where my groom, a knight in a rented cutaway, was to claim me, there was no Grantland! I whispered to my escort to slow down. There was I, waiting at the church—I knew just how the poor girl in that old song felt!

"After an eternity, the door swung open and out flew the groom—coat tails flapping, with brother John in his wake. He had arrived at the zero hour. Exhilarated with the reunion with John, Mr. Rice apparently had almost forgotten his own wedding!"

—Well, let Kit have her inning. Truth of the matter is, I hadn't almost forgotten the occasion. I had hovered around that church for nearly an hour before Kit and her entourage arrived. And Kit, from the moment I slipped that gold band on your finger, you've been my constant sidekick—at least in my thoughts—no matter how many the miles that have often separated us.

Our honeymoon was spent catching up with the Cleveland team, which had gone to Louisville, Kentucky, where the Indians were playing some exhibition games en route north. We caught up with them in the town that let loose the Kentucky Derby back in 1875—five years before I was born—and then proceeded to Cleveland with the club to open the 1906 season. Napoleon (Larry) Lajoie, Cleveland's playing manager, presented Kit with a huge barrel of china. For a bride about to set up light housekeeping in a Cleveland flat she hadn't yet picked out, my bride had enough chinaware to stock a hotel.

Cleveland was a good baseball town—still is. The Indians roared off to what seemed an insurmountable lead in 1906. Then the injury landslide started and the roof caved in. Lajoie, our star second baseman, was painfully spiked but continued and hit .355. However, Larry couldn't do it alone—Chicago and New York edged us out.

That fall the *News* upped me to 60 dollars a week. Several weeks later I was offered 70 dollars a week to return to Nashville. I accepted and in the spring of 1907 Kit, our brand-new baby, Florence, and I moved into my mother's house. I remember Kit berated me as we climbed the porch steps. It seems I was carrying Floncy under one arm like a football. She wasn't much larger.

The following four years—from 1907 through 1910—were my toughest. Luke Lea was starting a new paper, The *Nashville Tennessean,* with my friend, ex-Sewanee coach Herman Suter as editor. Suter had lured me back home. My only assignments were:

1. To get out two pages of sports daily and four pages on Sunday, with no assistant.
2. To write a column of verse and paragraphs on the editorial page, after the manner of F. P. Adams, Burt Leston Taylor, Judd Mortimer Lewis and some others. This was seven days a week.
3. To cover the theatre—Nashville being a one-night stand—practically each night.

This meant being at the office at 8:00 A.M. and returning home about 2:00 A.M. It also meant around 30,000 words, excluding some 20 sets of verse each week, but verse, usually, was easier to write than prose. I knew many stretches of 18 hours a day, with 12 hours a day the rule. I wonder what the Newspaper Guild would have said about that.

As a youngster, Keats and Shelley had been my particular

favorites; but as I hit 20, I had discovered a fellow named Rudyard Kipling. The meter and jungle drums inherent in Kipling's verse captured my ear and my imagination and never let go. My dear and departed pal O. B. Keeler of the *Atlanta Journal* could recite my stuff by the yard—but whatever verse I've written, more than 6,000 pieces, I've forgotten almost as quickly as I wrote it. Believe me, it just flowed.

I recall two things vividly about the year 1908. One was that I coached the Vanderbilt baseball team—and a rugged bunch we were. Trying to work on a newspaper and coach at the same time requires a bit of doing, but we muddled through to a pretty fair season. The second bit of personal history was the death of my old friend Joel Chandler Harris at the age of 60. The death of "Uncle Remus" jarred me. He had been a cornerstone of the *Constitution* in Atlanta for nearly 30 years. I wrote these lines for the next day's paper.

UNCLE REMUS
(*Upon the death of Joel Chandler Harris*)

There's a shadow on the cotton patch, the blue has left the sky;
    The mourning meadows echo with the south-wind's sigh;
And the gold of all the sunshine in Dixie's turned to gray
    But the roses and the violets shall hide his face away.

The Little Boy is lonesome and his eyes are filled with tears;
    Beyond the mists he only sees the shadows of the years;
The light now lies behind him with his best friend gone away;
    But the softest winds in Dixie at his heart will kneel to pray.

The people of the woodlands—the fur and feathered clan—
    The bear—the fox—the rabbit—will miss him more than man;
But the rose that sways above him in his blossom-tented tomb
    Shall turn its crimson lips of love to kiss away the gloom.

The shadow's on the cotton patch; the light has left the sky;
    A world will bow in sorrow at his message of good-bye;

And the gold of all the sunshine in Dixie's turned to gray;
But the sweetest flowers of the South will hide his face away.

Since graduating from Vanderbilt in '01, I'd done a bit of officiating—refereeing football and basketball games in and around Nashville from 1907–10, plus the shot at coaching the ball club. But I hankered for some participant sport that might fit in with my strange hours. I had covered several golf tournaments at the Nashville Golf Club—including the Southern Amateur in 1909 when Jack Edrington of Memphis defeated Yale's Ellis Knowles, one of our finest veterans today.

The flight of the ball intrigued me. I picked up a club and started swinging. The club pro, Charlie Hall, a squat figure who could hit the ball a mile, took me in tow and, at hours when sensible men were punching time clocks, I'd be out there taking lessons from Hall. I'd found a sport I could stick with—a sport destined to stick with me.

Through the intervening years I've played many more poor rounds of golf than good ones. From the first, the old football injuries to my back and ribs didn't help my swing. Certainly nobody ever confused it with Harry Vardon's, Walter Hagen's, Bob Jones' or Sam Snead's. However, when I used to get around more I shot some good rounds . . . two 68's and a 70 in tournament play. Much more important, however, is what golf gave me in informal companionship with so many champions and "names" of the sporting, business and political world. I've got almost as many columns while playing a round of golf with this or that person as I've gleaned from the press box.

When, in 1910, I received a letter from Mr. Henry L. Stoddard in New York, offering me 50 dollars a week to join his paper, the *New York Evening Mail*, I hesitated. The salary was a comedown. Kit said, "Go ahead!" If I had what I imagined it took to crash the big town, now was the time to show it. Leaving

Kit and Floncy behind in Nashville, I took the train north.
Arriving in New York, I found the offices of the *Mail* at Broadway and Fulton Street and, hat in hand, found Mr. Stoddard.
He came to the point.

"Rice,'" he said. "I've been reading your verse. I never knew
a sports writer worth fifty dollars a week, but in your case I'll
risk it!"

I stumbled out of Stoddard's office and the first person I met
was a young fellow fresh in from San Francisco—Rube
Goldberg, the cartoonist. Rube introduced me to another member of Stoddard's new staff, Frank (F.P.A.) Adams.

"Hello, Rice," he said. "Where are you living?"

"Nowhere's, yet," I replied.

"Come with me," he said. "I'll dig you up a room in the flat
I'm in."

Within the hour, I had a roof over my head at 616 West
116th Street. I wrote Kit that things were fine and proceeded
to feel my way around the big city. The following February,
Kit and little Floncy arrived, bag, baggage—and Nap Lajoie's
china. Following a short hunt, we secured a comfortable apartment at 450 Riverside Drive, our New York home until we
moved to 1158 Fifth Avenue around 1930.

That was quite a neighborhood. Walter Trumbull, one of
journalism's great editors and sweetest fellows, who through
the years managed desks all over town, lived in the same building with us with his wife, Marjorie. Other tenants included
Deems Taylor, Milton Sills (the movie actor) and young
Charley Hughes (son of the Chief Justice). Then there was Max
Foster, Irvin Cobb and his wife, and their little daughter "Buff."
I now see where Irvin's granddaughter, Buff Cobb the 2nd, is a
television star.

Dick Tully, of Bird of Paradise fame and his novelist wife
Eleanor Gates—she wrote "Poor Little Rich Girl"—were neigh-

bors, as was Herb Swope. Harry Hershfield lived at 119th Street, and several blocks south lived illustrator Arthur William Brown and his wife Grace. Heywood Broun had just bought a big old house in the 80's. I recall it didn't have any furniture, but a little thing like that never bothered Heywood. Yes, and near us a brilliant, moody fellow named Damon Runyon was standing New York on its ear with his writing. Damon used to "wander by" our place around midnight to drink coffee and talk by the hour.

The *Evening Mail* batting order comprised some heavy hitters . . . fellows like Broun, Jimmy Sinnott, O. O. McIntyre and F. P. A. Homer Davenport lampooned on the editorial page while Goldberg—still at it with King Features—handled cartoons for the sports side.

McIntyre started out on the copy desk. A long, gangly fellow, he saw enough in editing other writer's copy to convince himself he could do as well—or better. Francis Albertanti, always the promoter, took McIntyre to the Majestic Hotel and locked him in a room, where he began to write—and how he wrote. Albertanti used to enjoy taking Odd down to Chinatown to watch the evangelistic man try to reform "whores, 'pipe'-smoking Chinks and bums." Those were fantastic days in New York—when a young fellow named Irving Berlin worked tables at "Nigger Mike's" in the Village. Whenever Mike would have a bad day at Gravesend Racetrack, he'd come back and "fire" Berlin. Jimmy Kelly—now dead—of the famed Jimmy Kelly's on Sullivan Street would bring Irving back to Mike and get him rehired.

Our sports editor, an ex-Olympic swimmer named Fred Wenck, was a long-suffering soul with a saint's temperament. When he got sore, however, he really blew. One afternoon, Wenck, feeling the front desk was choking him on space, grabbed his typewriter and heaved it across Fulton Street into

St. Paul's Chapel cemetery. He then quit and later became owner
of the New Rochelle-to-Port Washington ferry franchise—and
prospered. Whenever any of the *Mail* sporting-page crowd
made the trip, we rode on a pass as friends of Fred Wenck.

New York around 1912 was a maelstrom compared to the
more sedate way of Nashville. At times I was homesick for the
home town and those I had left—particularly my mother.

> I'm coming back
> Some day, some day—will I be too late?
> Have I come too far—have I lost the track
> That leads again to the rose-rimmed gate?

The too frequent theme of a sad-voiced verse? Perhaps.
Often I vowed to myself and to Kit that we were going back
to Nashville. But somehow, I knew I wouldn't.

> But we have set our soul ahead
> Upon a certain goal ahead
> And nothing left from hell to sky shall ever turn us back.

Kit, Floncy and I had made the big step, a step destined to
take me to the press boxes and behind-the-scenes rooms of the
nation and the world.

II

The Flaming Heart . . . Cold Brain and Firm Command

CHAPTER FOUR

The Four Masters— and Some Others

In over 50 years of wandering about I have run across four master pitchers—pitchers you might label "super great." I have seen at least four other great ones.

These four happen to be "ancients"; three of the next four are what you might call "moderns." Believe me, however, I have no special tie with the past that makes me see everything that's old—that occurred when I was a youngster—as necessarily better than what's come since. Around each curve in life I fully expect to meet and to love a "great champion." I often find old favorites annoying when they carp and haggle over minute details of events that weren't even clear when they occurred 30 or more years ago. If I didn't look ahead to greater deeds in this speeded up age, I believe I would have withered away long ago.

Incidentally, my first baseball hero was a fellow who never did make the grade in the big leagues. I played baseball with him at Vanderbilt. His name was Joe Sherrill, a gangly sort who must have stood 6 feet 2. He had a shock of black hair and he didn't weigh more than 155 pounds. I was a freshman and substitute shortstop; Sherrill, a senior, was our Number 1 pitcher, a righthander. You must appreciate that back in the 1890's there were precious few baseball heroes to thrill the youngsters who lived away from the big-league cities. There were no wire services to pump out the deeds of Ruth, Cobb, Hoyt, DiMaggio, Williams, Mantle and all the rest for the edification of youngsters from here to Tokyo. We built our own heroes, often from our own contemporaries. And as I say, Joe Sherrill was mine. For a collegian, he had the poise, guts and speed of a champion.

I sat on the bench one Thursday and marvelled as Vanderbilt beat Georgia and watched Sherrill strike out 16 men. I think he gave up two hits. The following Saturday, I watched him defeat Georgia again. I don't remember how many men he fanned but he pitched a one-hitter. This was a good '98 Georgia team that had recently walloped Pennsylvania's strong nine.

Sherrill graduated that June and went straight to the Southern League. In his first assignment he struck out 17 men in seven innings. Then his arm went lame. He never pitched again. He became a doctor. Had his arm remained in one piece, Sherrill would have become a pitching immortal. But that's water long since over the dam.

So who are my Four Masters? In no special order they are: Cy Young, 511 victories; Walter Johnson, 416 victories; Grover Alexander, 373 victories; Christy Mathewson, 373 victories.

The four who are merely great: Rube Waddell, Bob Grove, Carl Hubbell and Herb Pennock. The last three belong to the modern era. Oddly enough, the top four are right handers and the second four southpaws.

They were all friends of mine, but I knew Mathewson, of the New York Giants, better than any of the others. I first met Matty in 1905, when we were both 25. But I didn't really get to know him well until 1911 when I came to the *New York Evening Mail.*

A graduate of Bucknell University, Matty was just a little bit better at all games than anyone else. He played chess and checkers and poker better, for example, and usually drew in most of the pots. He was smart looking and well dressed.

I played a lot of golf with him—from New York to St. Louis. We had a funny argument in Pittsburgh on one trip during the 1911 season. I had Mike Donlin for a partner against Matty and Merkle, Fred Merkle, the old Giant first baseman. I had about a three-footer on the first green when Matty spoke to Merkle just as I stroked and missed my putt. Naturally, I squawked.

"What's the matter?" Matty asked. "We play baseball with thousands yelling and cheering. Yet somebody talks and you can't putt."

"They are entirely different games," I said.

"That's a lot of bunk," Merkle said. I said nothing.

This particular match was at the hilly Schenley Course in Pittsburgh. On the second tee, Matty was at the top of his swing when I spoke to Donlin. Matty lunged and topped his ball into the ravine. He glared at me. Merkle was also at the top of his swing when I spoke again. Merkle's ball followed Matty's into the ravine.

"What's this," Matty asked, "a golf match or a talking duel?"

"I thought you said it didn't matter," I replied. Both quickly agreed to keep quiet if I would. They found golf needs silence just as baseball needs noise.

Mathewson was as fine a companion as I ever knew. That

night in Pittsburgh after the match, he asked me to have dinner with him at the Pittsburgh Athletic Club where he was slated to play a chess match. He was to meet 12 opponents. After dinner, walking back and forth from table to table, he won all of his matches, as I recall.

Mathewson had an unusual but sound idea concerning the alibi. "An alibi is sound and needed in all competition," he said. "I mean in the high-up brackets. One of the foundations of success in sport is confidence in yourself. You can't afford to admit that any opponent is better than you are. So, if you lose to him there must be a reason—a bad break. You must have an alibi to show why you lost. If you haven't one, you must fake one. Your self-confidence must be maintained."

I think there is something in this—but never for the amateur or week-end star. To me, that would be a one-way road towards becoming a complete and insufferable fool. However, devote your life and your living to a sport—be it baseball or golf—and this approach might stand up. Had Sam Snead had more of it after blowing that horrible 8 on the 18th hole in the '39 Open at Philadelphia, he might have won the Open title years ago. Hogan, on the other hand, has a good deal of this attitude although I'm not sure he realizes it when discussing his own game.

Matty's philosophy concerning the alibi went farther, which, to me was the saving grace of his primary thesis. "Always have that alibi," he continued. "But keep it to yourself. That's where it belongs. Don't spread it around. Lose gracefully in the open. To yourself, lose bitterly—but learn! You can learn little from victory. You can learn everything from defeat."

He was the smartest—all the way around. In the 1905 World Series against the Athletics, during the six days he pitched and won three games, all via shutouts, Mathewson was the greatest pitcher I ever saw. The games were played in October. I believe he could have continued pitching shutouts until Christmas! The A's got 13 singles off him in three games.

"In those games," Matty said later, "I had everything you need. Almost as much speed as Johnson, a curve that broke as I wanted it to, and perfect control."

The next two years, in 1906 and 1907, he had a bad arm. He worked on his fadeaway. In 1908 he won 37 games for the Giants and saved at least 12 others, being responsible for at least 50 Giant victories. He was either pitching or in the bullpen all year.

"When I pitched that extra play-off game against the Cubs," he told me much later, "my arm was so sore and stiff I needed an hour's warm-up. I could barely lift it."

In that game, Cy Seymour's failure to play deep for Joe Tinker, as Matty wanted him to do, cost the Giants the flag— for Tinker's triple was the decisive blow.

I recall another thing about Christy Mathewson. Since he pitched most of the time, he learned to coast. He would get four or five runs ahead and then loaf. "Let the infielders and outfielders do part of the work," he'd say. He could loaf and then tighten at a moment's notice. He had no interest in the earned run department. "The game alone counts," he remarked. "I'd rather win nine to seven than lose one to nothing. So when I get ahead, I try to rest my arm." This would have meant nothing under the modern situation where a lead of three or four runs can be wiped out in an inning. It was different in the day of the dead or unrubbered ball.

In 1908, when Matty won 37 games, with any breaks he could easily have won 43 or 44.

Mathewson, Grover Alexander, Cy Young, and Walter Johnson were entirely different types.

Matty, friendly and companionable with his friends, was aloof with others. For example, he and Babe Ruth were opposites. Here are two examples. Matty was explaining something to me one day in a hotel lobby in Chicago when a stranger came up, interrupted us and asked for his autograph.

"Can't you see that I'm talking to a friend?" Matty asked coldly. The stranger walked away, apparently sore.

"I owe everything I have to them when I'm out on the mound," he said. "But I owe the fans nothing and they owe me nothing when I am not pitching."

Under the same conditions, when I was talking to Ruth, he turned on the stranger and said, "Sure, I'll give you an autograph; but, you big so-and-so, sit down and wait till I'm through talking to my friend." The stranger said, "Sure, Babe, I'll wait for you." And he did—and left smiling.

Alexander, a partly sick man, had unbelievable control. Cy Young had a puzzling delivery—four different ones plus speed and stamina. Johnson had blinding speed. If Walter had ever been wild or had tried to brush a few hitters away from the plate, I don't believe they would ever have hit him, except by luck. One week end when Washington played New York, Johnson shut out the Highlanders or Yankees three times in four days. He pitched 56 consecutive innings without permitting a run.

They were discussing Walter in various papers, asking what he had. I wrote a piece of verse which only the departed O. B. Keeler remembered. It closed with these two lines—

> How do they know what Johnson's got?
> Nobody's seen it yet.

Johnson was a big, shy man who rarely had much to say. I never heard him protest to an umpire when he was pitching. Matty, Alexander and Young also rarely complained.

Denton True (Cy) Young, with his vast body, turned his back completely on the hitter with something of a swivel-chair delivery. He never let the ball go until he spun back, almost completely, making his pitch extremely difficult to follow.

"I had four different deliveries," he told me. He won more than 30 games in five different seasons en route to his 511 winning games.

One night during the 1939 World Series, I introduced Cy, in Cincinnati, to a crowd of baseball writers. "He won five hundred eleven games," I added.

"You are wrong," Cy immediately retorted. "It was five hundred and twelve games I won. I won one they wouldn't allow me, but I won it."

Cy had a grand time fanning with the writers. "How many innings did you say you pitched?" Bob Considine asked. "Over seven thousand three hundred and something," Cy replied. "Good night," Bob said. "I'm afraid I'll have to be going." The actual count was 7,377.

Of the four men, Alexander was the keenest control artist I ever studied. He was a victim of alcohol, a true alcoholic. Yet he won 30 games or more for three years—his earned run average was the lowest of them all—around 1.65 year after year.

Johnny Evers told me he almost cried each time he had to hit against Old Pete. "I knew in advance it was a hopeless job," he said.

Alex could throw a ball into a tin cup. I have never seen such control. He would pitch a game in an hour and fifteen minutes—rarely longer than an hour and twenty minutes. He wasted no time staring at the batter or rubbing the ball in his hands, as so many pitchers do today. He pitched like Gene Sarazen plays golf: no fuss and feathers. I remember one year when he pitched 16 shutouts, working mostly in Philadelphia's bandbox park where a soft fly was a home run.

Each of these four had some definite form of greatness to give: Cy Young, his 511 victories—Walter Johnson, his 3,497

strike-outs, 113 shutouts, and 416 victories, most of the time
with a weak club—Mathewson, three famous 1905 World Series
shutouts, 37 wins and 12 saved games in 1908—Alexander, his
373 victories and his stingy earned run mark with a bad club,
the Phillies. With the modern Yankees, Alex would have won
40 games many, many times. Alex and I came to the big league
the same year—1911, my first baseball season in New York. He
won 28 games as a rookie that season.

These pitchers are baseball's greatest. Among them, they
won 1,673 games, an average of more than 400 games each; and
two of them—Johnson and Alexander—worked for weak clubs.

Waddell, Grove, Pennock, Hubbell and Plank were magnificent, but in my book not quite like Young, Johnson,
Alexander and Mathewson. Dizzy Dean? As good as anybody
for a short span. He didn't pitch long enough to be rated with
these others, who worked so many years. But Dizzy, christened
Jay Hanna, was not only a great pitcher. He had more native
color than one of his native Ozark sunsets.

In 1931, Diz was a bush rookie up from Texas for spring
training with the Cardinals. That day they were playing an
exhibition game with the Athletics, who had whipped the Cards
in the 1930 Series. Gabby Street, the Cardinal manager, quickly
figured Dizzy was more than he could handle. Around the fourth
inning, the A's had the bases full, nobody out and Simmons,
Foxx and Mickey Cochrane coming up.

"Wish I was out there," Dean said. "Those monkeys
wouldn't score."

Catcher Jimmy Wilson, sitting that game out, winked at
Street. Street winked back. "All right, Diz," he said. "You're in
there! Go to work."

Without any warm-up, Diz proceeded to strike out Simmons, Foxx and Cochrane.

Branch Rickey earmarked Dean back to Houston, Texas.

That same evening, Wilson recognized one of his silk shirts on Diz.

"Say, Dean," Jimmy said, "isn't that my silk shirt you're wearing? Where'd you get it?"

"Listen, Jimmy," Dean replied. "You wouldn't want the world's greatest pitcher to wear one shirt for a month, would you?"

"What's the answer to that one?" Wilson said to me later.

"There is no answer to anything Dizzy says," I told Wilson.

"Or anything he does," Wilson replied.

In 1929, Paul, Diz and father Dean started for Texas riding in two separate, battered old jalopies. Diz, the true pioneer, led the way by a few hundred yards.

"When a freight train came by and separated us, I went on. I musta left Pa and Paul behind," Diz recalled later. "They finally turned 'round and went back home to Arkansas. I went on to Texas. We didn't see each other again for years. I joined the Army and had to be bought from Uncle Sam when Rickey discovered I was the best pitcher in the country."

It was at spring training in 1933 when Dizzy announced to all within hog-calling distance that he owned a kid brother "back on the farm" whose high, hard one was even faster than his own. A year later, in '34, he again hollered that "Me and Paul" would win 45 games. Diz proved better than his word. Between them, they won 49 (Diz 30; Paul 19) for the swashbuckling Gas House Gang—and four more from Detroit as the Cards won the World Series four games to three.

Paul (Daffy) always had his big brother's interests at heart. Riding on the train with the Cardinals during that hectic '34 season, Diz and I were sitting on one side with Paul across the aisle swigging a bottle of pop. The train suddenly roared into a long tunnel.

"Diz," exclaimed Paul. "You tried any of this stuff?"

"Just fixin' to," replied Diz. "Why?"

"Don't!" cautioned Paul. "I did and I've gone plumb blind."

Struck on the toe by a line drive off Earl Averill's bat in the 1937 All-Star game, Dean was cut down at 26. Favoring the toe, he pitched without his full stride and injured his shoulder. When bursitis developed, Dean's effectiveness dimmed.

Branch Rickey, shrewdest David Harum ever, peddled Dean to Phil Wrigley for a modest 125,000 dollars. It was as a Chicago Cub in 1938 that Diz made his immortal remark when I questioned him about the arm.

"Well, Grant," he said, feeling his right shoulder, "it ain't what it was . . . but then, what the hell is?"

At times lately, I'm forced to agree with one of my dearest confederates, Dizzy Dean, Pitcher-Philosopher Emeritus.

(While Mr. Henley isn't looking)

Out of the blight that smothers me
  Deep as the pits from hole to hole,
I thank whatever gods there be
  For what is left of my wrecked soul.

In the fell clutch of grip and stance
  I've often winced and cursed aloud.
Where heelprints often meet my glance
  My head keeps bloody, but unbowed.

It matters not the sacrifice
  Which makes the duffer's wife so sore.
I am the captive of my slice,
  I am the servant of my score.

CHAPTER   FIVE

Golf's Advance Guard

When I started hitting a ball at the Nashville Golf Club in 1909, I never dreamed that golf would open as many doors of friendship, provide as much grist for my typewriter and engender as many kernels of philosophy, as has this game, born in the British Isles somewhere around 1600.

With the possible exception of croquet "for blood" and billiards, golf is like no other game. You are attacking an inert ball. Also, you are on your own. You are the referee. Nine times out of ten you must call the penalty on yourself—if a penalty is to be called. You can play the game by the rules or you can cheat. You are meant to play the ball as it lies, a fact that may help to toughen your own objective approach to life.

Golf gives you an insight into human nature, your own as well as your opponent's. Eighteen holes of match or medal play

53

will teach you more about your foe than will 18 years of dealing with him across a desk. A man's true colors will surface quicker in a five-dollar "Nassau" than in any other form of peacetime diversion that I can name.

Golf lends itself nicely to the 19th hole, a period of refreshment, happy talk and commiseration. I've got a host of columns from the locker room . . . not only about and with name golfers but about and with headliners of every sport and business. Peeled down to his shorts, a highball in one hand, an attested score card in the other, it's hard for a man to be anything but himself.

Three amateurs, from 1907 through 1916, played leading roles in the golf destiny of this country—Jerry Travers, Chick Evans and Francis Ouimet. They won both our Amateur and Open titles. Travers was first on the scene. Not physically equipped to reach and hold any sustained height, he nevertheless won our Amateur crown four times—in 1907, 1908, 1912 and 1913—and the Open in 1915. New York born, Travers rates as one of the greatest competitors who ever played any game. He had Ben Hogan's concentration. Unable to use a driver, he used a Number 1 iron off the tee. Never long but poker-straight, he crushed opponents with his approaching and putting.

Alex Smith, who trained and taught them both, told me that Travers was an even greater competitor than Walter Hagen. "I always know whether Hagen is winning or losing," he said. "I never knew how Travers stood from watching him."

Chick Evans, the Chicago marvel, was playing title golf in 1906 and still plays superb golf today—48 years later, the length of our friendship. Chick, with his extra-long hickory shafts, won the Open in 1916 at Minneapolis Minikada Club, setting a new record of 286 for 72 holes. He won the Amateur that same year at Merion Cricket Club, Pennsylvania, and again in 1920 at the old Engineers on Long Island. A truly fine iron player, Chick had the sweetest foot action I've ever studied. Had he been able to putt with the killing coolness of Travers, there would have been no stopping him for at least ten years.

Our third great amateur before the age of Jones was Francis Ouimet of Boston. As a young ex-caddie, Ouimet was most responsible for golf's sudden boom in America.

By 1913 the United States had outgrown its knee britches in practically all sports except golf. Thanks to a big Indian named Thorpe, we had kicked the stuffings out of the field in the 1912 Olympics at Stockholm. We had taken England's measure in tennis, yachting, boxing and polo. But the Scotch and British dominated at golf, with Harry Vardon and Ted Ray, two of John Bull's finest. Vardon had won the British Open five times and was to win it again in 1913. Ray took it in 1912.

Backed by the *London Times,* this pair came to America during the summer of 1913 and toured the country giving exhibitions before record crowds at record fees. Vardon, a well built fellow with his publicized overlapping grip, was the complete stylist. Ray, however, was a ponderous, stoop-shouldered bear of a man who affected a walrus mustache, a Sherlock Holmes pipe and the ability to lunge into the ball with more brute strength than anybody this side of "Brisbane's gorilla." Neither man was a talker but Vardon, possessed of biting intelligence, could be civil. As for Ray, he was usually as dour as an elephant with a sore foot.

I covered the Shawnee Open that year in which Johnny McDermott, the American champion, was paired with Vardon. McDermott, a great golfer with a tragic fate awaiting him only weeks away, was at his crest. Vardon would hit an iron approach 12 feet from the cup. You could see McDermott's chest expand as he hit one nine feet from the pin.

McDermott won this big tournament, leading the field in a runaway by something like 12 strokes. When the cup was presented to McDermott he welcomed the two star Britishers but concluded with this statement.

". . . but you are not going to take back our cup!"

Vardon and Ray were insulted. The golf committee called McDermott back to apologize. McDermott offered an apology if he had hurt their feelings. But turning to Vardon and Ray, he added, "But you are not going to take back our cup!"

That 1913 Open, played at the Country Club of Brookline, a Boston suburb, was, nevertheless, considered a shoo-in for either Vardon or Ray with any American including Ray, our defending champion, about 100 to 1 in any wagering. Into this picture walked an unassuming Francis Ouimet, a 20-year old local, as Boston as the cod and just as cool. At the end of 72 holes of medal play over the rough par 71 layout, it was Vardon, Ray and Ouimet—all tied.

More than 3,000 braved a steady drizzle for the playoff. The smart money expected Ouimet to crack wide open. Instead he cracked the two British rocks with a precise 72, defeating Vardon by five strokes and Ray by six. The match was written up as The Shots Heard Round the World—and advanced golf's popularity with the masses at least 10 or 20 years. Ouimet had fired the imagination of thousands of youngsters who had known only baseball, football and perhaps basketball. Kids began swinging a battered mashie iron as well as a bat.

A decade later, Hagen and Jones were to create an entirely new industry—the wholesale machining of golf clubs and equipment for the golf-happy masses who turned to the game following World War I. But Ouimet made that first big dent into the sports consciousness of America.

Another figure I must include here is Australian-born Walter J. Travis, who began playing the game at 36 and won the United States Amateur crown in 1900, 1901 and 1903 and the British Amateur in 1904—when an antagonistic Travis outgamed and outshot the supremely antagonistic British at their own game. A slight figure, the cigar-chewing Travis under pressure had the physical and mental toughness of a mule skinner.

"What is your secret?" I asked Travis one day.

"I never hit a careless shot in my life," he replied. "I bet only a quarter but I play each shot as if it was for the title. I concentrate as hard for a quarter as I do for a championship." He was hard boiled, grouchy and tough but I liked Walter Travis immensely.

Another great contributor to American golf in those early years—tougher and rougher even than Travis—was Charles Blair MacDonald who won our second Amateur title in 1895 and went on to envision many of our oldest and finest courses. A transplanted Scotsman, MacDonald was a fiery, fierce man in all argument and debate. He knew and bowed only to the Royal and Ancient of Saint Andrews but he laid out the National, Lido, the Yale and some of our finest midwestern courses. He was the advance guard of the championship courses we know today.

A parting salute to the Vardon and Ray team was given me by Tommy Webster, the brilliant British cartoonist and wit. Following that historic 1913 Open, the pair of them sailed for home where they were immediately booked in three consecutive tournaments. Webster followed Ray in that third tournament where the lumbering giant finished up by crawling the last two holes. Tommy asked Ray what he was going to do the following week.

"Do?" exploded Ray. "I'm going back home tonight and have a bloody good sit down!" For two weeks back at his club, Ray refused to leave his chair.

Those pioneering professionals prior to World War I were

a hard-bitten but colorful lot. They trail-blazed golf in a day when iron clubheads, tricky hickory shafts and rough-hewn courses often teamed with strong drink to outlive, outfight, outcuss and outscore the devil himself. If golf had been a social game, they roughed it up with a rasp.

As burning as any of the early greats, I won't forget our first American gamecock McDermott, the first homebred to check and stop the supremacy of the Scotch and the British. A fighter, McDermott would wager any amount on himself in practically any match he played. The fire of his own intensity burned out the little fellow and following that 1913 Open, McDermott went mentally astray and vanished into a home. Years after he was put away, Johnny was brought to a well-known Staten Island course where he shot a 70. He hadn't seen a golf club in years.

CHAPTER SIX

Walter Hagen,
the Incredible Man

Five years before I met Walter Hagen, I was at the Druid Hills golf course at Atlanta. I was playing in a foursome with George Adair, a fine player and father of Perry Adair, who, with young Bobby Jones, was one of the most precocious golfing youngsters in the South.

Adair's partner lunged at his drive, topping the ball off the first tee. Walking down the fairway, the fellow was moaning.

"Why all the fuss?" asked Adair. "You didn't really expect to hit a good one, did you?"

"As a matter of fact, no," laughed his partner. "It's just that I was hoping so hard."

Because golf exposes the flaws of the human swing—a basically simple maneuver—it causes more self-torture than any game short of Russian roulette. The quicker the average weekend golfer can forget the shot he has dubbed or knocked off line

—and concentrate on the next shot—the sooner he begins to improve and enjoy golf. Like life, golf can be humbling. However, little good comes from brooding about mistakes we've made. The next shot, in golf or in life, is the big one.

Walter Hagen, a dazzling ornament to the history of sport, had the soundest golf philosophy I've ever known. More important, he applied it.

"Grant," he said, "I expect to make at least seven mistakes each round. Therefore, when I make a bad shot I don't worry about it. It's just one of the seven."

I saw Hagen make 19 mistakes during one round in a North and South Open at Pinehurst in 1924. He finished with a 71, ultimately winning the tournament. A mistake meant nothing to him. Neither did defeat. He scorned second place. "The crowd remembers *only* the winner. I'd as soon finish tenth as second," he said.

This faculty of being able to forget the bad shots ties in closely with the art of relaxation, a gift Hagen utilized to greater advantage than 99 per cent of today's circuit-swinging pros, who, except for Jimmy Demaret, are a grim, foreboding band. Relaxation—the art of breathing deeply and approaching the next shot with unhurried objectivity—was Hagen's big secret. He refused to take himself too seriously.

It was in 1912, while I pounded out my column, "The Sportlight" (a title that Frank Adams suggested), that a young caddie named Walter Hagen was pounding the fairways of the Country Club of Rochester. In those days golf was pretty much restricted to the exclusive social centers around Westchester County and Long Island. I liked to play the game and enjoyed writing about it—which cut little cheese in New York. Golf got scant notice in the metropolitan papers, and Francis Albertanti, then our assistant sports editor, disparaged its importance like most editors.

Albertanti hailed from the lower East Side. He knew fights

—and how to publicize them. In fact, he later became Tex Rickard's press agent. He also composed a two-column slug that remained in type for years—Albertanti's gesture towards tennis:

Tilden Beats
Richards Again.

But in Albertanti's book, golf was something played by un- employed sheep herders and "coupon-clipping stiffs." It didn't belong on the sports pages.

Theophilus England Niles, the *Mail's* managing editor, called Albertanti into his office one day to ask why golf wasn't receiving space.

"Golf? What's golf?" asked Francis.

"Why, it's a game—an important game," replied Niles. "A lot of big businessmen are playing it."

"Then put it on the financial page," retorted Albertanti.

Francis Ouimet's dramatic victory over Vardon and Ray in 1913 helped to give golf popular appeal, but it remained for Hagen to supply the human interest, to put the throbbing kick into the game. Color, no matter how it's spelled out, means gold for the newspapers. Hagen had more color than a lawn full of peacocks.

Blessed with a pair of strong, quick hands, Hagen was trying to choose between golf and baseball as a career. Extraordinarily keen at shagging golf balls, on the fly or on the bounce, young Walter caught the eye of Andy Christie, the club professional. Christie promoted the youngster to the pro shop, sweeping and cleaning up, but before long Hagen's hands were busy wrapping, straightening and mending hickory shafts and burnishing iron clubheads.

In 1912, the National Open was to be played at nearby Buffalo, and Hagen, then Christie's assistant, asked if he might enter.

"Not a chance," replied Christie. "I don't mind giving you three days to go up there and watch and perhaps learn something. But I'm not letting any twenty-year-old kid make a fool of himself in that fast Open crowd."

One of America's all-time greats, Johnny McDermott, won that Open, but when Hagen returned from his short sabbatical, he told Christie, "They're not the players I'd expected."

A year later, at the Country Club in Brookline, Massachusetts, Hagen arrived—this time with his clubs. Years later, Ouimet told me about Hagen's entrance.

"There was a crowd of us, including McDermott, the defender, in the locker room when this black-haired youngster came in and blithely announced, 'The name is Hagen. I've come down from Rochester to help you fellows stop Vardon and Ray.' "

Ouimet did the stopping, but Hagen outscrambled and outscored every American pro except McDermott, whom he tied for fourth place!

In 1914, I suggested I cover the Open at Midlothian (Chicago). The desk was unenthusiastic. Although some 350,000 people were playing golf in America at that time, probably less than 5,000 of them were around metropolitan New York. Hagen won that 1914 Open without any assistance from me. Dressed in raiment that out-Astored Mrs. Astor's horse, the "veteran" of 22 led the field from wire to wire, canning an eight-foot putt on the last hole to defeat Chick Evans by a stroke.

In 1915, I got to cover Hagen at Baltusrol, where he was to defend his Open title. Although Jerry Travers, a master of amazing concentration, won that Open with his driving iron and a phenomenal putter, Hagen took his lumps in insouciant stride. From the first, he impressed me as a young man of charm and unbelievable self-confidence. He disported himself, even then, without the slightest fear of failure.

But the first true mark of Hagen's greatness I discovered at

Deal, England, in '20. After winning our Open title again in '19, Hagen decided to cross the Atlantic and attack the barren burns of the long Deal course. His target: the British Open. In America, Hagen's rather lofted shots, sensational recoveries and icy green-work enabled him to win the Open twice, plus a flock of other titles. However, those native-born pros who knew Britain's terrain and squallish weather predicted that Hagen's "basically unsound" swing would collapse like the pig's house of straw. "The wind alone will do it," they said.

Commenting that "there are no bunkers in the air," Hagen was his usual supremely confident self as he set sail to find the pot of gold at the end of the British rainbow. Quoted and mis-quoted all over the place, he found the big crowd dogging his heels when he teed off in his first round at Deal. Hagen shot an 83! In 53rd place following that round, he was never a factor.

As Walter came up to the big board to post his score, you'd have thought he was leading the pack. He might have packed up and quit, as others had done before him. But he marched up to the board, and, turning to the crowd said, "There it is! But I'll be back." No alibi, no excuse of any sort. The next year, at St. Andrews, he finished sixth. In '22, at Sandwich, he won—the first American to do it. From 53rd to 6th to 1st—in only three years. From then on, through his fourth and final Open victory in 1929, Hagen was the most respected opponent Great Britain knew during those days when John Bull was at his absolute golfing peak.

All told, Hagen won 11 National and International crowns —a record second only to Bobby Jones'. He won the U.S. Open twice, the British Open four times and the PGA five times.

Archie Compston, the raw-boned Britisher, humiliated Ha-gen in a 72-hole exhibition match a week before the 1928 British Open. A stint before the Hollywood cameras and the subsequent boat ride had rusted Hagen's game more than he had realized when he agreed to the match. Walter was guaranteed 500 guineas, the equivalent of 2,500 dollars, for that appearance— the first time an American pro was paid real money for extra- curricular shooting in the British Isles. Compston drubbed Hagen 18 and 17! While the British press chortled over Hagen's "downfall," Walter retired to a secluded seaside course, where he went to work in earnest. A week later, he won the Open at Sandwich. Compston finished third, three shots behind.

During one round in that championship, Hagen's drive wandered far off and into the heaviest kind of rough. As he approached his ball, a British lord standing nearby remarked, "That's a terrible spot. I doubt that you can play it."

"I put it there," replied Hagen—then made one of his mir- acle recoveries.

Down the years, many stories have been told about Hagen's insistence on entering the clubhouse by the front door to change his clothes—thereby setting precedent. Walter didn't change the social system of the British Isles, but his easy grace and deportment helped soften it somewhat. Hagen had an eye for style and plush, and a skilled mechanic's ear for a perfectly attuned engine. He liked to be driven from his hotel to the first tee by a liveried chauffeur, preferably in a Rolls Royce. And if a gorgeous blonde was hanging on his arm as he alighted, that was all right with him, too.

Following World War I, our pros began beating the day- lights out of their British competition with a routine regularity that became depressing for the British. The London press asked Hagen why.

"There are two reasons," replied Hagen. "First, we have more tournaments at home. There's no substitute for competi- tion. Secondly, and perhaps more important, in America the golf professional—in fact, the professional athlete—is respected far more than he is over here. He is encouraged to rise in the

social as well as in the financial scale, and this gives him greater
confidence in himself and in his work. We American professionals are proud of our calling."

The British change slowly, if at all. But Hagen, by his tact,
deportment, style and over-all color, did for the professional
golfer what Babe Ruth did for the professional ball player.

After winning a tournament, Hagen was often invited into
the clubhouse, where he was the picture of debonair charm.
The Hagen "polish" and unaffected ease was as real as it was
apparent. Walter set the example and the others followed. But
he was not the pushy type and never sought an invitation. With
the then Prince of Wales tagging Walter's footsteps, somehow
he didn't have to.

Walter enjoyed his association with British titles and gentry,
but he knew how to laugh at himself. Before the Open matches
at Troon in 1923, Hagen, as leader of the United States forces,
was riding high.

"Our boys were hitting the ball pretty well at that," he remarked. "I was enjoying a highball when I was paged. It seemed
that Sir Alexander Walker, Captain of the Troon Club, desired
me to come to his home at seven that evening. I told my boys
I'd be unable to join them, since I was dining with Sir Alex—at
his home.

"When I rang his bell that evening the butler condescended
to let me enter. He then left me standing in the hall. Finally I
heard a gruff old bark, 'Hagen!'

"I followed the growl and arrived in the old gentleman's
study, where I found him propped in a leather chair. Looking
me over, he finally spoke.

" 'Hagen,' he said, 'I've had word that your fellows have
been practicing from the brush-covered part of the tees. We
want those tees in good shape for the matches. See that it doesn't
occur again. Good night!' "

Hagen's confidence in Hagen was, as I have said, amazing. He and Joe Kirkwood, the trick-shot artist, stopped on a tour at New Orleans, where they were to play two local pros. Hagen couldn't get a bet.

Finally he asked what the course record was. It was 69.

"I'll bet a thousand dollars I break it," he said.

A local group got together and raised the thousand. On the last hole, Hagen planted his second shot within 12 feet of the pin. Arriving on the green, he spotted his betting opponents in a worried-looking huddle. Hagen walked up to his ball and looked back at the group. He needed that shot for his 68.

"Miss this putt for one thousand dollars?" he cracked. "Not a chance!"

After he tapped his ball—in fact, while it was still rolling— he held out his right hand towards the betting group. "Gimme," he said.

He was golf's greatest showman. He "staged" many shots that looked hard but were not. But he could make the hard ones with the easier chances.

In one Los Angeles tournament in the mid-1920's, Walter whacked his tee shot on the ninth hole to the green, some 60 feet beyond the cup. It was raining, and the huge green was full of uneven slopes.

I was standing in the huge crowd, behind the ropes. Walter beckoned me to join him on the green. "You know," he remarked, "I've been studying this putt. There's just one way to get my ball within twenty feet of the cup—I've got to hole it." Which he did.

I can't tell you how many times I've seen Hagen arrive at the club house only ten minutes before starting time, still in his night-club uniform, dinner jacket and all. He'd saunter through his change, knock over a Scotch and turn in a 70 without batting an eye.

I followed Walter in a big California tournament one morning after a rough and turbulent all-night party in some downtown deadfall. He topped his tee shot . . . he topped his second . . . he topped his third, which luckily ran up on the green 40 feet from the pin . . . and holed out for his par 4. He finished out that nine with a 39. As Hagen approached the tenth tee, a fellow asked if he hadn't seen the golfer at a night club at 6:00 A.M. "this morning."

"Probably," said Walter.

"My Lord, where have you been since?" the man asked.

"Sleeping," replied Hagen. He then finished in 33 for his 72, ultimately winning the 72-hole show.

During the Florida boom in '26, Hagen defeated Bob Jones 12 and 11 in a 72-hole challenge match—36 holes at Sarasota and 36 at St. Petersburg. Bob's nerves were badly shaken by watching Hagen's ball disappear into the palmettos—only to hear a crash and see the ball come whistling out and land stiff to the pin.

"After Hagen's off-line tee shots, there were too many holes I knew I couldn't lose—holes I lost to a birdie or par. I simply couldn't keep my game going," said Bob later.

On one short hole, Hagen was 20 feet from the cup, and Jones, also strong, was nearly 60 feet beyond the pin. Jones holed his long putt for a 2. Hagen turned to the gallery. "What do you think of that?" he smiled. "Bob gets a half after all." Then Hagen sank his putt.

Hagen was the first golfer to make a million dollars—and the first to blow it! I recall when he made a world tour—Japan, Australia, India—all over the map. He had 5,000 dollars on his person, or within quick reach, when he left. He won 14,000 dollars in several big tournaments. But when he returned to the old U.S.A., he had to borrow a dollar from his manager, Bob Harlow, to pay his taxi fare. Money—a dollar or 10,000 dollars—meant nothing to Hagen. In one year, before 1929, he made and blew more than 300,000 dollars—and without a regret. I was riding in a high-priced car with him in Los Angeles. He had a liveried chauffeur.

"You see this car?" he asked. "You see my driver?"

"What about it?" I replied.

"Just this. I haven't got a dime—not even a dime," said Walter. "But I'll still get by."

Hagen's appraisal of his own swing was uncanny. Like a sleight-of-hand magician, he knew exactly what his hands were doing at all times, although the bystander was often mystified.

"Even as a kid I tried out everything possible in swinging a club," he said. "For example, I think I was one of the few who 'blue-printed' my hands throughout the downswing. At the finish, I could turn my hands for a slice or a hook—whichever was preferable under the conditions.

"Also, I learned to figure each hole as it came—to look for the bad side, where you can find real trouble, or for the safer side, where the penalty is lighter. I like to make my mistake on the right side, where I can lose only one stroke. You've seen me make a lot of mistakes, but you've seldom seen me worry over 'em," continued Walter. "They've usually been on the safe side."

Had a golf glove been the vogue when Hagen was at his peak, I doubt that he would have worn one. Most of today's pros worry more about their glove than they do about their hands. Not Walter. His touch was such that he figured, correctly, that the human skin gives more "feel" than the best glove ever devised. He never had a callous—a testimony to the basic correctness of his grip. He was also old fashioned about shoes. Until the advent of knickers forced him into oxfords, Hagen preferred high-laced shoes for the support they gave his ankles.

I followed Walter in perhaps his bitterest match—and certainly one of his greatest. It was at Pelham, New York, in the final round of the PGA championship in 1923, in a match-play final with Gene Sarazen, the defending champion. Gene had come into sudden fame in 1922 by winning the U.S. Open at Skokie. He was then 21 years old, at the top of his game, and with the hackles of a gamecock. He had just beaten Hagen in a challenge match.

This particular match was dog-eat-dog all the way. In one spot, Sarazen asked for a ruling from the referee.

"Why don't you read the rules—or can't you?" snarled Hagen. Sarazen missed the putt and lost the hole.

"I'm glad I missed that," said Gene, "so when I beat your brains out today there'll be no alibi."

Hagen had a ten-inch putt. He looked at Gene, expecting him to concede it.

"Hole it," said Gene. "I'm giving you nothing but hell today."

That's the way it went. They finished the 36 holes all square. They halved the 37th with two birdies. At the 38th (the second), a partial dogleg, Hagen hit one of his greatest tee shots—a 290-yard hook that stopped hole-high, 20 yards from the cup, with a shallow sand trap intervening.

Sarazen hit a wild hook, and his ball crashed into a tree at the out-of-bounds mark. The ball was finally located in a wheat field—in bounds, but in wheat up to Gene's neck. I was standing next to Hagen when Sarazen played the almost impossible shot. From the wheat, the ball rocketed out and finally stopped 18 inches from the cup. I looked at Walter. He looked like a man who had just been bludgeoned. He then popped his short approach into the trap at his feet, and Sarazen won.

But this I'll say for Hagen. He had won five PGA matches going into that final in the 1923 PGA. He then proceeded to win in 1924, 1925, 1926 and 1927, and he went to the final round in 1928. That means that Hagen won 34 of 36 matches from the greatest golfers in the world—29 of those matches in succession. It was one of the finest chapters in golf's long history, an incredible performance. Hagen was the match-play king, and that goes for all time. He had no equal when it was man-to-man. To win 34 of 36 matches from a field comprising such giants as Barnes, Sarazen, Armour, Hutchison, Mac Smith, Diegel, Cooper, and many, many others was fantastic—but Walter did it!

My old friend Tommy Webster, sports cartoonist for London's *Daily Mail* these many years and one of Hagen's dearest pals, likes to tell a "Hagen in Paris" anecdote. Following an especially colorful victory in England, Walter hopped over to Paris, where he was booked for several exhibition matches. On this particular morning at St. Cloud, he threaded his way towards the first tee amid the "oohs," "aahs," and "magnifiques" of the French gallery. Walter had been out on the town all night, and his head was bigger than a pumpkin.

"Well, sir," related Tommy, "The Haig finally gets his ball teed up, addresses it a bit shakily—and whiffs! That French crowd is as silent as one of their cathedrals. Shocked, an official then announces, 'Meestaire Hagen . . . he is indisposed . . . he is a seeck man!'

"We took Walter back to the club house, wrung him out and ordered a jug of black coffee as long as your arm. After pouring a quart of it down his gullet, Hagen was quite sober. He then went out before that French gallery and shot a sixty-six!"

One night—it was in 1935, during the Masters tournament in Augusta, Georgia—Hagen, pushing 45, and I got into an old-fashioned fanning bee. We found the sun shining in our eyes. As Hagen stopped at the desk to get his room key, an idea struck him.

"Suppose I phone the leaders and tell 'em I've been arrested and ask them please to come down and get me out," he chuckled. "Then we'll start even."

He had to tee off in about two hours. "Grant, follow me this morning and I'll show you some *new* golf," he said.

Then he went to his room, showered and shaved with the straight razor he's been using for at least 30 years. Incidentally, that razor is another testimony to Hagen's uncanny touch. To handle the straight-edge as Hagen does when the boat is rocking badly after a long night—well, the average fellow would cut his throat. I struggled through nine holes with Walter at Augusta that morning. He dubbed about every kind of shot imaginable. But he always had the Big One left—an approach or a long putt. He butchered exactly 14 shots—hooks, slices, topped balls, the works! But he was out in exact par, 36. How was that again? He had seven one-putt greens. That proved to be Walter's final salvo. He finished poorly.

"When a fellow gets along in years, it's not his tee shots that go. Why, Ruth could still hit home runs when he was an old man," Hagen remarked later. "It's the putting that goes first, and do you know why? The legs. They're not up to that hydrant immobility needed for the solid stance. When the eight-footers begin to look like eighteen-footers and they don't drop for you consistently any longer—that's when you know you're old."

I wonder if Ben Hogan felt something of this in losing the '54 Masters play-off to Sam Snead—not from tee or fairway, but on the greens.

Hagen was a great putter. (The greatest five, in my book, are Walter J. Travis, Jerry Travers, Bob Jones, Hagen and Horton Smith.) But Hagen's following will remember him much longer for his color, his sparkling wit, his impeccable dress, his manners and charm under all conditions, than they will for his putting.

As long as I've known Hagen—40 years—I've found him

without inhibitions of any sort. Whether he's with the King of England or a broken-down caddie, Hagen has never changed his manner to suit the occasion.

Hagen was golf's super-salesman. Like Rockne, Dempsey, Ruth, he basked in the roar of the crowd. He had that personal spark, that magnetism that transmitted from club champs or chumps to his own eminent self. He tugged on the imagination —which made him wonderful copy. He seldom let his public down. When he did, it was something like Ruth striking out— with a magnificent flourish, stark drama.

Before World War II, during the Open at Canterbury, Cleveland, I gathered such golfers as Ben Hogan, Sam Snead, Byron Nelson, Jimmy Demaret and others for a dinner. I wanted Hagen—matter of fact, he was the star attraction. I asked Freddie Corcoran, the energetic manager of the PGA's circuit swing, to pick Walter up at a nearby club. The anecdote is Freddie's.

"I arrived and spotted Hagen in the bar," relates Corcoran. "Walter was wearing a handsome white sharkskin suit, silk shirt, purple tie and the inevitable carnation in his buttonhole. He was immaculate. As we were leaving, Hagen decided we had to have 'one for the road.' While we waited for our drink, some old grad spotted Walter and commenced to make a fuss over him. He had a tall rum drink with fruit in it. In his enthusiasm, he jostled Walter, spilling the drink and fruit salad all over him. Hagen never batted an eye. Instead he called to the bartender, 'See here, this fellow needs a drink! Mix him another, will you?' "

Through the years, Hagen has had a lot of drinks with a lot of people. He always seemed to have a drink in his hand. But few people ever saw Hagen when he had more than he could carry. Another thing—Hagen could play with a highball. He always accepted a fresh drink when the round was repeated.

But next day you could spot the majority of Walter's drinks—hardly dented—behind a nearby bookcase or rubber plant.

Freddie Corcoran also tells what is probably the most revealing anecdote about Hagen.

"I recall my first year with the PGA tournament grind, in 1936," says Corcoran. "It was in Los Angeles, and I was half crazy trying to iron out all the last-minute details. Everything was balled up. I was walking down the first fairway when Hagen joined me. He knew I was worried.

" 'Freddie,' he said, 'relax. Don't worry—don't hurry. You're here on a short visit. Be sure to smell the flowers!' "

That's the Hagen philosophy, and I'll give him credit. He's lived it now for more than 60 years. Walter Hagen—a great competitor, a colorful golfer—a great fellow.

CHAPTER SEVEN

Bobby Jones
the Incomparable Youth

One lovely spring day in 1915, I stood with Alex Smith and Long Jim Barnes, both Open champions, watching a 13-year-old kid playing his approach, a mashie shot, to some green now lost to a long-ago past. The youngster hit a good, crisp shot to within ten yards of the cup. Immediately he threw his club in disgust.

Barnes' eyes opened. "Who is that boy?" he asked.

"His name is Jones . . . Bob Jones," I replied. "I've known him since he was a three-year-old. He's the son of a good friend of mine . . . Bob Jones, Senior . . . a fine lawyer here in Atlanta . . . I played baseball against him while he was at Mercer and I was at Vanderbilt."

"It's a shame," Alex said, "but he'll never make a golfer . . . too much temper. Why, that was a fine shot for anybody."

"I disagree," replied Barnes, "this kid will be one of the world's greatest in a few more years. Look at him—broad-shouldered with big, strong hands."

"I've got to agree with you, Jim," I said. "At thirteen he's already playing in the low seventies. He isn't satisfied with just a good shot. He wants it to be perfect—stone dead. He has a great ambition to play every shot in the bag right.

"But you're correct about that temper, Alex," I continued. "He's a fighting cock . . . a hot head. That one fault could prove his biggest hazard. If he can't learn to control it he'll never play the kind of golf he'll be capable of shooting."

From 1917 to 1923, seven long years, Bob Jones went to war with his temperament . . . his eagerness to be perfect. He won that war but only after seven years of bitter disappointment during which time he kept losing to opponents to whom he could spot several shots. Jones was 21 years old before he had himself conquered and could apply full concentration to the act of hitting a golf ball correctly.

I followed Bob, usually with his father. Those were the wilderness years—from 1916 through 1922. But when Jones finally found the rainbow—and the pot of gold at the end of it—by winning the Open in '23, he was on his way! From '23 through '30, "the fat years" as my departed pal O. B. Keeler called them, Jones won 13 national titles, four U.S. Open titles, five U.S. Amateur crowns, three British Open titles and one British Amateur title. This last was in 1930 when he stormed golf's bastions to sweep the Big Four—and then called it quits with major championship golf—perhaps the toughest test of mental and physical stamina in sports.

As you may know, there are three types of golf—golf, tournament golf and major championship golf. And the psychological hazards, pits and deadfalls in the last category are terrific—as cruel as they are unrelenting.

The record will always treat Walter Hagen with deference, as it will Ben Hogan. Sir Walter, over a longer competitive stretch than Jones, won two Opens, four British Opens and five

PGA titles—another incredible mark. And Bantam Ben, after a late start, has been coming fast.

But there was this difference about Jones. He was a young amateur, who graduated from Georgia Tech and Harvard and later entered the law business with his father. Unlike the tournament-tough golfers of today, Jones—from '23 through '30—played in only three or four tournaments each year.

In all that time, Jones had but one sour tournament. That was in 1927, in the Open, when the deep furrowed traps and the skimmed, slippery greens of the Oakmont course at Pittsburgh got Bob down. No one broke 300; Jones finished 11th. That year Oakmont had been lengthened to 6,915 yards, a man beater for distance, and had been so devilishly trapped that you couldn't see the greens for the bunkers. After holing a long putt for an eagle 3 on the first, Jones played the next two conventionally in par 4. Came the fourth hole, a par 5, and I saw the shot that killed off Jones.

This hole measured 550-yards. Bob hit his longest drive of the day, then played his second shot, a fine Number 1 iron, through a narrow opening to the trap-guarded green. The ball almost hit the green but caught the bunker on the near side and snuggled in an ankle-deep furrow, an all but unplayable lie. Jones studied the half-hidden ball. This was before the advent of the sand wedge. Four niblick explosions and 30 muttered oaths later, Bob finally blasted the ball onto the green and sank a good putt for a 7. After that he kept trying to steer the ball away from those deadly Oakmont traps . . . traps trumped up to eat pars and even bogies.

But back to Jones, the youngster, for a moment.

When Bobby was five he started swinging a golf club. His family lived just off the 13th fairway at Atlanta's East Lake course. The boy would amuse himself watching foursomes play by, then scuff about with an old ball and a cut-down club. At the age of seven, he was swinging a midiron with better form than the average club champ.

Who started him? Himself. But the fellow he often pestered was the club professional, Stewart Maiden. Bobby would watch Maiden impart his wisdom to a pupil, then go off to one side and practice. The boy had a large head on a smallish body and the head served as a perfect anchor for those shots that later would flow so flawlessly from his clubhead. As a result, by the time the kid was 12, he had hung up a 70 at East Lake. He had grown from a rather sickly-looking kid into a chunky, broad-shouldered youth with thick, powerful wrists and big, strong hands. At 12 he could drive 240 or 250 yards.

When Jones arrived at Philadelphia's Merion Golf Club for his first crack at the Amateur title in 1916, he was 14½ years old. I was then 36 and writing my column for the New York *Tribune* syndicate, having left the New York *Mail* in 1913 at the invitation of Mr. Ogden Reid's offer of 280 dollars a week.

I needed no crystal ball to perceive that young Bob Jones was to become an immediate hit with the galleries—the ladies particularly—with his dark blue beret, his big blue eyes and his winning smile. But there was nothing wistful, in the old Jackie Coogan tradition, about the kid. He was only 5 feet 4 inches tall but weighed a solid 165. Hounded by a devilish temper, the youngster was an adept club thrower. Bob and I had breakfast together the morning of his first match round. Having qualified the previous day with a miserable 90, he was to meet Eben Byers, a very sound golfer and a former Amateur champion in 1906—ten years earlier. Byers, also hot tempered, wasn't averse to wrapping his own hickory shafts around the neck of the nearest tree.

I mentioned this fact to Bob, who said little but kept eating. Impetuous as he was impatient, Jones was champing when the veteran Byers arrived considerably late. On that first tee, not

20 yards from the swarming clubhouse porch, Jones was boiling but keeping his mouth shut.

I recall one hole, particularly, in the battle of tempers that followed. It must have been the fifth. Byers was straight down the middle. Jones hooked way off the fairway into deep rough. After a short delay, Byers hit his second shot and started walking ahead.

Jones, deep in the morass, called out, "Fore, Mr. Byers!"

"I'm sorry," Byers responded. "I thought you had picked up."

"Picked up, hell!" fired Jones. "You just watch this one."

The recovery shot stopped about four feet from the cup for a birdie 3. That was a large measure of satisfaction for the hot-blooded Georgia kid. He won 3 and 1, because as Jones put it later, "Byers ran out of clubs first."

That evening after finishing my overnight—those Georgia papers were thirsty for Jones copy—I had my own qualms about Bob's going very far. He had all the shots, but his temper was on the verge of throwing him. Next day, however, a self-controlled, strong-willed Jones went out and defeated Frank Dyer 4 and 2 and it was this round that earned him the first of the tremendous galleries that were to become a Jones trademark. In the third round, it was Jones against the defending champion, Bob Gardner. It was a tremendous round—Gardner finally winning on the 31st green! The only way Gardner was going to beat Jones that day was with a horsewhip. Certainly, it took every shot in Gardner's extensive bag to stop Jones who, though wild with many of his long shots, made a series of miraculous recoveries that had the gallery goggle-eyed. That Amateur went to another great fighter, slim Chick Evans, who in 1916 also won the Open. From that round right through Bob's final round at Merion in 1930 when he won the Amateur to complete The Big Four—U.S. Open and Amateur plus British Open and

Amateur—the tourney marshalls had to call out the guards to keep the thundering herd at bay.

It was in 1917 that young Bob and his Atlanta pal Perry Adair were sent north to play several War Relief charity matches in and around New York City—all under the aegis of the USGA. Bob's dad wrote ahead asking me to sort of keep an eye on the youngsters. Kit, of course, insisted they stay at our apartment at 450 Riverside Drive. Those were interesting evenings. While Floncy scampered about and Kit burst her buttons to entertain Bob and Perry, I'd bang away at the typewriter getting out my column. Our living room reminded me of a set from *You Can't Take It With You.* We enjoyed having two partly grown-up "sons" about the place. How Kit, Floncy and I relished their stay. One evening I took the entire brood to Coney Island— a great trip. We didn't miss a ride! It was during their stay that Bob and I became acquainted in a way few persons with a gap of 20-odd years between them ever do.

The clincher, I think, the final damper on Jones' temper, occurred four years later in the British Open in '21. Bob was stopping with Lord Northcliffe. Playing spotty golf, he took 46 shots to reach the turn in the third round. He unravelled a 6 on the tenth and on the short eleventh needed his putt for a 6. He picked up his ball—equivalent to throwing in the towel. Northcliffe's paper, the *Daily Mail,* blasted him—and rightly.

All of Bob's friends—his dad, O. B. Keeler, his ever-faithful Boswell, and myself among others—had admonished Bob concerning his temper. But it took the British Open to expose it to Jones in a manner he never forgot. He had committed the unpardonable, and the thought of it rankled him throughout the next nine years—years, incidentally, when the Bobby Jones deportment remained at a magnificent standard.

The boy had become a man—at 19.

If temper had been Bob's major flaw, a minor one concerned diet. His appetite between morning and afternoon rounds was voracious. A fighter, football player, even a baseball star—with the eternal exception of Babe Ruth—goes light on the chow going into battle. I'd remarked as much to Bob. Nevertheless, he continued to cover the noon menu pretty well —including the pie a la mode. During those on-trial years leading into the Open in 1923 at the Inwood course on Long Island, he was being beaten off in the final rounds more often than not. And Jones was becoming a touch fatalistic about these defeats.

"Fate, hell!" I replied when he mentioned the subject following his thumping at the terrifically hot hands of Jess Sweetser in the 1922 Amateur at Brookline, Massachusetts. "You eat like a ditch digger at noon and then wonder why you don't quite have that extra "feel" in the afternoon. Many a hearty lunch has cost thousands of golfers a good round later on . . . where even death was the result. Heart attack . . . bunk! The nerve center of the body and the digestive center are only an inch or so apart. They can't both work well at the same time."

However, I think it was Bob's closest confidant, O. B. Keeler, who convinced Jones that a drastic switch in his noon meal might mean more than a hot putter. From 1923—the year he won the Open for his first major title—until the end, eight years later, Jones stuck to a lunch of crackers and milk. During that span, in which time he picked up 13 major titles, it was strictly a case of Jones against the field.

Looking back on the Bob Jones story there were, in my opinion, two critical shots in Bob's career. The first came at Inwood (Long Island) in the 1923 Open. The big ones had been escaping him—somehow—and when I saw him in New York on his way out to Inwood for a few practice rounds he was in an, "I'll give it one more try" frame of mind. Tournament golf hadn't been kind to Jones, and the 18 or more pounds he dropped

That's me, 3rd from left in front row, at Spout Springs Country School, 18th District, Nashville, Tenn., about 1888. I must have been in the 3rd or 4th grade.

The Rice family in 1896. L to R: Bolling, Dad, me, Mother and John. Dad died in '17, Mother in '42—at 80—Bolling in '52 and John in '53.

Football heroes at Wallace Prep in Nashville, about 1896. I'm 2nd from left in back row. I was never a great player. I loved the game but was too light.

Seven years after graduation from Vanderbilt I found time to coach the Black & Gold '08 Team. We weren't "tops" but we could make the double play.

Here's Cobb at 16 when he was playing semi-pro ball.

Floncy, a champion in her own right.

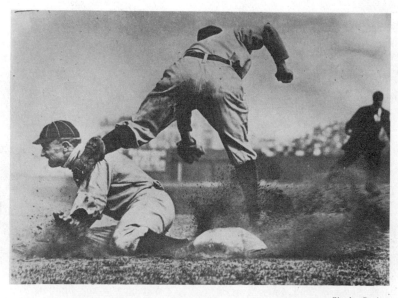

Charles Conlon

Shot by Charles Conlon with an early Graflex, this hook slide by Cobb stealing 3rd base, caught TY at his finest. Note his spiked shoe far wide of base.

Baseball scribes in 1912 at Polo Grounds. Seated, L to R, are Sam Crane, Fred Lieb, Damon Runyon, Boze Bulger, Sid Mercer, me and Walter Trumbull. John Wheeler and John B. Foster behind with Harry Stevens, father of the hotdog and grandson, seated.

With Jess Sweetser and Jerry Travers (center), two all-time Amateur kings.

Watching a dog fight in France in '18 None of it was very pretty.

The Haig playing from where he liked it best—the deep rough, about 1925.

Scribes & Pharisees in 1915 at Yanks Training Camp, Savannah. (L to R) Rice, Ed Curley, "Bunk" MacBeth, Bill Slocum, Fred Van Ness, Harry Schumacher and Fred Lieb. I can't recall the fellow in the derby.

With Bobby Jones at Amateur Championship at Merion, Pa., when he was about 15. Bob had begun fighting two things--a voracious appetite and a hot temper.

With Bernard Darwin of the London *Times,* in 1919. Darwin, tremendously gifted, wrote the most exciting golf I ever read with George (N. Y. Sun) Trevor a close 2nd.

Harris & Ewing

Two champs, Benny Leonard and Exterminator and his owner, Willis Sharpe
Kilmer at Binghamton, N. Y., 1930.

At the White House in '21 with my pal Ring
(Short Pants) Lardner, Pres. Harding and Sec.
of State, Fletcher.

Bob Jones and Bud Kelland watching National Open at Baltusrol (N. J.) in 1936.

Alex J. Morrison

With Hal Sims and Jack Wheeler, during a match at Lakeside, in California about 1940. Our 4th must have really belted one!

HOLE	YDS.	PAR	Where Strokes are Taken / Strks.	Watso	Rice	Martin	Cushman	HOLE	YDS.	PAR	Where Strokes are Taken / Strks.	S. Alon	Rice	Martin	Cushman
1	503	5	2	5	4	6	4	10	181	3	18	3	3	4	5
2	235	4	14	3	3	5	3	11	375	4	3	6	4	6	5
3	167	3	17	4	4	2	4	12	299	4	9	4	3	4	4
4	326	4	10	5	3	5	7	13	312	4	11	5	4	5	5
5	328	4	16	5	4	5	6	14	385	4	13	5	5	6	6
6	205	3	8	5	5	3	4	15	461	5	7	5	4	6	7
7	380	4	6	6	4	5	6	16	446	5	5	5	5	6	5
8	365	4	12	5	4	6	6	17	488	5	1	6	6	5	7
9	387	4	4	7	4	5	6	18	208	3	15	6	4	4	4
	2896	35		42	35	42	46	Total Out	3155	37		45	37	46	48
									2896	35		42	35	42	46
									6051 Handicap	72		87	72	88	94

An old score card I dug up, dated 1915, for a Newspaper tourney at Scarsdale, N. Y. I managed a 72, good enough to take the marbles.

At Shelby before Dempsey-Gibbons fight, a group help Bide Dudley figure expense account. Broun, far left, was nattier here than I ever saw him.

Dempsey stalked Gibbons for 15 rounds at Shelby but could never quite tag the elusive, jabbing vet.

With Tex Rickard at Hot Springs in '27, As a golfer, Tex remained a top promoter.

International News Photo

The Babe as I knew him in '19. Terrific south-paw pitcher, he was blossoming into the game's greatest slugger, getting his great frame into his swing with a rhythm wonderful to behold. Red Sox manager Ed Barrow switched Ruth to the outfield, when he wasn't pitching. He was in 130 games, hit .322, pitched 8 victories and hit 29 homers, an un-heard of mark at the time.

Jake Ruppert gloried in Ruth while Judg Landis had, on occasion, to check him.

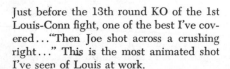

Just before the 13th round KO of the 1st Louis-Conn fight, one of the best I've cov-ered..."Then Joe shot across a crushing right..." This is the most animated shot I've seen of Louis at work.

I don't know what's going on here! Anyhow the principals are Mrs. Morgan Belmont, Dempsey and Harold McGraw.

With Tunney at Miami Beach in January '28. Six months later Gene defended his title by knocking out Tom Heeney and retired.

A favorite shot of one of my favorite people, Helen Wills, when she really had it in the early 1930's. Helen wasn't particularly quick but was sure graceful.

Tommy Hitchcock, polo's all-time greatest, taken in 1939 at Meadow Brook, in his 19th season, his 17th as a 10-goaler. Tommy died in a P-51 crash in '42.

Jim Thorpe, No. 1 American as he looked at Stockholm in the 1912 Olympics.

...and as he looked 32 years later, in '44 wi his grandson. Jim was our greatest "natura

Acme

At Artists & Writers tournament at Palm Beach in '29, with Rickard, Lardner, Tunney and Rube. A few days later Tex died of a burst appendix.

"The Babe's" first game of golf following '32 Olympics at Los Angeles—with me, Gallico, Pegler and Braven Dyer...as strange a 5-some as ever cluttered a course.

At the Louis-Pastor fight, Sept. 1939 at Detroit. I'm the one with the bad cold. GM president Bill Knudson, Bud Kelland and an unidentified character wait for "the main." Joe KO'd Pastor in the 11th.

during a big tournament with little but stark disappointment at
the end of 72 holes had him edgy. There was something in the
world besides Amateur pay-as-you-go golf. At 21 he was beginning to think of law and the practice with his dad's firm.

"You never looked better," I lied.

That '23 Open field was a roaring good one. But at the close
of 72 holes, two Bobbies—Jones and Cruickshank—were tied.
Cruickshank, the wee Scot with the thoroughbred's heart, had
come through the thickest fighting and the meanest prisoner-of-
war incarceration in World War I where he served with valor
as a member of the famed Black Watch. Among other tests, he'd
seen his brother blown to bits right beside him in France.

When Jones and Cruickshank teed off in the 18-hole medal
play-off, Cruickshank was a 10–7 favorite. Jones had "blown it"
on the last hole the preceeding day when, needing a sloppy 5 to
win on a par 4, he blew a horrible 6. Bob didn't sleep that night.
The next morning both men marched off that first tee determined to win on their own shots . . . not the other fellow's
errors. That's the way it was played. Attack . . . attack . . .
with but three of the 18 holes halved. On the 18th tee the match
was even.

It was Cruickshank's honor. Hitting into a headwind, Bobby
tried to keep the ball quail-high, below the breeze. He hit a
half-topped drive that hooked into the rough. Jones' drive was
long and hugged the right side, finally landing in a soft spot
at the edge of the rough. Cruickshank then played the only
possible shot—a recovery short of the lagoon guarding the
green.

What to do? Should Jones play it safe from his own poor
lie and shoot to tie the hole—and bank on wearing down his
little adversary in extra holes—or would he give it the big
gamble, going all-out to win or lose the title on the strength
of one attacking shot? Bob studied the ball a moment before

grabbing his midiron, a treacherous club even on a good lie. The club flashed back and down; the clubhead tore into the ball. It drilled straight into the swarming storm clouds, a speck of white arrowing over the lagoon and drilling onto the green 190 yards away . . . then up . . . up to within five feet of the cup. That settled it! Bob Jones, Open champion, was on his way.

The other vital shot—a putt—occurred six years later in the 1929 Open at Winged Foot Club at Mamaroneck, New York. Jones was leading Al Espinosa by four strokes with four holes to go. Then Bob blew, sprinkling 7's around like Rockefeller with a pocket full of dimes. At the 72nd hole he needed a 4 for a tie. Jittery, he left himself a mean 12-foot side-hill putt. With the angel of doom looking over his shoulder, Bob took his Calamity Jane putter, finally stroked the ball . . . and made it! Next day in the 36-hole medal play-off with Espinosa, Jones won by 23 strokes.

"If I'd missed that putt and had lost a tournament already won," commented Jones, "I hate to think of what might have happened to my confidence. And without confidence a golfer is little more than a hacker."

Gene Sarazen, as tough as they come under pressure, still regards Jones' winning of the '29 Open as one of "those miracles."

"You cannot take a seven and win—anytime—during seventy-two holes of title play," Gene declared. Jones took four 7's in that Open and still won it. He could piddle away strokes when he was leading. So did Hagen. But the ability to come through under pressure, when the blue chips are down, is the sternest trademark of The Champion.

A perfect example of Jones dogging it as a front runner occurred in the spring of 1930, his last competitive year. That was the year Bob enjoyed the greatest success any golfer— including Hogan—has known. Bob was then just 28 years old and was getting ready to quit the tournament grind . . . a grind that was wearing him out mentally and physically. It was at the Southeastern Open at Augusta. I was following him along with Ty Cobb. It was the last round and Jones, having scores of 72, 72, 69, was leading the field in a relaxed lope.

As Jones reached the 16th tee his nearest foe, Horton Smith, had just finished. The grapevine came back that Bob was 18 strokes in front . . . with Hagen, Sarazen and the other limelighters of the day finishing nowhere.

Bob lay down for a few minutes to take a rest. Looking at him, Cobb was indignant.

"But Ty, with pars from here on in I'm eighteen strokes ahead," said Jones.

"Then win by eighteen strokes!" snapped Cobb.

Jones finished carelessly with five strokes over par for the three holes—for a 71. He still finished 13 shots ahead of runner-up Smith, an all-time margin for big tournament. Cobb was disgusted.

One of Bob's strongest connections was Stewart Maiden, his old teacher who had watched him from babyhood. Maiden, a silent, dour Scot, never wasted two words when one would suffice. Whenever trouble dogged him in later years Jones returned to Maiden. Jones described the following as perhaps his finest lesson.

"I had been wild on all my long shots," he told me one day in 1927, the year he won the third of five U.S. Amateur crowns. "Everything—driver, brassie, spoon. I went after Stewart.

" 'Hit a few,' he said.

"I did. They were wild. He waited until I'd finished; then he got up, but as he was leaving he turned and said, 'Hit the hell out of 'em!'

"Maiden had seen it all. I had been steering the ball, afraid to swing too hard. I hit the next ball as hard as I could and it was as straight as a string—dead on the target. I had no more trouble after that."

The year 1930 was a memorable one for Jones; he won the Grand Slam—or as the late George Trevor wrote, he "—stormed the impregnable quadrilateral of golf." I'll give odds, here and now, that it will never happen again.

The day before that 1930 Amateur at Merion, I played a round with Bob. He was in fine mental form. Walking down the seventh or eighth fairway, Bob became expansive.

"Granny," he said, "I've suffered at this game a lot of years. Among other things, I've discovered a man must play golf by "feel" . . . the hardest thing in the world to describe—but the easiest thing in the world to sense—when you have it completely. . . . Today I have it completely. I don't have to think of anything . . . just meet the ball. But during championships, I've had to rivet one, two and sometimes three check points in my mind, usually on each shot. Hell, there are a hundred check points if you want to be technical, but I find I can hold onto no more than three at the most and still meet the ball!"

"And what are your three checks, Bob?" I asked.

"Dragging . . . rather than lifting that clubhead back, bringing my left hip into action at the start of my downswing, and keeping my left arm close to my body—from inside out—for the completion of the shot. Today everything's falling into one piece—perfect. But it seldom happens—at least with me—and very seldom in title play."

Bob Jones' swing was in one piece at Merion during that Amateur. He wrapped up Gene Homans in the final, 8 and 7, for his fourth and final conquest of the Big Four.

When Jones returned to golf as host for the Masters Tournament at Augusta in 1934, his concentration and determination, his old keenness were no longer with him. He could still go out and murder par on occasion, in friendly play at so much a side.

But that shot or mental discipline, so paramount in championship play, had fled.

After Bob quit the title trail, our close friendship rekindled with, at times, a distressing vengeance. During Bob's competitive years, O. B. Keeler practically lived with him—in fact, dedicated his journalistic life to Jones. But with title shooting behind, O. B. began hitting the circuit with the wonderful "Ma," O. B.'s ever-loving.

When he could get away from his law practice for a few days, Jones still enjoyed travelling. During the early and mid-1930's, we made more calls than two sailors, often with authors Bud Kelland, "Socker" Coe, Frank McClain and our wonderful actor pal, Frank Craven.

It was during the summer of '33, the year the Amateur was played at Cincinnati, with George Dunlop beating Max Marston for the title. Anyhow, Bob and I landed there straight from covering a fight in Chicago. We were both tired when we were given the absent Odd McIntyre's suite at the old Hotel Sinton.

"Let's have a quiet dinner up here and then hit the hay," I said.

"Granny," said Bob, "that suits me!"

After filing my story, we were about to order dinner when we decided to ask Pop and Mom Keeler to drop in for a cocktail. Paul Gallico, covering for the New York *News*, stopped by as did one or two others. When we finally sat down to dinner— along about 10:30—there were at least 15 of us.

Suddenly realizing we hadn't asked Dan Horgan, our host, up for a snort, I called and Dan arrived. Because it was getting towards that hour, Dan called the Supper Room and got the orchestra up, including the loudest trap drummer in the business.

Well, the quiet meal for two had, through the process of osmosis, or spontaneous combustion, developed into a house party. When guests began calling, complaining they couldn't sleep, Dan invited them over. The entire guest list, it seemed, accepted. It was dawn when we swept out the last remains. Somehow that type of thing wasn't unusual whenever Bob and I combined forces.

In 1936, when I covered the Olympic Games at Berlin, Bob and Mary Jones joined Kit and me aboard the *Europa*. We wanted to revisit England and Scotland before the Games. Bob and I were looking for something different in London hotels and a Philadelphia friend told me of a little hideaway on Half-moon Street, near Buckingham Palace, that was a dream. "Real English with none of the American glitter." Somehow, at the boat train, the Joneses and Rices became separated, and by the time they arrived at the hotel in a hack, my bride was out on the sidewalk sitting on her trunk. She informed Bob what my friend could do with his "real English" hotel. I calmed her, after a fashion, but two days later we were at the Claridge.

I'll never forget the expressions of both Kit and Mary on the boat over when each showed on deck in similar tailored suits— both gray. But it was just a patch on Bob's and my expressions six days later. I agree with that *South Pacific* song—"There Is Nothing Like a Dame." But spare me, forever more, from dames in gray suits.

I knew Bob was popular, sure, but I had no idea his name had spread so far. It had been six years since his retirement. He hadn't been in Europe since 1930.

At Glen Eagles, Bob had a hankering to play St. Andrews, the scene of two of his great British victories—the '27 Open and '30 Amateur. He phoned over and said he would be on hand the next morning, asking the St. Andrews pro not to tell anyone he was coming. That pro swears on a stack of Scottish Bibles that he told no one. But when Bob stepped on the first tee at 9 o'clock the next morning, at least 5,000 were present. They came swarming in like locusts. By the time he reached the 18th green, up by the ancient clubhouse, at least 10,000 spectators were on hand. One bewhiskered, venerable old Scot, smoking a large pipe, said to Mrs. Jones—not knowing who she was—"Isn't it graund . . . isn't it graund . . . Bobby's back." Tears were coursing their way through his beard.

Bob had a 3 for a 31 going out. On the short ninth he took a Number 7 iron with the wind but his old caddie insisted on a 5. The shot carried over the green into a matted gorse and Bob took a 6. Even with this blow he finished in 70.

Later, after watching the Games at Berlin for several weeks, Bob, Mary, and Kit went on. Wherever they stopped, Munich, Vienna and Budapest—where Bob played a round or two—it was the same. Flowers for the ladies and receptions and dinners. According to Kit, you'd have thought a king was making the tour.

It was at the Augusta National in '41. I watched Bob come up the 18th fairway towards the green—out of contention of course but still the smiling gallant competitor and host. Then I thought about Bobby and Cobb, Georgia's great gifts to the roll call of Champions. Returning to the Press Tent, I pecked out the following verse:

Augusta National, Augusta, Ga., April 3

Echoes of the Red Clay Hills
(A Personal Reminiscence)

The low, lost winds come whispering, over the red clay hills.
They sing to me through Georgia pines the song of remembered
thrills.
They bring back ghosts from a vanished year—phantoms beyond
all reach.
When Bobby Jones was the king of golf—and Ty was the Georgia
Peach.

Still pink and white down April lanes, the dogwood calls me home.
And the peach blooms beckon around the world, no matter where I
may roam.

The blue wistaria gleams once more, but still I turn to the day
When Emperor Jones gave the world his dust—and Cobb took the
   right-of-way.

Spring is back in the red clay hills where the sun of the south still
   shines.
And I follow the ghosts of youth again through the trail of the lonesome pines.
Where I turn the hands of the old clock back to the glint of the
   great twin star,
When Ty was king of the hoof-spiked pack and Bob was the czar of
   par.

Lean, bronzed and skilled, I watch them form—the winners from
   coast to coast—
Stars of the game who have murdered par—stars who have earned
   their boast—
But winds through the pines come whispering back through many
   a Georgia glen—
"How'd you like to see Bobby and Ty, back at their peak again?"

Well, it's now ten or more years later and the Bob Jones of
today, physically speaking, is a far cry from the Jones of 20 years
ago. A spinal ailment has all but riveted him to a wheel chair.
But the mental—the really important—side of this great and
gracious gentleman shines through with nary a flaw. In this
respect he calls to mind another thoroughbred, the late and
great Lou Gehrig, the Iron Horse, whose dynamic body was
short-circuited and snuffed out by another and even more tragic
spinal disease.

For nearly 50 years "young Bob Jones" has afforded me
a host of worthwhile copy . . . more important, a glorious
warmth of companionship.

May we both continue to travel the same path . . . from
here to eternity.

CHAPTER EIGHT

War Clouds

When the United States declared war on Germany in April 1917, I was 37 and had been banging away for the Tribune Syndicate for four years. Quite a string of papers were using The Sportlight column, and my pay amounted to 300 dollars a week. In December of that year, I handed over all my securities, totalling about 75,000 dollars, to a lawyer friend for safe keeping. (If I didn't come back, at least there remained a tidy chunk for my two girls.) Then I enlisted as a private in the Infantry.

On December 5, 1917, a bitter cold day, I pulled out of New York, headed for the balmy old South. It was five above and snowing when our train chugged into Greenville, South Carolina. We were marched to Camp Sevier and issued gear—a pup tent and miscellaneous paraphernalia. My tent had a rent in it as big as a frying pan. The next morning when I awoke I found myself up to my ears in snow and mud. The cold I got that first night in the sunny South lasted until the Armistice.

Why I chose the Infantry I'm not sure, except that Kipling

had made it all sound romantic and tough. But we didn't remain
a foot-soldier regiment long. In a short time we were changed
over and rechristened the 115th Field Artillery. (In a neighbor-
ing field, with the 114th, was a redhead named Larry Mac-
Phail.)

Our Commanding Officer was Brigadier General Gus
Gatley, known throughout the service as "Good God Gus." One
of the roughest-talking generals since the days of the Continental
Army, Gatley later headed the artillery section of the famous
Rainbow Division in France.

The majority of our outfit consisted of Southern farm boys.
The fact that I was older than most and knew my left foot from
my right probably had a lot to do with my becoming a Sergeant
drill instructor, and then a candidate for officer training. During
the two months of study in preparation for the written exam required for commission, I was fortunate in getting to know Colonel John Geary, a big Irishman with a desert-rat mustache.
Geary had come up through the ranks. He had a sharp sense of
humor and he understood the enlisted man far better than most
officers.

The officers' training course was loaded with mathematics.
Do you know how to compute the weight of a liter of air? I
didn't then, and I still don't.

"Colonel," I said one day, "I haven't opened a math book
for more than fifteen years. I'm not up to this foolishness."

"No, Rice, you're not—but you will be," grinned the Colonel. Geary helped me to qualify for my commission—in fact,
without him I never would have made it. He had been the
athletic officer at the Presidio in California, and after I was
pinned a second lieutenant he put me to work.

One morning Geary called for me.

"Lieutenant," he said, "I've got two jobs for you."

"Colonel," I replied, "I am already mess officer, telephone

sentry, athletic officer and liaison officer of this outfit. I need more sleep, not more jobs."

"In this Army," replied Geary, "it's not *how many* jobs you have—it's *what* jobs!

"We need a VD officer," he continued. "Also, that patch of trees over there must be cleared for a baseball field—for a game two weeks from today. It's got to be ready. Gatley ordered it."

Colonel Geary's "patch" was a solid green forest.

"Colonel," I said, "I would make the worst VD officer imaginable. But I will have the baseball field ready, provided I get the necessary help."

"Commandeer whatever you need," he said.

The next morning I had 280 men working that forest with picks, axes, saws and dynamite. The noise of hundreds of stumps being blown to kingdom come was vibrant. In the midst of the flying debris, General Gatley appeared.

"You've got every goddam man in the regiment!" he roared. "Who gave you the authority?"

"Colonel Geary, Sir," I replied.

We played that ball game two weeks later against the 114th.

One morning the entire company was in the field working on a problem involving sighting in cannon for range, deflection and the rest. My enlisted man and I were in a cluster of turpentine pines. It was hot. Our "four-inch howitzer" was a sawed-off pine log. The problem was valid to almost everyone but me. Stripped to the waist, my NCO was hard at work when Colonel Geary appeared.

"Son," he asked, "when does the parade go by?"

"Sir?" said my man. "What parade?"

"There's *always* a parade," smiled Geary. "Get the shirt on. If it's right, get it all on."

Moments later, Gatley arrived on the range. Striding up to my battery, he surveyed the picture.

"Lieutenant," he said, "what command are you about to give?"

"Point blank, fire," I replied.

"Why?" he asked.

"Sir, at point-blank range I can't miss the target."

Pleased, Gatley told me as much. "What about the problem?" he then asked. "Do you know what you're doing?"

"Sir," I answered, "I haven't the slightest idea."

"Just as I thought," observed Gatley. "Well, I've got something more important for you to do. The morale of this outfit needs a boost. I want you to write me a song—something the men can sing."

I never got around to writing that song.

❈   ❈   ❈

Gatley was a Spartan leader. Some of the old-timers in that outfit who had served with him in the Philippines told a yarn that charcterized this rugged soldier. Gatley's mountain artillery was scaling a high Philippine mountain ridge, bringing up disassembled guns by mule. The animals were threading their way high on the mountain pass when one mule, with more curiosity than sense, stopped, stretched his neck over the side and promptly fell into the ravine 1000 feet below—gun and all. Charging up, Gatley looked over the side, then roared, "It serves you right, you inquisitive S.O.B.!"

One day, walking down the company street, I saw a young recruit sitting in the gutter. One look told me he came from the Tennessee mountains. With his eyes swollen with tears, he was the most homesick pup I ever saw. Looking up at me with a vacant expression, he drawled, "Is this France?" He'd never been more than ten miles from home before.

In April 1918 our outfit sailed from Hoboken, New Jersey, aboard the old *George Washington*. Weeks later we arrived at Brest. I started for the front with my bunch but didn't get very far before an order came through reassigning me to Paris and *The Stars and Stripes*. Alec Woollcott, Will Irvin, F. P. Adams, Harold Ross and others were putting out a daily paper for our soldiers. I shied at the assignment, but it wasn't until four months later that I managed to get orders cut reassigning me to the 115th, then up near the Belgian border at Souilly.

After I came home, Kit showed me a letter written to her by Irvin on the day I left Paris for the front:

"Dear Kit: I saw Granny off to war today. I never saw such a 'departure for the front.' He marched out of here with the biggest back pack I've seen on a mortal, let alone a mule. He was packing enough equipment to quartermaster half the boys at the front."

I was pretty loaded down at that—blankets, fry pan, burner, extra shoes, rifle, that infernal gas mask, socks, shelter half, ammunition—I shed stuff like a moulting turkey sheds its feathers, until, by the time I'd relocated the old 115th, I was wearing one raincoat—period.

As a soldier I was no great shucks. As an officer I didn't crowd MacArthur. However, I saw and experienced enough of the filth, suffering and horror of war to realize it never can account for anything that a slice of good Christian faith can't outstrip every time. I saw youngsters hurtling through the skies over France in small fighter planes, and I watched more than a few of them come down in flames. I saw kids and old men slugging through the mud to the front, and the heart inside me twisted as I watched those lines of the walking wounded threading their tortured way back again, leaving so many of their buddies dead where they had fallen.

To A Doughboy

I watched you slog down a dusty pike,
One of many, so much alike,
With a spirit keen as a breath of flame,
Ready to rise and ready to strike
Whenever the fitting moment came;
Just a kid with a boyish grin,
Waiting the order to hustle in
And lend your soul to the battle thrill,
Unafraid of the battle din
Or the guns that crashed from a hidden hill.

I watched you leap to the big advance,
With a smile for Fate and its fighting chance,
Sweeping on till the charge was done;
I saw your grave on a slope of France
Where you fell asleep when the fight was won:
Just a kid, who had earned his rest
With a rifle and helmet above his breast,
Who proved, in answer to German jeers,
That a kid can charge a machine-gun nest
Without the training of forty years.

I watched the shadows drifting by
As gray dusk came from a summer's sky
And lost winds came from beyond the fight,
And I seemed to hear them croon and sigh:
"Sleep, little dreamer, sleep tonight;
Sleep tonight, for I'm bringing you
A prayer and a dream from the home you knew;
And I'll take them word of the big advance,
And how you fought till the game was through
And you fell asleep in the dust of France."

I don't think many men come out of a war with their ideals
and idols exactly the same. In my case, I found war to be a quick
distillation of life's tribulations, all wrapped up in a red, raw
bundle. In war, however, the good in a fellow surfaces—or sinks

—much quicker than in civilian life. In many ways, the same applies to sport. Thinking on these things one night, I scratched out the following by candlelight.

The Battle Line

Wars may be on again, wars may be over,
So far as the guns are concerned,
But life is a fight—not a dream in the clover,
No matter what road you have turned.
Fate is a party who ducks from the fighter
That faces him squarely and grins,
But, oh, what a wallop he takes at the blighter
Who trembles when trouble begins!
For it's Trouble that toughens that fiber all through,
The best little trainer the world ever knew.

Perhaps we are through with the lung-burning gases,
On which I am betting no cent;
But even if shrapnel or bursting bomb passes,
There still is the bill for the rent;
There's poverty, bitterness, worry or sorrow
To lead a left hook for the glim,
And it may come today, or it may come tomorrow,
So you might just as well keep in trim.
And it's Trouble that strengthens the point of the jaw,
The best little trainer the world ever saw.

When the Armistice was finally flashed around the world on November 11, 1918, I was at Third Corps Headquarters at Souilly, on the northwest coast of France, near the Belgian border. Everybody, from buck private to brigadier, immediately got drunk—on anything and everything, from cognac to sterno.

I wound up at Angiers, France, with thousands of troops who, suddenly, had nothing to do except think and dream about home. One day we were slogging around on a drill field near an ammunition supply depot, cursing the mud and the boredom, when I heard a voice explode, "There's Grant Rice!"

I knew that voice. It belonged to Jack Wheeler, my press-box crony from the old New York *Herald*. Now an ammunition supply officer, Wheeler was standing with another newspaperman, Frank Knox, owner-editor of the Manchester (New Hampshire) *Union Leader*. A colonel at that time, this was the same Knox who later became Secretary of the Navy.

"What are you doing here?" asked Jack.

"I'm not flying an airplane," I replied. "I want to go home."

Somehow, along with Knox and Wheeler, I got orders cut to go home. We moved down to St. Nazaire, a port in the south of France, and there we sat on our haunches, waiting and hoping for those heaven-sent orders assigning us to a ship. Jack and I lived in barracks; Knox lived downtown. But we kept the contact flying, and lo and behold, our ship finally hove into port. She was the *Ryndam* of the Holland-America line. Knox was the ranking officer on that boat. (I realize the correct terminology is "ship," but "boat" she was to me.) We were Knox's adjutants, and as such were detailed to supervise deportment of troops. There were nurses on the *Ryndam*, and we had aviators, too. The fly boys were quick to take over. We had to issue—and back up—an order for all aviators to be in quarters (their own) by 9:00 P.M.—which didn't make us very popular. I also recall that the cook on that boat had been J. P. Morgan's chef on his private yacht, so we had no complaints about the food. Brandy, on Knox's orders, was verboten, but everybody aboard seemed to have his own supply, with the possible exception of Knox— who was seasick for most of that long, deadly ride.

I use the word "deadly" in its literal meaning. A flu epidemic broke out less than three days after we pulled anchor. It was a heart-rending sight, watching those men and boys dying like flies—knowing they were sinking but struggling that much harder to get home. Jack and I spent most of our time making out final papers on the listed dead—a list that grew daily.

For those who were fit, we tried to put on a show with soldiers in the roles of singers and dancers. It wasn't too successful; we seemed to have nothing but whistlers and screechers, the kind you hear at any ball park.

A thankful, subdued Lieutenant Rice landed with an equally subdued Lieutenant Wheeler at Newport News, Virginia, on a drizzly day in February 1919. We both bee-lined for New York. I had scarcely thrown down my gear when I learned that the lawyer with whom I had entrusted my securities in 1917 had just committed suicide by swallowing poison. Apparently he had reinvested the money I left with him and had lost the entire bankroll. Eighteen years after starting, I was back at scratch. I blame myself for that poor fellow's death; I shouldn't have put that much temptation in his way.

Wheeler and his bride, Elizabeth, and Kit, Floncy and I went up to Lake Placid for several weeks. There we succeeded pretty well in getting the misery and stench of war out of our systems—for a little while. For dreams have a habit of jerking you back into your past. My days were about to be caught up in the fantastic boom of business and sports, the Golden Twenties. But for years my dreams were of France and of those who made a crossing much bigger than those of us who had made the long voyage home to the U.S.A.

GHOSTS OF THE ARGONNE

You can hear them at night when the moon is hidden;
  They sound like the rustle of winter leaves,
Or lone lost winds that arise, unbidden,
  Or rain that drips from the forest eaves,
As they glide again from their silent crosses
  To meet and talk of their final fight,

Where over the group some stark tree tosses
  Its eerie shadow across the night.

If you'll take some night with its moonless weather,
  I know you will reason beyond a doubt
That the rain and the wind and the leaves together
  Are making the sounds you will hear about:
The wintry rustle of dead leaves falling,
  The whispering wind through the matted glen;
But I can swear it's a sergeant calling
  The ghostly roll of his squad again.

They talk of war and its crimson glory,
  And laugh at the trick which Fate has played;
And over and over they tell the story
  Of their final charge through the Argonne glade;
But gathering in by hill and hollow
  With their ghostly tramp on the rain-soaked loam,
There is one set rule which the clan must follow:
  They never speak of returning home.

They whisper still of the rifles' clatter,
  The riveting racket machine guns gave,
Until dawn comes and the clan must scatter
  As each one glides to his waiting grave;
But here at the end of their last endeavor
  However their stark dreams leap the foam
There is one set rule they will keep forever:
  "Death to the phantom who speaks of home!"

III

Dame Fortune Is a Cockeyed Wench

CHAPTER NINE

The Big Fellow, Babe Ruth

The first time I saw Babe Ruth was in April 1919. Ruth was taking his turn in batting practice at Tampa, Florida, the spring-training camp of the champion Boston Red Sox. Since covering my first World Series in 1905, I'd seen a lot of swingers. But never a swinger like this!

Babe blasted one pitch clear out of the park into a ploughed field. I gauged that trip as about 500 feet—not bad, even without a publicity man around to check the distance with a tape measure. While Ruth hit, I watched, and Ed Barrow, the Red Sox manager, talked.

"Ruth was our main holdout," said Barrow. "He's been signed to a three-year contract. At twenty-four, this fellow can become the greatest thing that's happened to baseball. He's a fine southpaw pitcher—he can become a great one. But the day I can use him in the outfield and take advantage of his bat every day—well, they'll have to build the parks bigger, just for Ruth."

After bombing about ten shots, Ruth circled the bases,

mincing along with short, pigeon-toed steps—a base-circling
trot destined to become as celebrated as Man O'War's gallop.
When Ruth came over to mop his face in a towel, Barrow introduced us.

"You sound like you got a cold," said Ruth.

"I have, sort of," I replied.

Taking an enormous red onion out of his hip pocket, Ruth
thrust it into my hand. "Here, gnaw on this," he said. "Raw
onions are cold-killers." While Ruth talked I gnawed, with tears
streaming from my eyes.

From the start, Ruth and I hit it off. Absolutely honest, the
Babe from first to last said exactly what he thought. The Chicago
White Sox, he felt, had a smart, hustling club, and Boston would
need the breaks to stick close.

"Babe," I said, "I was watching your swing. You swing like
no pitcher I ever saw."

"I may be a pitcher, but first off I'm a hitter," said Babe.
"I copied my swing after Joe Jackson's. His is the perfectest.
Joe aims his right shoulder square at the pitcher, with his feet
about twenty inches apart. But I close my stance to about eight
and a half inches or less. I find I pivot better with it closed. Once
committed . . . once my swing starts, though, I can't change it
or pull up. It's all or nothing at all."

Throughout a career that spanned 20 years, Ruth never
changed the basic fundamentals of that gorgeous, gargantuan
arc—a swing that captured the imagination of the crowd nearly
as much as the man behind it. To watch Ruth go down, swinging
from the heels, often sprawling from the sheer violence of his
cut, was almost as exciting as seeing him blast one out of the
park.

Of all the sluggers that the advent of the lively ball has
spawned, Babe was the only one I ever knew who never shortened or choked his grip when the count reached two strikes. He

gripped his bat with the knob of the handle "palmed" in his right hand. So perfect was his wrist snap—and the other reflexes that go into the perfectly timed swing—that he could wait on the pitch until the last split second and "pick" the ball practically out of the catcher's mitt. Ted Williams is about the only other long ball hitter I know who has this amazing faculty.

The Babe liked plenty of lumber in his war clubs. Many of his bludgeons weighed 42 ounces—about a half-pound more, than the average bat.

That spring the Red Sox and McGraw's Giants played a four-out-of-seven exhibition series at Tampa. In '18 the Giants had finished second, behind Chicago, and in '19 John J. felt he had a hustling club that was really going places. A Giant rookie that spring was Jim Thorpe, the big, amiable Carlisle Indian. McGraw said Thorpe couldn't hit a curve ball, but I still feel the main reason he got rid of Jim was that Thorpe was turning his team inside out—in friendly wrestling matches.

I hung around for several games to watch Ruth hit and play left field. The New York writers were pop-eyed; the Boston boys had already oiled up their best adjectives for him. In the first game he hit the longest ball I ever saw—some six miles over the right center-field fence and into the infield of an adjacent race track.

Bill McGeehan, of the New York *Tribune*, who didn't impress easily, wrote: *The ball sailed so high that when it came down it was coated with ice . . . a drive that would have rattled off the clubhouse roof at the Polo Grounds.*

My own notes includes this gem: *No less than 134 automobiles chugged through the gate and surrounded the playing field in a gleaming cordon. This gave Ruth a shining target to shoot at, but the Babe still prefers the old-fashioned fence— over which today's winning smash traveled like a runaway comet.*

That Giants series put the exclamation mark on Ruth, the home-run hitter, and practically wrote his finis as a pitcher. That was O.K. with Babe. Ruth, the outfielder, no longer would have to muscle his way in.

"It was sorta rough at that," he commented years later. "I came up as a southpaw pitcher—and pitchers aren't supposed to hit—or to clutter up the batter's box *trying* to hit during practice. I saw no reason why I shouldn't take my licks. I'd get them, usually, but there were times I'd go to my locker next day and find my bats sawed in half."

That '19 season was one week old when I opened my column with this verse:

Son of Swat—Babe Ruth

When you can lean upon the ball
And lay the seasoned ash against it,
The ball park is a trifle small,
No matter how far out they've fenced it.
Past master of the four-base clout,
You stand and take your wallop proudly—
A pretty handy bloke about,
I'll say you are . . . and say it loudly.

I've seen a few I thought could hit,
Who fed the crowd on four-base rations;
But you, Babe, are the Only It—
The rest are merely imitations.
I've seen them swing with all they've got
And tear into it for a mop-up;
But what they deem a lusty swat
To you is but a futile pop-up.

Somewhere amid another throng,
Where Fate at times became unruly,
I've heard Big Bertha sing her song
Without an encore from yours truly.
Yes, she had something—so to speak—

A range you couldn't get away with,
But when you nail one on the beak
They need another ball to play with.

Boston finished in sixth place as Chicago's brilliant team roared in, despite the fact that Ruth hit 29 homers. In January 1920, when owner Harry Frazee of the Red Sox was heavily in debt, he sold Ruth to Jake Ruppert's third-place New York Yankees for 125,000 dollars outright, plus a 350,000 dollar loan. The transaction remains baseball's all-time bargain.

A word anent baseball's only scandal, the '19 World Series between Cincinnati and the Chicago White Sox, who overnight became known as the Black Sox. Installed as heavy Series favorites for the best of nine games—a short-lived concession to post-war fervor—eight Chicago players sold out to the gamblers. I covered that Series with Ring Lardner, Jack Wheeler, Runyon and the rest of the New York crowd.

Chicago was at least 5 to 3 to win it all and could easily have been an even more lopsided favorite. Their pitching staff featured Ed (Knuckles) Cicotte, who had won 29 games that year; Claude (Lefty) Williams, 23 and 11; and Dickie Kerr, practically an also-ran with a 13–8 record.

"Champ" Pickens, organizer of the Blue and Grey football game at Montgomery, Alabama, years later, was in our party. The eve of the first game in Cincinnati, "Champ" walked into my room and said, "I've just been offered five to four on Cincinnati by a professional gambler."

"How much of it did you take?" I asked.

"Take, hell! This Series is fixed," replied Pickens, tossing his ticket on the bed. "You can have it—I'm going to the race track."

Cicotte was knocked out of the box in the first game, the Reds winning 9 to 1.

Williams opened the second game against the Reds' "Slim" Salee, and it was a pitching duel for three innings. Williams "blew" in the fourth, giving three bases on balls and three runs, the Reds winning that one 4 to 2.

I was sitting next to Lardner when Ring started pounding his typewriter furiously. He kept humming, "I'm Forever Blowing Bubbles." His bitter parody of that song, dedicated to Williams, opened with, "I'm forever blowing ball games. . . ."

Kerr, never implicated in the "fix," won two games, his first a 3-hit shutout, but there just weren't enough Kerrs to go around. I felt as though I'd been kicked in the stomach. The investigation lasted through the '20 season, the guilty ones being banned from organized ball for life.

And so it remained for this great, overgrown kid, Ruth, to lead baseball out of the wilderness and back into the aura of respectability. It was at the Princess Martha Hotel in St. Petersburg in 1930, after Ruth had signed a contract calling for 80,000 dollars a year for two years, that Colonel Ruppert commented, "Who are we kidding? I could pay 'Root' two hundred thousand dollars a year and he wouldn't be overpaid."

In 1920, the year following the Black Sox scandal, baseball needed a Superman, a man who could capture the imagination of the public—who could restore America's faith in baseball. Babe fit the bill. The public wanted to see the ball smashed out of the park—where there couldn't be any question of inside baseball—and the game's leaders moved to help. The ball was given a shot of rabbit juice, and in '20 Babe's big bat boomed for 54 homers. He alone realigned the game on the order of the long hit—the big inning. Lifting the Yankees aboard his shoulders, Ruth immediately became the heartwood of what was to become "Murderers' Row." In '20 the Yanks, again third, outdrew the Giants—in the Polo Grounds, to McGraw's chagrin. In '21, '22 and '23 the Giants and Yanks tangled in the World Series

—'23 being the year Ruppert's team moved from the Polo Grounds into their own million-dollar home across the Harlem River, "The House That Ruth Built."

Concerning Ruth "the kid"—he seldom mentioned his childhood. Actually Babe recalled little about it himself. He was in St. Mary's Industrial Home at Baltimore from the time he was seven or eight until he was seventeen, when Jack Dunn, the old Orioles manager, took him from Brother Gilbert and signed him to a contract calling for 600 dollars for the 1914 season.

Johnny Evers, keystone of Chicago's immortal Tinker-to-Evers-to-Chance combine, once told me an anecdote that Ruth told him.

When Babe was about seven, it seems he tapped the family till. "I took one dollar," said Babe, "and bought ice cream cones for all the kids on the block. When my old man asked me what I'd done I told him. He dragged me down cellar and beat me with a horsewhip. I tapped that till again—just to show him he couldn't break me. Then I landed in the Home, thank God!"

Some years ago, Tom Meany, writing a book on Babe's life, ran into a tout who sold his daily tips, in printed form, at the New York tracks, and who had spent his childhood with Babe at "The Home."

"You know," he said, "either Babe's gone soft or I've gone nuts. But I hafta laugh when I hear that place mentioned as 'The Home.' All I know is that there was guys with guns on the walls. . . ."

Small wonder, then, that for a youngster who had known only the roughest kind of treatment, life as a baseball hero was a case of Christmas every day.

Down the years I've always had a fondness for the horses —the kind that run. And in my wanderings I've come across a lot of tracks in many climes. But I've never been burned as badly as Babe was during the winter of 1925—the year of his

giant bellyache—when he visited Charles Stoneham's Oriental
Park at Havana and tried beating the ponies. John McGraw
was also down there that winter having a go at 'em. In less
than two weeks Ruth blew between 30 and 50 thousand dollars.
That cured him. College football also intrigued him—but for
only one game as a betting medium.

"I bet five thousand dollars on them Harvards," he told me.
"But the Yales win it. I'm off that football business, too."

In March of 1933—my third year with the Bell Syndicate—
I headed South for spring training, stopping en route at Bob
Woodruff's shooting preserve in south Georgia. When it came
time for me to pull out, Woodruff gave me his car, chauffeur
and a luggage compartment loaded with game.

"I'll throw a Florida dinner in your honor," I said. "We'll
feast on Woodruff's eighteen-carat birds, basted with Coca
Cola."

"If you do," replied Woodruff, "I wish you'd invite Walter
Lippmann and his wife. They're down near Bradenton, and
they're good friends of mine."

The dinner—to which Babe was also invited—was a huge
success, until the dignified Mrs. Lippmann asked Babe to describe the homerun he "called" in the '32 Series against the Cubs,
a four-straight rout for the Yankees.

"It's like this," boomed Babe, bigger than a freshly laun-
dered barn in white gabardine and puffing on a huge cigar.
"The Cubs had (censored) my old teammate Mark Koenig by
cutting him for only a measly, (censored) half share of the
Series money.

"Well, I'm riding the (censored) out of the Cubs, telling
'em they're the cheapest pack of (censored) crumbums in the
world. We've won the first two and now we're in Chicago for
the third game. Root is the Cub's pitcher. I pack one into the
stands in the first inning off him, but in the fifth it's tied four to

four when I'm up with nobody on. The Chicago fans are giving me hell.

"Root's still in there. He breezes the first two pitches by— both strikes! The mob's tearing down Wrigley Field. I shake my fist after that first strike. After the second, I point my bat at these bellerin' bleachers—right where I aim to park the ball. Root throws it, and I hit that (censored) ball on the nose —right over the (censored) fence for two (censored) runs.

" 'How do you like those apples, you (censored, censored, censored),' I yell at Root as I head towards first. By the time I reach home I'm almost fallin' down I'm laughin' so (censored) hard—and that's how it happened."

The Babe's baccalaureate finished, a battered Mrs. Lippmann mumbled that they'd have to be leaving. A minute later the Walter Lippmanns were history.

"Why did you use that language?" I asked Babe.

"What the hell, Grant," snorted Babe. "You heard her ask me what happened. So I told her!"

As a golfer, Ruth was a long but not a terrific hitter. I was with him at Clearwater, Florida, when he bet Babe Didrikson 50 dollars a tee shot. She outdrove Ruth by at least 20 yards—for 200 dollars—before he was convinced. But nobody ever enjoyed the game—or cussed it and himself—more than Ruth. His special meat was match play, man-to-man competition.

One morning in '38, Babe and I had a date to play with Dizzy Dean at Belleair, in Clearwater. Having recently started the game, Diz was pretty wild with his woods and long irons.

"I got a bushel of bets riding with Dean today," bellowed Babe. "I'm giving him strokes on ten different bets—from one to ten shots—and I expect to collect on 'em all."

"Diz may be wild, but not that wild," I warned.

As we reached the club, Babe spotted Pat Dean, Dizzy's handsome bride.

"Pat," said Babe, "come on out with us this morning. The walk will do you good."

Puzzled, but appreciative of Babe's invitation, Pat accepted. Diz said nothing. He hit a good drive, then smothered two shots. After another sloppy shot by Diz on the second hole, Pat commented, "Dear, you're ducking!"

"Ducking, hell!" exploded Dean. "Who asked you on this rabbit shoot anyhow?"

Followed the fireworks. Ruth howled. Pat stalked off. Dean couldn't hit a shot the rest of the round. The Babe never collected an easier hatful.

McCarthy's Yanks were headed north in 1934, Babe's last year aboard. At Atlanta, always an important exhibition stop, Ruth suddenly developed a huge hankering for chicken Georgia style. I called Bob Woodruff and in the course of our conversation mentioned Babe's fresh craving for chicken.

"I'll send my car over," said Bob. "Take it and look over these spots." He named a number of attractive places, and Bob Jones added a few more. Clare Ruth, Babe and I covered the list and ultimately chose a small hideaway several miles from town. The proprietor promised he'd prepare four of Georgia's finest hens for Babe's dinner. As we were leaving, Babe admired the front lawn, swarming with spring flowers. He plucked one and handed it to Clare.

"They're pretty daisies," he remarked.

"No, dear, they're daffodils," commented Mrs. R.

"They're still daisies to me," replied Babe. Any flower, from a dandelion to a white orchid, was simply a "daisy" to Babe.

Ruth showered after the sixth inning. Returning to our little hacienda, we were greeted by the beaming proprietor, flanked by a retinue of darky waiters, shining and popeyed.

"The chickens—they are prepared," said our host proudly.

"Chickens hell!" exclaimed Ruth. "I want beef steak!"

He got it.

The following day Babe visited his friend Bob Jones. Bob III, now manager of the Coca Cola plant in Pittsfield, Massachusetts, was then a youngster. We were fanning a highball in Bobby's living room when young Bob roared in with the neighborhood kids in his wake.

"That's him!" cried Bobby III. Babe grabbed an old bat from one of the youngsters, found it was cracked and tore it apart.

"Bobby," said Babe, "I want your old man to buy you a *good* bat. Make him promise."

Had Santa Claus visited 32–50 Northside Drive that day, he would have had to wait his turn.

Babe's love of kids was sincere. In many ways he was a big kid himself. I was in his room for dinner on the eve of the World Series in Chicago in 1932. (He always ate in his room before games because he would have been mobbed by fans and autograph hustlers in the hotel dining room.)

"I've got to go for a short trip, Grant," he said.

"Where are you going on the night before a World Series?" I asked.

"I'll tell you, but if you print it I'll shoot you. I'm going to take a baseball to a sick kid on the other side of town. I promised his mother and father I'd come. He's pretty sick."

The place was 20 or 30 miles away—over an hour to get there and another to get back. No publicity.

Babe was known by more motorcycle cops than any athlete who ever lived. They enjoyed giving Ruth an escort to the Stadium or helping him to get away after a game. They were usually there, like the Travelers' Aid, whenever the Babe needed a lift home to Riverside Drive after a late party.

One morning Babe asked me to pick him up for our golf game at Leewood, in Tuckahoe. "Sure," I replied, "but what happened to your car?"

"I lost it," said Babe.

"Lost it?" I said. "You had it last night."

"That was last night," replied Babe. "I wrecked it somewhere in Westchester and left it."

So he had. The cops had driven him home.

Another time, when Babe was roaring along by dawn's early light, the law stopped him, checked on his condition and suggested he be driven home.

"Why you (censored)!" roared Babe, and punched the cop on the nose.

"Now I *know* you're drunk," said the cop. "Move over! I'm drivin' you home."

I was with Babe one evening when he turned down a one-way street—the wrong way. "This is a one-way street," said the cop.

"I'm only drivin' one way!" yelled Ruth.

"Oh, hello, Babe! I didn't know it was you," replied the cop. "Go anywhere you please—but take it easy!"

And so it went.

I once had Babe on a national radio hookup, with Graham McNamee in charge. A short script had been prepared for Ruth to read—pretty much on split-second timing. He worked it over and was practically letter-perfect. Came the big break, with orchestra lending background music. At the last minute, Babe's carefully rehearsed script became scrambled. Before I could throw a halter on him, he was off and running. McNamee was frantic; the orchestra leader was frantic; the producer was frantic—as Ruth rambled on.

At one point the Babe was supposed to refer to the Duke

of Wellington's historic remark that the Battle of Waterloo had been won on the playing fields of Eton. Babe managed to come out with this gem:

"As Duke Ellington once said, the Battle of Waterloo was won on the playing fields of Elkton."

Later I asked Babe how he could louse up one short statement so completely.

"About that Wellington guy I wouldn't know," he replied. "Ellington, yes. As for that Eton business—well, I married my first wife in Elkton (Maryland), and I always hated the goddamn place. It musta stuck."

The network got a load of Ruth at his purest that night. But it certainly wasn't NBC's conception of a tight program.

One evening Babe and I were having a few drinks in the grill room of the Chatham Hotel. Suddenly he looked at his watch. "Jesus!" he cried. "I gotta run!" In a flash he'd grabbed his cap and coat and was flagging a cab. Alarmed, I asked what the trouble was.

"Trouble?" yelled Ruth. "Why, 'Gangbusters' is on!"

Moe Berg, the eminent linguist, Princetonian and major-league catcher, once said: "Ruth isn't a man; he's an institution." Ruth was a man who loved crowds. And the crowds always swarmed to see Babe hit. The Yankees from 1926 to '34 were a terrific aggregation, each man big in his own right. But it was Babe the crowds came to see. Each Yankee exhibition-game contract carried this clause in heavy type: "It is understood and agreed that Babe Ruth will play." He seldom missed a curtain call.

I've seen the great ones, from Cobb through Williams, but Ruth was the only ball player I have known who could turn out capacity crowds every time. He did this in every city the Yankees played. When the Yankee Stadium was dedicated in April

1923, more than 74,000 people turned up—to see the Yankees, sure, but more important, to see Ruth cavort around "The House That Babe Built."

He was the greatest single magnet sport has ever known. Jack Dempsey was top man in his game. But Jack fought in defense of his title only six times in seven years. Babe played each day, six months a year, for nearly 15 years. He lured packed stands in the big cities and he drew them out in the bush. I know, for I followed him from 1919 to his final game in 1935. Big league, bush league, the great cities, small hamlets—at the ball park or train depot—always capacity.

I've ridden in cars with Babe in cities all over the map. Everywhere, the mobs would wave or call his name, and Babe would answer, "How're you, Mom!" . . . "Hello, Pop!" "How can they miss this silly mug?" he used to ask.

Whether it was playing baseball or golf, hunting, fishing or sitting around a room drinking and punching the bag, I can recall no one who got as much joy out of sheer living as the Babe.

Friendship—pure, warm, unadulterated friendship with no holds barred, ever—is the key to the Babe Ruth I most treasure. For the 30 years I knew Babe—until cancer killed him in 1948— I never saw Ruth really sore at anybody. Oh, I've seen him lose his temper—at himself—on a golf course, when he'd bury his club in a bunker after missing a shot or lash his putter after a missed putt. (Once he wrapped the clubhead around his leg so hard he thought he'd broken his ankle and roared like a hopped-up elephant.) But Ruth, the man-boy, was the complete embodiment of everything uninhibited. He couldn't possibly fail —that was Ruth's credo. And when he found that baseball, particularly the Yankees, had no managerial berth for him, he was deeply hurt. But in remarks or actions, the Babe was kindly —so kindly.

Ruth established many records, most of them Homeric, and

no pun intended. It will be a long time before any slugger breaks his all-time homerun mark of 714. And, at the risk of sounding disloyal to the game, I hope it's an eternity before some youngster, teeing off on today's jet ball, smashes Babe's mark of 60 homers in one season: This I hope for Babe, wherever he is, kicking his heels around on some king-sized cloud.

CHAPTER TEN

Jack Dempsey,
the Man from Maumee Bay

In sport, you'll find there are great defensive stars and brilliant offensive competitors. Among the great offensive athletes I've studied I must include Ty Cobb, Bill Tilden, Babe Ruth, Harry Greb and Jesse Owens. But I found the greatest attacking, or pure offensive, star one June day in 1919 in Toledo, off the hot and steamy shores of Maumee Bay.

His name was Jack Dempsey. I had been in France during 1917 and 1918, so had seen no prize fights in that period. When I first met Dempsey, he was burnt purple. He had trained down to 180 pounds in getting ready for Jess Willard, the 250-pound giant. Dempsey was then 24 years old. He was keen and lithe, almost as fast as Cobb. It was his speed, speed of hand as well as foot, that made him such a dangerous opponent.

Dempsey was the oddest mixture of humanity I've known. In the ring he was a killer—a superhuman wild man. His teeth

116

were frequently bared and his complete intent was an opponent's destruction. He was a fighter—one who used every trick to wreck the other fighter.

Yet, outside the ring, Jack is one of the gentlest men I know. I've seen him in his restaurant at times when some customer, with more enthusiasm than good sense, would grab his vest or part of his shirt—strictly for a souvenir—with no kickback from Jack. I've known the man closely for more than 30 years and I've never seen him in a rough argument or as anything except courteous and considerate.

Looking at Dempsey and Willard in 1919, it was hard to give Dempsey a chance. Dempsey, slightly over 6 feet, weighed 180. Willard, at 6 feet 6, weighed 250 at least.

Willard looked on Dempsey as a little boy. The night before the fight Bob Edgren and I called on Jess. He thought the fight was a joke.

". . . outweigh him seventy pounds," Willard said. "He'll come tearing into me . . . I'll have my left out . . . and then I'll hit him with a right uppercut. That'll be the end."

Next day when the first round opened, Dempsey circled Willard some 25 or 30 seconds. He was a tiger circling an ox. Finally Willard couldn't wait any longer. He jabbed at Dempsey with his left, and the roof fell in. Jack ducked under Willard's left, threw a right to the body. At the same time he nailed Willard on the right side of the head with a smashing left.

"I knew it was all over then," Jack said later. "I saw his cheek bone cave in."

Jack rubbed his own wire-stubbled jaw reflectively. "Funny thing about this fight," he continued, "was that Kearns (Dempsey's manager Jack Kearns) claimed he had bet ten thousand dollars to one hundred thousand dollars I'd knock out Willard in the first round. That's what I did. The referee had raised my right hand, awarding me the fight. Willard's head was hanging over

the lower rope. He was practically unconscious from several
knockdowns. I left the ring. The fight was over . . . or it should
have been. I must have been twenty-five yards from the ring
when they called me back. That was the biggest shock I ever got
. . . when I was told the bell had rung three seconds too
soon . . . Suppose it had? My hand had been raised and I had
been given the fight by the referee."

—Willard, bleeding like a half-butchered ox, was unable
to answer the bell for the fourth round.

"I sure recall my end of that purse," recalled Dempsey.
"For three rounds I collected twenty-seven thousand five hundred dollars my first big payday. Willard did all right too. His
share, win, lose or draw, was one hundred thousand dollars."

Lining up Georges Carpentier for the Dempsey vs. Carpentier fight, at Boyle's Thirty Acres, Jersey City, for July 1921, was
a shrewd piece of work by Tex Rickard. Tex "sensed" more and
better gate-building tricks in one minute than today's promoters
can dream up in a year. I realize that television has taken a lot
of the steam off the need for a "live" gate—what with TV rights
selling for great chunks of cash. But the fact remains that Rickard, yes, and Mike Jacobs, had the kind of promotional touch
that would have them storming the gates today instead of taking
in the fight through a camera.

Carpentier, with a gaudy if superficial war record, had returned to Paris in one piece—and hungry. He was a pretty fair
light-heavyweight, but they couldn't have ballooned the Frenchman into a bona fide heavyweight, except in the papers, with two
sandbags for added ballast. At any rate, Rickard—knowing the
public's love of a hero and villain tangle—cast Dempsey, the
scowling, wire-bearded "draft dodger" as the villain, with apple-
cheeked Carpentier, the amiable, personable soldier boy, as
the hero. Pictures of Dempsey, riveting battleships in patent
leather shoes—all at Kearns' behest—flooded the sports pages,

along with those of Carpentier, practically winning the war singlehanded.

That fight was the first to be broadcast—with Graham McNamee describing the action—and it had the whole nation taking sides for or against Dempsey.

Carpentier landed in America several weeks before the match. He had never seen Dempsey. He was a Frenchman on a holiday, a good-will emissary.

Dempsey trained at Atlantic City; as for Carpentier I'm still not certain that he did train. He was never on exhibition to the press—never on a scale—about the only time we'd see him was on a rubbing table or sauntering into a restaurant.

The story of that fight—badly overplayed, but eaten to the last adjective by the public—was actually ordained days beforehand. But the culmination of Carpentier's mental and physical unpreparedness was seen near his dressing room just before the fight at Boyle's Thirty Acres—not by me, but by Kit and Sophie Treadwell McGeehan, W. O.'s wife and a fine reporter in her own right. It happened this way and here it is in Kit's words.

"Sophie McGeehan was covering the color story for her paper," reports Kit. "A lot of New York's carriage trade was there and that was part of the story. Well, it had started to rain before the bout. I spotted a little exit to somewhere and we decided to get in out of the rain. We were in this little room, sitting on a rubbing table and complimenting ourselves on our abode when a cop entered and said to us, 'Ladies, where do you think you are?' We told him we were out of the rain. 'You've got to leave. You're in the Frenchman's dressing room!' replied the officer.

"At that moment down the corridor came Carpentier. Dressed, he was as white as a sheet . . . thin . . . and, Oh Lord, but he looked frightened. And several steps behind, wear-

ing trunks and a heavy red sweater, and unshaven, came Dempsey—big, tough and bristling. He dwarfed the cops guarding
him.

"I looked at Sophie who, of course, was staring. Studying
the contrast between the two men, she said, 'That poor French
boy. Why he'll be murdered!' We returned to our seats and
waited for the Angel of Doom to claim Carpentier."

It was all over in four rounds, but had Dempsey wanted to
put the slug on Carpentier, I think he could have nailed him
in the first round. From ringside, all French ships at sea received this cabled flash: "Your Frog flattened in fourth"—for
a new "high" in international diplomacy.

I recall another "visitor" who came to America to strike-it-
rich against Dempsey—Luis Angel Firpo. When hurt, Firpo
truly lived up to his "Wild Bull of the Pampas" monicker; but
in recline, after a meal, he looked more like a great bum in the
park.

My first glimpse of the South American was two weeks before the fight—at the Polo Grounds, September 14, 1923. His
camp was at Atlantic City. When I arrived early one morning,
Firpo was tackling a light breakfast: a huge steak smothered with
lamb chops. After finishing, he walked over to a couch and lay
there like a python who'd just swallowed a calf. He seemed
dopey and indolent. I compared his camp to Dempsey's at
Saratoga. There the order of the day was mayhem, with the
massive George Godfrey as Jack's Number 1 sparring partner
at 1,500 dollars per week, and I wondered at the fight that was
about to be perpetrated on the unsuspecting public. Fifty-dollar
ringside seats were being gobbled up for 100 dollars each. Firpo
had a couple of two-bit sparring partners whom he outweighed
by a ton and belabored at will. He sure didn't spend much on
that camp, except on food.

Firpo Knocked Out In 2d Round After Flooring Dempsey

Woman Heads Line All Day To Be Crowded Out

The woman who headed the long line waiting for general admission tickets to the Dempsey-Firpo fight all day yesterday did not get to see the bout, despite her long vigil.

When the line was broken up by the frantic thousands seeking the bleacher seats she lost her place. An hour later, when the tickets actually were being dispensed, she was on the outer rim of the crowd and could not get within half a block of the window.

125,000 Throng Polo Grounds; 85,000 in Arena

Larger Army Than Gallieni Led Out of Paris to First Marne Struggles to See Battle of Fistic Giants

Champion Is Hurled to Knees, Then Clear Out of Ring, but Drops Challenger 4 Times in First

Title Nearly Lost By Seeming Fouls

Argentine Battered Down by Fighting Fury in 4 Fast, Slashing Minutes

By Grantland Rice

In four minutes of the most sensational fighting ever seen in any ring back through all the ages of the ancient game, Jack Dempsey, the champion, knocked out Luis Angel Firpo, the challenger, just after the second round got under way last night at the Polo Grounds.

Dempsey slashed his way to victory with a right and left to the jaw that lifted the Argentine giant from his feet and hurled him headlong to the floor with the crash of a mighty oak falling from great heights.

At ringside my typewriter was next to Jack Lawrence's. During the final prelim bout, we were discussing the main.

"They're two big guys," said Lawrence. "If somebody goes through the ropes I hope it's Dempsey. At least he's lighter than that truck Firpo."

Just before the bout started, I moved down four seats, next to Bob Edgren of the old New York *Evening World*. Well, for the record, Lawrence got his wish. It was Dempsey who came hurtling through the ropes in that madhouse first round. He landed, back first, on top of Lawrence, who had put up his hands to protect himself. But nobody, including Lawrence, had to help Dempsey back through those ropes. He was all for helping himself—but fast!

Dempsey never cared to talk about that fight at any length. To him it was his closest call.

"Rickard asked me to carry Firpo for four or five rounds . . . to give the customers a run for their money," Jack said. "I told Tex to go to hell, that Firpo was too strong and hit too hard to play with. I told Rickard I'd put Firpo away in the first round— if I could.

"You know, before the fight you had told me that Bill Brennan had said Firpo threw rocks at you . . . that he had a rubber arm . . . that he'd sock you from a good way off. Well, in the first round I got in a little too close and Firpo's first shot —a full right—caught me on the chin. I almost went down but kept punching. I was dazed. You wrote, and others did the same, that I hit him when he was just getting up. At that time I wasn't fighting for any championship or any million dollars. I was fighting to keep from being killed. I would have hit him at any place I found him.

"The wallop that sent me through the ropes was a half punch and half shove," continued Dempsey. "It was nothing like that opening right hand he nailed me with earlier."

"What was your first thought as you went flying through the air out of the ring?" I asked.

"To get back up and in as quickly as I could," he said. "I might say that no one at ringside tried to help me. They put up their hands to break my fall. It was all instinctive."

I don't think there was ever a moment in any fight that Dempsey thought in terms of defense. He had a method of weaving and moving about that was partly defense but it always led to attack or headlong assault.

Dempsey was not a bad boxer. He wasn't as good in this respect as Tunney, Corbett and Louis were; but he was none too easy to hit with a good punch. He knew most of the tricks.

Dempsey was head and shoulders over Rocky Marciano as a boxer. He had to be to go 15 rounds with Tom Gibbons when Gibbons was hungry and able. That brings up the Dempsey-Gibbons title match at Shelby, Montana, in some ways Dempsey's most demanding fight. As a promoter's dream, the Shelby fight—that and the Sharkey-Stribling fight in 1929 at Miami Beach—were both pure phantasmagoria.

Mike Collins, a fight manager of sorts out of St. Paul, had a string of fighters barnstorming through Montana in 1923, working any town where there were a few dollars to be made. Collins met Loy Molumby, head of Montana's American Legion, and in a short time they were cruising all over the state in a flimsy old airplane . . . shooting off horse pistols and calling for wine. In the course of their meanderings they ran into a man named Johnson, who, among other things, was Mayor of Shelby and president of the local bank.

With the talk flaring around fights and fighters, somebody had the glorious idea of staging a heavyweight championship fight right there in Shelby! It would cause a land boom, make it a city overnight. Collins called his pal, Eddie Kane, Gibbons' manager back in St. Paul, and propositioned him.

"Listen, Mike," replied Kane. "You get Dempsey out there
. . . anywhere . . . and Gibbons will fight him for nothing.
All you got to do is pay Dempsey. What do you think of
that?"

That, they liked. Next they wired Jack Kearns, Dempsey's
manager, offering him 300,000 dollars "to defend his title against
Tom Gibbons at Shelby on July 4th."

Kearns wired back: "Send 100,000 dollars now . . . 100,000
dollars in a month and 100,000 dollars before Dempsey steps
into the ring and it's a deal."

The first 100,000 dollars came easily enough and seeing they
meant business Kearns and Dempsey headed west and set up
training quarters at Great Falls, Montana, about 70 miles south
of Shelby. Eddie Kane went direct to Shelby and set up Gibbons'
training camp there.

Late in June, I boarded a Pullman in Chicago with a crowd
of other writers—Broun, Runyon, Bide Dudley and Hugh
Fullerton were there—and we were off by way of the Great
Northern, to the wild and wooly West, by God! Great Falls, we
discovered, was a fair-sized town. Visiting Dempsey at his camp
among the cottonwoods, I found him in high humor. I recall it
was June 24th, his 28th birthday. His dad was there and so
was his cousin, Don Chafin, a raw-boned husky from West Virginia and a paid-up life member of the famed Hatfield clan.
The camp mascot was a cub timber wolf. Jack was giving himself daily facials with some sort of bear grease that had tough-
ened his face to the general texture of a boar's hide. It was
Jack's first title defense in two years but he looked to be in great
shape. Even walking, he seemed to slither along, snakelike, his
muscles glinting in the sun.

I don't recall just what I expected from Shelby, the fight
site, but I wasn't impressed. A town of perhaps 2,000, it was
little more than a crossroad in the middle of a desert. There

were few houses and a building or two that passed for hotels. Press headquarters and living accommodations were in one of the Pullman cars shoved over on a siding.

Gibbons, meanwhile, was training hard and looking forward to what I thought was certain annihilation. His wife and two children were with him. It was a case of Papa Bear, Momma and the kids, all up there in a stark little house on the crest of a barren little hill with not so much as a shrub as far as the naked eye could see.

I remember Hughey Fullerton spotting a Blackfoot brave in war regalia, including paints and eagle feathers. Trying out an Indian dialect, Hughey asked him, "Who Big Chief like? Dempsey or Gibbons?"

Much to Fullerton's astonishment, Big Chief replied, "Sir, I happen to like Dempsey. Gibbons has the skill as a boxer. Dempsey has the power. Power usually prevails over skill." He was a Carlisle graduate brandishing an English course.

Mayor Johnson, Molumby and friends were beginning to realize the facts of life . . . and were having a rough time scraping up that second 100,000 dollar installment—with still a third to come. Kearns, meanwhile, remained adamant. After Johnson all but hocked his bank, Kearns had 200,000 dollars.

"You've got to pay Dempsey every cent, or you won't see Dempsey at all!" was the ribald chant on Shelby's Main Street.

Included in my Sportlight column were occasional pearls under the subhead, "Campfire Songs from Shelby."

> *In the wide open spaces where men are men*
> *The slogan today is, "Never again!"*
>
> *In the wide open spaces, loud rings the fuss,*
> *"Germany's lucky compared to us."*
>
> *In the wide open spaces, they cry bereft,*
> *"Yes, we have only bananas left."*

I arrived back at Dempsey's camp about four days before
the bell rang. Dempsey was enthusiastic. "Grant," he said, "we're
really shootin' today. . . . Think you'll enjoy it."

George Godfrey again was Dempsey's Number 1 sparring
partner. Had he come along ten years later, this Negro might
well have been a world's champion.

Godfrey was under instructions to do his best. He weighed
about 230; Jack about 190. From the bell, the two tore at each
other. Godfrey threw a full right, a real bomb that grazed Jack's
chin, bringing blood. Jack retaliated with a left hook that
knocked Godfrey down into such a heap he broke two ribs. So
much for the shooting. "Big Ben" Wray, a 7-foot 2-inch "cowboy"
had lasted 28 seconds with Dempsey a fortnight earlier. Jack's
left hook broke Wray's right jaw . . . all of which left Wray,
his head in a plaster cast, taking nourishment through a straw.
I recall the doc removed two teeth to admit the feeding tube.

Meanwhile, owing to Kearn's vacillations about the purse,
special trains, alerted to bring in crowds from San Francisco
and Chicago, had been forced to cancel. The night before the
fight, slated for Independence Day afternoon, was the most
harrowing in Shelby's history. Still claiming the last possible
ounce of flesh, Kearns "officially" called off the fight seven times.
Endeavoring to keep fresh, up-to-the-minute bulletins pumping
over the wires, Broun, Runyon and the rest of us had long since
gone nuts.

At the 12th hour, Kearns again reversed his field, decided
to gamble on the gate "take" and declared the fight was on. In
a matter of minutes Shelby's main drag erupted into a madhouse.
Cowpokes, their spike heels kicking up the alkali dust, bought
drinks for millionaires and the millionaires mingled with Blackfoot Indians, many of them in full tribal gear. Drifters, motorists
from Louisiana, society ladies and wild dames. Hollywood stars
and sheep herders—they were all there, along with Mrs. Raymond T. Baker, the former Mrs. Alfred Gwynne Vanderbilt, and

One-Eyed Connolly. I recall Mrs. Baker's private Pullman car, The Palm Beach, reclined on a nearby siding and I spotted Mae Murray peering at the revelry from the sanctuary of her own private car. Against a background of blaring bands, the snake dance lasted clear through the night. Yes, it was prohibition, but that night everybody packed a bottle.

And looking down on it all from his little family shack on a bare hill sat Tom Gibbons, like Teufelsdröckh, the attic watcher in *Sartor Resartus,* and had his share of philosophical cogitations. I thought about Tom. More, I thought of his sweet wife. Her man, a family man 34 years old, was about to face Dempsey, "the Killer," and for nary a thin dime!

The fight was scaled at 50-dollar ringside and the huge wooden bowl erected for the bloodletting was built to hold some 50,000 customers. But the final count was a trickle over 7,000 when the Main finally went on.

Dempsey and Gibbons went 15 rounds like two featherweights. I've never witnessed as much sheer speed in a heavyweight bout. At the finish, the decision was clearly Dempsey's, but Gibbons, a wildcat that steaming afternoon, remained dangerous all the way. Dempsey resorted to every boxing trick he knew and as the bout unfolded, he knew plenty. But he couldn't nail a scowling, stabbing Gibbons, who fought the fight of his life . . . for nothing.

"He never hurt me, really, after the first round," Gibbons said. "But Lord, how that fellow can hit! It was in the first round. Dempsey shot a straight right punch. . . . I saw it but couldn't duck it, entirely, and took it on the top of my forehead. That's the thickest part of a man's skull . . . but Grant, I didn't come out of a daze until the fourth round.

"I'd like to fight him again, for money," concluded Gibbons. ". . . but don't let anybody ever tell you Dempsey can't box. He knows all the tricks."

I was having breakfast with Jack and Max Baer one February morning back in 1931 at the Warwick Hotel. The day before, Jack had refereed the Baer–Tommy Loughran fight at Madison Square Garden. Max had been decisioned in ten rounds.

"I've been looking at left jabs all night," Max said. "Lefts . . . lefts . . . lefts . . . that's all I've seen!"

"The funny part," said Dempsey, "is that you could have stopped that 'Lefty' in the first round."

"How?" Baer said.

"Take off your coat," replied Jack to big Maxie, 6 feet 3 and 220 pounds. Max shucked off his coat and faced Dempsey.

"Now lead with a left, just as Loughran did," said Jack. Max led . . . and there was an immediate yelp. "You broke my arm," Max howled as he backed away, holding it.

As Baer led with his left, Dempsey had dropped his huge right fist across the right biceps with paralyzing force. The left arm became useless for 30 minutes.

"I'll show you another punch," Jack said. He spun Baer and then socked him.

"You can't do that," Max said. "It's illegal."

"They'll only warn you the first time," Dempsey said.

Jack Dempsey was and remains the most restless man I ever knew. When he was in his middle 20's, he couldn't sit still for two minutes. He was all over the room, always in motion. After he quit fighting to settle down, he settled down all over the map. Buenos Aires one week, Toronto, Canada, the next and on to Boston or Dallas or San Francisco—refereeing wrestling matches and prize fights or representing some company in an advertising drive. He also took a flier with various circuses . . . and he loved the work. In one circus he had a chimp that always waited for him. He'd give the chimp a cigar and a bottle of Coke. The monk would drink the bottle, smoke the cigar and jam the cigar in the bottle for a stopper. He was Jack's pal.

Even today, the sight of a restless Dempsey cooped up in some hotel room reminds me of a caged tiger. I've always loved animals, particularly wild animals. In other years, I don't know how many hours Gene Fowler and I spent studying the tigers, elephants, lions and big snakes at zoos in New York, Chicago, St. Louis—or even the 'gator farms in Florida. During the late 1930's I envisioned a short-lived plan for transporting pairs of jungle beasts to Florida and turning 'em all loose in the Everglades. I believe they would have thrived. When the Florida dream fizzled, I was for doing the same general thing with the Brazilian jungles and had the late Martin Johnson enthused over it—until World War II knocked that out the window. I still think my plan had more merit than that, or any war.

The tiger, particularly, contains more grace and less waste motion in one flick of his paw than most of us possess in our entire physical makeup. For pure animal grace, the sight of Sam Snead murdering a tee shot; Babe Ruth swinging from his heels; yes, and Jack Dempsey raining savage destruction on a foe—these remain for me the acme of tigerish reflexes in human form.

Some years ago while in Sarasota, Florida, on the spring baseball beat, I spent a morning on the Ringling Brothers' circus lot. In a short time I was back with the menagerie watching my old friend, the tiger, prowl his caged beat. Studying him, I compared the fellow to Dempsey. These lines began to take shape on that March morning with the thermometer pushing the eighties.

To A Caged Tiger

I've watched you stalking back and forth, the hurt look in your eyes,
Seeing, far off, the jungle grass, the blazing Indian skies,
The matted snarl of underbrush that sweeps the covered loam,
The hidden places that you knew, and looked upon, as home.

There you could move on silent paw to track your luckless prey—
There you could find the jungle thrill that knows the right of way;
Part of the ancient plan that came with life's first flame of sun,
Lord of the kingdom that you ruled, where might and right were one.

I've watched you in your steel-bound cage, but you are not alone,
O, hapless captive with your dreams that seek the outer zone;
Don't look with envy on the lot of those who cross your view,
The world today is chain or cage, for all except a few.

For we who watch your restless step can understand your dreams
Of far-off shores and jungle grass and sunlit, singing streams,
Chained to a desk, or out of work, drab captives of some fate
That shuts the Great Adventure out, beyond the city's gate.

Tiger—the Indian sun is hot—the jungles' echoes call—
Tiger—I know just how you feel—with chain and cage and wall—
On restless feet you'll dream your dreams—and stay within your
      cage—
With restless heart I'll dream with you—and write another page.

I once asked Dempsey why college athletes never made
good fighters. "Football is just as rough," I said. "They star in
those games. But seldom in boxing where the big money is."

"They're too smart," Dempsey said. "The fight game is the
toughest game on earth. When I was a young fellow I was
knocked down plenty. I wanted to stay down. I couldn't. I had
to collect that two dollars for winning—or go hungry. I had to get
up. I was one of those hungry fighters. You could hit me on the
chin with a sledge hammer for five dollars. When you haven't
eaten for two days you'll understand.

"Few college fellers ever get that low. I had one early fight
when I was knocked down eleven times before I got up to win.
You think I'd have taken that beating if I had had as much as
twenty-five bucks with me? No chance."

He would have.

And speaking of money, when he finally earned it there's

no telling how much of it he gave away. One week it amounted to 1,700 dollars, just handouts to bums. He was and is one of the most liberal of men.

Dempsey has two lovely daughters—Barbara and Joan, both now married. He has watched over and guarded them like four mothers. His care of them has been complete.

Gene Fowler, the writer, knew Dempsey back in Denver as a kid. "He never liked to fight then," Gene said. "He was the nicest kid in the neighborhood. He has been one of the greatest fellows I've known. Whatever a real gentleman is—that's Dempsey."

Jack had steel fists and an iron jaw. Some experts have written that Marciano punches harder or with more explosive force than Dempsey. Gene Tunney says this statement is ridiculous. Marciano has at least one asset that matches Dempsey. Dempsey could take it—to a full degree. So can Marciano.

"There are two things that count in ring success," Dempsey once told me. "The big punch and the ability to take a big punch. Any real champion must have both."

I recall at Chicago in '27 . . . in the fourth round I think it was. Tunney had Dempsey in trouble. He looked groggy. "Why didn't you follow up that right hand?" I asked Tunney later.

"Because I know Dempsey," Tunney replied. "He can recover quicker than any man I ever fought. He's dangerous with a five-second interval."

Two months before his return match with Tunney, Dempsey fought Jack Sharkey in the Yankee Stadium. It was the night of July 21, 1927 . . . and this, Dempsey hoped, would be a tight tuneup for the revenge bout with Tunney.

That night Sharkey, at 25, was as good a fighter as he ever would be. And when he was right, Josef Paul Zukauskas (Sharkey's square name) was plenty good. Dempsey, at 32, was something else again. Stories from Dempsey's camp at Saratoga reported Jack was soaking his left arm—the one that sired the hooks that smashed Willard, Carpentier and Firpo—in nightly applications of hot salves. The betting odds established Sharkey as the favorite.

Sharkey, in fine trim, was becoming cockier by the minute. One day while he was being rubbed down after work, Sharkey asked me to drop into his room.

"Come in here a minute," beckoned Sharkey. "You know," he said when the door was closed, "I could'a had this fight with Tunney. . . . Rickard offered it to me."

"Why didn't you take it?" I replied. "By the looks of you, it might have been a short cut to the title."

"Tunney can wait," said Sharkey. "I know I can lick Dempsey, and by beating him I figure it'll be a better buildup for Tunney."

Nearly 80,000, shelling out more than 1,000,000 dollars, made another Rickard promotion pay off that night. Names from the entertainment world dotted ringside. I recall bumping into Byrd and Chamberlin, trans-Atlantic heroes of that year, en route to working press.

Instead of charging his foe in customary fashion at the opening bell, Dempsey suddenly played it cute waiting for Sharkey to make the first move. Sharkey did—almost tearing Jack's head off with a left and right.

"I must have hit him five punches in quick succession," said Sharkey later. "What a sucker I was. The old champ is staggering. All I need is one more punch. But I remembered how they cheered Dempsey and booed me when we were introduced. So with Dempsey groggy, I turned to the mob and yelled, 'Here's your bum champion! How do you like him?'

"When I returned back to Dempsey he had recovered enough to clinch and save himself. That's how I lost the fight."

When hurt, Dempsey, at 20 or 32, would have used a tire iron on his tormentor if one happened to be at hand. But that reaction was inexplicably slow to ignite against Sharkey. Had the once hungry but now opulent Dempsey gone soft—and cautious? For six rounds Sharkey knocked Jack all over that ring. Instead of jabbing and moving . . . jabbing and moving—the way he'd defeated Jimmy Maloney and many others—Sharkey, despite orders from his corner, threw caution overboard and punched flatfooted, shooting for a knockout. An over-confident Billy Conn tried the same thing in his first fight against Joe Louis in the Polo Grounds 14 years later. As the bell ended the sixth round, a battered, bloody Dempsey whipped two shots to Sharkey's face. As referee O'Sullivan pried the men apart, the crowd jeered Sharkey and cheered Dempsey.

Dempsey opened the seventh with two sharp rights to Sharkey's belly—right on the belt line. Stunned and hurt, Sharkey, instead of covering up and riding out the storm, looked appealingly at the referee. O'Sullivan warned Dempsey, but the suddenly rejuvenated Manassa Mauler tore into Sharkey's belly again with palpably low shots. Sharkey again turned to the referee, gesturing pain. Wham! That dreaded left hook landed flush on Sharkey's jaw. Down he went, in a distended heap, half crawling and clutching his groin—his head grovelling the canvas. O'Sullivan, himself dazed for a monment, seemed to be deliberating whether to start counting or award the fight to Sharkey on a foul. He finally picked up the count from the timekeeper, Kid McPartland. At 10, little Joe Humphrey climbed between the ropes and raised Dempsey's hand. Bedlam broke loose with straw hats sailing into the ring and cries of "Foul!" and "Quitter!" booming through the Stadium. Hammering away at my morning lead, I wasn't sure whether I was working a heavyweight fight or a riot.

Two months later in Chicago's Soldier's Field, nearly 105,000 paid 2,658,660 dollars to see an all but washed-up Dempsey try to regain his crown from Gene Tunney.

I mentioned Dempsey's fight at Shelby, and the Sharkey–Stribling fight at Miami Beach six years later, as two historic nightmares. Dempsey, unwittingly, played an important role in the Florida venture.

The Jack Sharkey vs. Young Stribling fight at Miami Beach in February of '29 foreshadowed the dead-ahead depression. Carl Fisher, the "inventor" of Miami Beach, had fellow Hoosier and publicist Steve Hannagan and his partners Joe Copps and Larry Smits booming Miami Beach. This fight was blueprinted as a heady publicity adjunct.

Once the preliminaries were under way, a ruptured appendix killed Tex Rickard. He was a good friend of mine. Money was never his main interest—it was just stuff to move around. He loved publicity and wanted to be known as the greatest promoter of all time. That was all. In this he was and will remain safe. He was the greatest.

When Rickard died, Bill Carey, one of the head men of Madison Square Garden, was handed a tube of sunburn cream and rushed into the breach. As a portion of Rickard's "property," Dempsey was pressed into service as Rickard's stand-in. Dempsey was to get 50,000 dollars or 100,000 dollars for promoting the fight.

Bill Carey—a gentleman and everybody's pal—was perhaps the greatest booster professional ice hockey ever had in New York. As a fight promoter, however, Bill knew as much as an elephant knows about contract bridge . . . or a kangaroo knows about golf. He began spending money so fast and with such a lavish hand that Dempsey soon saw there would be nothing left for him. So—Jack agreed to work for nothing. "I was afraid I would have to pick up the check," he remarked.

All correspondents, plus droves who didn't know a typewriter from a milk can, were admitted—free—to the day and night revels. Carey had leased Fisher's mansion right on the beach at the head of Lincoln Road and, as I recall, several writers were wounded in the rush for rooms overlooking the Atlantic Ocean. Four hotels, including the Drake as base of operations, were utilized to handle 435 newsmen from all over the world. For nearly seven solid weeks it resembled New Year's Eve in Babylon—and I don't mean Long Island.

Meanwhile, Dempsey, now working for nothing to save a little money, was engulfed. So were all others trying to steer affairs back to sanity. The tidal wave was on, beyond control. Everybody within 50 miles of The Beach became one of Carey's freeloaders. Headquarters for the press gang became head-quarters for everything—with the beach itself serving as the front lawn. I recall Harry Grayson got an old ex-manager pal, Gus Wilson, then running a restaurant-bar in New York, to act as maître d'hôtel for the press. It was prohibition, of course. But with Gus, if you ordered a gin fizz, you got a gin fizz! Beer costing Carey one dollar a bottle was used to water the geranium plants. How many cases of champagne, gin, bourbon and scotch were consumed I don't know. But I do know that Nat Fleischer, in charge of auditing, signed a check for 32,100 dollars for booze alone. That was one of the thirstiest mobs ever. There must have been two drunks to every square yard of beach. And the majority of the crowd had no connection whatsoever with the fight.

I went to Miami three weeks early. The New York *Tribune,* for whom I was operating, told me not to cover the fight. They thought it a phony—no good. However, I had promised Harry Staton, the manager of the Tribune Syndicate, that I would cover his 50 or more papers. I was writing two separate columns —one for those who wanted the fight covered, another for the *Tribune.* Meanwhile, the rest of the sports-writing fraternity was beating out copy—of sorts.

A week before the fight, it was apparent that they were going to take in more than 400,000 dollars on a sellout and still lose big money. Meanwhile, Lionel Levy, the young architect who had built Madison Square Garden, was putting the final touches on his open-air wooden arena in Flamingo Park.

Back in New York, Bill McGeehan, the *Tribune* sports editor—and one of the best ever—decided to come down and investigate. Bill had been roasting Carey daily in his column. When he arrived, Bill expected Carey to have him tossed out. I introduced them, "Mr. Carey, Mr. McGeehan."

Carey beamed his welcome through his milk-bottle lenses. "And by the way, Mr. McGeehan," he said, "what business are you in?" That was the only time I ever saw McGeehan stopped cold. He fled the camp. He refused to write a word. Harry Cross then followed to "cover" McGeehan. In a few more days that brilliant if at times baffling youngster, Don Skene, arrived to cover both the boss and Cross. Following Bill's precepts, both refused to write a word. At the 11th hour the New York desk suddenly wired all four of us to file 1,000 words or more. Mc-Geehan, Cross and Skene—wherever he was—filed nothing. I wavered and weakened after a plea from Staton, my boss.

During that final week, Al Capone, from his island home, decided to make character . . . and threw a demure cocktail party for all visiting writers. I didn't attend but Scarface was strictly Emily Post. Capone managed to spread his peculiar good will the night of the fight by scattering 100-dollar bills among the ushers. They got paid even if Dempsey didn't.

The actual fight should have made big money—200,000 dollars anyway. It lost. During all the buildup I'd had a room at the Flamingo Hotel—at the straight daily rate. I could look over the situation with a clear conscience, but that didn't help Carey and the Madison Square Garden Corporation. Sharkey won when he might well have lost. Later Jack told me, "Strib-ling hit me with a full right over the heart. It hurt a lot. I fell in to grab him. He beat me to it by grabbing me first and holding on until I was ready to go on. Had our positions been reversed, I could, in fact, I would have murdered him."

Stribling could have been a great fighter. He wasn't. He was a fine boxer . . . a good puncher . . . fast and strong. But he was the oddest ring fighter I ever knew. He was dead game—out of the ring. He was seldom as game in the ring during a tough fight . . . Schmeling, Sharkey, Berlenbach, Ad Stone are a few samples. Yet he would drive a shaky aircraft in front of a hurricane . . . or a motorcycle through a heavy wall. I have seen him do it. He was killed on that motorcycle.

Shelby, Montana, and Miami Beach are two memories that will never be forgotten. The Miami Beach fight came just before the famous market crash. That's where it belonged. But looking back and reflecting on that golden, crazy age—from 1919 to 1930—I'm convinced, more than ever, that no decade in history has produced the likes of Ruth, Dempsey, Jones, Hitchcock, Man o'War, Weissmuller—my all-time swimmer—and Bill Tilden. They had that indefinable but 18-carat touch called "color," that put them above the greats of any age. Call it crowd appeal, class, warmth, personality—whatever it was they had it!

Over the Hills

Weary the years that have passed since then,
Who dreamed as the star dust fluttered down
Of fame that fluttered beyond the years,
Of glory hooked to the sweep of cheers,
A kid who looked to the heights some day,
Over the hills and far away,
Over the hills and far away.

Weary the years that have passed since then,
Faint the dreams in a lonesome den,
The sullen tread of the crowd moves by,
Where stars are dim in a fading sky.
Where is the glory that ruled the fray?

Over the hills and far away,
Over the hills and far away.

Ty and the big Babe, Matty and Cy,
Dempsey and Tunney—Thorpe and the rest—
Where are the mighty who held the road?
Those who dwelt in the gods' abode?
Where are the kings who ruled the play?
Over the hills and far away,
Over the hills and far away.

CHAPTER ELEVEN

Gene Tunney,
a Study in Concentration

Tip to Young Fighters

Pardon—I don't want to bore you,
  You, and your half dizzy mates,
But look at the field out before you
  Where there's a million that waits.
The million I mention is money,
  It's yours for a hook and a jab,
For high-grade condition, offensive ignition,
  And maybe a right-fisted stab.

Pardon—you kids who are swinging
  The leather in clubs here and there.
Mugs who are too often clinging
  To less than a dollar to spare.
Those whom the flophouse is dating,
  All written down in the book,
Look—there's a million that's waiting
  For only a jab and a hook.

The Giants were playing at home and Heywood Broun, covering for the *World,* and I were in the press box at the Polo Grounds when Walter Trumbull, sports editor of the old New York *Post* appeared in our midst with a young fellow in tow. Trumbull introduced his guest, Gene Tunney, all around, and I recall that Broun made quite a fuss over the handsome youngster.

I had glimpsed Tunney several days earlier when he fought "Soldier" Jones, a tough trial horse in a supporting bout to the Dempsey–Carpentier fight at Jersey City. Tunney scored a knockout in seven rounds. He was known only as a soldier-boxer who had won the light heavyweight title of the AEF in France. However, he had not fought as a bona fide heavyweight and certainly looked no part of one.

"What are your plans?" I asked.

"My plans are all Dempsey," he replied.

"Very interesting," I said. "But why not sharpen your artillery on Harry Greb, Carpentier or Tom Gibbons before you start hollering for Dempsey?"

"I suppose I'll have to beat them on the way up," Tunney said. "But Dempsey is the one I want."

I said no more and turned my attention back to McGraw's Giants, who with George (High Pockets) Kelly at first base, were headed for their first pennant since 1917. I recall Tunney later volunteered that he was 23 years old. I couldn't help thinking that this forthright young fellow would make a fine insurance salesman but certainly had no business having his features and brains scrambled by Dempsey's steel fists.

In January of 1922, Tunney defeated Battling Levinsky for the light heavyweight crown but lost it the following May to Harry Greb in perhaps the bloodiest fight I ever covered. A great fighter—or brawler—Greb handled Tunney like a butcher hammering a Swiss steak. How the Greenwich Village Irishman

with the crew haircut survived 15 rounds I'll never know—
except that Tunney always enjoyed more and better physical
conditioning than anybody he ever fought. By the third round,
Gene was literally wading in his own blood.

I saw Gene a few days later. His face looked as though
he'd taken the wrong end of a razor fight. "You know," he said,
"I must have lost nearly two quarts of blood in there."

Abe Attell, the former fighter-gambler and long-time "character" in the fight game, probably saved Tunney from bleeding
to death.

"Abe was sitting near my corner—a spectator," continued
Tunney. "When he saw the shape I was in after the second
round, he ducked out to the nearest druggist and bought his
entire supply of adrenalin chloride. Hustling back, Attell slipped
the bottle to Doc Bagley. Between rounds Doc's long fingers
flew. A superb 'cut' man, he'd managed to stop the bleeding
only to watch Greb bust my face apart in the following round.
It was discouraging."

To me, that fight was proof that Tunney meant to stick with
prize fighting. I tried to tell Gene that Greb was too fast for
him . . . to go after a softer touch. But less than a year later
they fought again and Tunney won the decision in 15 rounds.
I scored that fight for Greb, but then Tunney met Greb four
times more without defeat.

In the buildup for the Rocky Marciano vs. Roland La
Starza title bout in September 1953, they were comparing La
Starza to Tunney and Marciano to Dempsey—all tom-tom beating. For two years, prior to this fight, La Starza should have been
"learning" against the toughest monkeys he could find, fighters
with the mauling, brawling overtones of Marciano. That's exactly what Tunney did preparing for his first Dempsey fight.
Instead, La Starza remained in comparative cold storage, a fact
that became cruelly apparent as the recent fight wore on. One

of the prime truisms of the ring remains—namely, if fighting is your business, fight!

Many people are under the delusion that Tunney fought comparatively little . . . that he rocketed into the championship. Gene fought 65 bouts before meeting Dempsey at Philadelphia—with several professional fights in '17 and '18 before he enlisted in the Marines in May, 1918. Tunney was no glamour boy; he came up and learned the hard way.

After knocking out Carpentier in 15 rounds in '24 and dispatching Tom Gibbons in 12 rounds in '25—along with a string of other tough babies like Jimmy Delaney, Martin Burke, Chuck Wiggins, Tommy Loughran, and Johnny Risko—Tunney again camped on Dempsey's trail.

The Tunney–Gibbons fight, staged at the Polo Grounds in June, '25, ended in a knockout by Tunney in 12 rounds. Following his fine stand against Dempsey at Shelby, Gibbons had put together an imposing string of victories along the barnstorming route—mostly by knockouts. But when Gene tagged him at the Polo Grounds, Gibbons, then 36 years old, decided he'd fought his last fight. He retired and subsequently became sheriff of St. Paul.

As for Tunney, he finished out the year with KO's over Jack Herman and Bartley Madden and a decision against rubbery Johnny Risko, the Cleveland baker. Then he spent the next ten months preparing for Dempsey at Philadelphia.

In 1925 Tunney fought another fight that has never been recorded. I was the matchmaker and promoter.

Jim Corbett, the old champion and the world's greatest boxer, had written a book called *The Roar of the Crowd*. I was in the business of making sport pictures for the Sportlight, and I finally sold Corbett the idea of boxing three rounds, for pictures, with Gene Tunney.

My "assistant" promoter was Frank Craven, the actor. At

that time Tunney had heard of Will Shakespeare and having met Craven he was quite keen about it all. He also knew of Corbett's reputation as a boxer and what Jim had meant from the viewpoint of science and skill. We arranged a spot in midtown Manhattan, atop the Putnam Building.

Anxious to pick up any possible tip from the old stylist, Tunney arrived at the appointed hour, ready to go and attired in trunks. Corbett took one look at them and said, "I'd like to wear long white trousers. I had a pair of good looking legs in the old days but they don't look so good now. I'm nearly 60 and they are kinda shrivelled."

They boxed three 2-minute rounds. Tunney was on the defensive. Corbett was brilliant. He feinted with his left—then punched with his left. A left feint . . . a left hook; a right feint . . . a left jab; a right feint; a right cross. He still had bewildering speed! He mixed up his punches better than practically any fighter I've seen since—with the possible exception of Ray Robinson.

After the exhibition, Tunney turned to me, "I honestly think he is better than Benny Leonard. It was the greatest thing I've ever seen in the ring. I learned plenty," he said.

At 59 Corbett was still the master.

That winter in Florida I played golf with Tommy Armour and Tunney. Gene would hit his drive, toss aside his club and run down the fairway throwing phantom punches—left and right hooks—and muttering, "Dempsey . . . Dempsey . . . Dempsey."

"He's obsessed," observed Armour. "His brain knows nothing but Dempsey. I believe Jack could hit him with an axe and Gene wouldn't feel it. I don't know if Dempsey has slipped, but I'll have a good chunk down on Tunney when that fight arrives."

I should have gone along much stronger with Tommy's hunch but in those days Dempsey, in my book, remained a killer

whose arsenal was simply too much for Gene, a skilled boxer
who lacked a real KO punch. It would take a stick of TNT to
dislodge Dempsey, the kind of dynamite a crude but willing
Firpo had thrown that night in the Polo Grounds three years
earlier.

Soon after his Florida vacation, Gene was in Hollywood
making a picture called "The Fighting Marine." He didn't allow
the greasepaint and glitter to interrupt his training or, more
important, his thinking. Each afternoon he'd work at the Hollywood Athletic Club where Harry Grayson, now NEA sports
editor, got to know him. An ex-Marine himself, Harry spent a
lot of time with Tunney. The more he saw him, the better he
liked him. Six months before the fight, Grayson picked Tunney
to beat Dempsey. He never recanted. Matter of fact, Grayson
was the *only* fight writer in America to go overboard on Tunney.
We all thought he was crazy.

With Municipal Stadium, Philadelphia, selected as the site
of the fight, Dempsey settled down to heavy work at Baeder
Field, Atlantic City. Tunney went first to Saratoga, then to
Speculator, New York, and finished off his last three-weeks work
at East Stroudsburg, Pennsylvania, down by the Delaware Water
Gap and only a pitch shot from Fred Waring's golf course at
Shawnee. Billy Gibson, Tunney's manager, had the ring pitched
next to the first fairway of the town course and commandeered
the clubhouse as Tunney's quarters.

During those roaring twenties, fight camps were colorful,
with a heavyweight's camp handling more daily paying customers than the average TV fight of today. The *Tribune* had
Bill McGeehan, Fred Hawthorne, Harry Cross and Rice beating
out copy, stethoscoping Tunney's scholarly breathing and blue-
printing Dempsey's primeval snorting.

Ring Lardner, writing a syndicated column, had two pas-
sions, Notre Dame and Dempsey. Both represented the West.

Ring hailed from Indiana . . . as did Rockne's Irish. Dempsey came out of Manassa, Colorado—also "West, by God!" Lardner looked at Tunney, a New Yorker, with cold contempt . . . just as McGeehan, a transplanted New Yorker by way of San Francisco, viewed Dempsey with complete intolerance. Why? He hated Kearns because Jack fed Dempsey "exclusives" to Runyon in the Hearst camp.

Tunney went into heavy training at Speculator, New York, about 40 miles west of Saratoga. His camp was pitched near a small river amid gorgeous scenery. Ring Lardner and I went up for a visit. As we arrived, Gene was coming over the brow of a hill with a fat book under one arm. He could have passed for a young college athlete studying for his Masters in English.

Greeting us enthusiastically, Tunney said he'd been rowing up the river and then reflected on his communing with nature.

Ring pointed to the book. "What's the title?" he asked.

"The Rubaiyat . . . ," replied Tunney.

Brimming with enthusiasm for nature, Gene commented that he hadn't been able to take his eyes off the scenery. Fixing Tunney with those solemn, prominent eyes, Lardner cracked, "Then why the book?"

Tunney, at Speculator, was in fine physical shape. Later, at Stroudsburg, Pennsylvania, where he'd gone three weeks prior to the fight, he looked wonderful and was boxing sharply. I told him as much.

As for Dempsey—banging away behind closed doors at Baeder Field—well, he didn't look or move like the Dempsey of the Firpo fight three years earlier. Wealth, opulence, a bride and a revamped nose hadn't exactly brought Jack anything approaching soul comfort. Also, he was fighting his old manager, Kearns. Having moved out of Dempsey's camp bag and baggage, Kearns was slapping him with six kinds of injunctions right up to the eve of the fight.

"Lawyers!" snorted Dempsey one afternoon when we were alone. "Honest, Grant, I'd be better off if I could get rid of the whole mob of 'em for one hundred thousand dollars. It would be cheaper in the long run. They're nothing but a pack of bums . . . every last one of 'em!" Thus was Dempsey's state of mind going into that first Tunney fight.

Concerning sparring partners, Jack never spared the horses. For this fight his main hired hand was Tommy Loughran, a particularly clever light heavyweight. Several days before the fight, a well-known fight manager and close friend of Dempsey saw Jack's last workout with Loughran. He saw Loughran out-box Dempsey for three rounds by a city block. He paid little attention to what had happened until Dempsey sent for him.

"How did I look today?" Dempsey asked.

"You looked fine . . ." the manager said.

"You are crazy," retorted Dempsey. "I was terrible. Tunney would have murdered me today."

They argued back and forth. Then the fellow left with the horrible realization that he had a 20,000 dollar to 5,000 dollar bet on Dempsey. "Jack don't like his chances," he thought. "I got to do something about this."

I saw him that evening in the lobby of the Ben Franklin Hotel. When I commented he looked extra pale, he told me his predicament. Next morning, however, when I encountered him, he looked positively beamish.

"It's this way," he smiled. "I'm walkin' around the corner last night. I'm treadin' that last mile . . . when I bunk into this character. He asts how I'm doin'. I tell him I couldn't be better.

"I tell him I'm just back from Atlantic City seein' that tiger, Dempsey, work. It's like finding gold in the gutter . . ."

" 'What's like finding gold in the gutter?' he says.

" 'My bet,' I says. 'I'm down at four to one on the Champ. Twenty thousand bucks to make five thousand. It'll be over in

two rounds. . . . Good return on my investment . . '. don't you
think?'

"'I'd like a chunk of somethin' like that,' he says.

"'How strong?' I says.

"'Strong,' he says.

"'Doubt I can help but I'll see what I can do,' I says. I
walk once around the block and bunk into my friend . . . he's
riveted to the spot I left him.

"'Got you down,' I says. 'It wasn't easy! You're in at four
to one at twenty G's.' I'd rolled him my whole bet . . . thank
God!"

Two days before the fight, the sports section of the Sunday
Tribune went ten solid pages. The *Tribune's* owner-publisher
Ogden Reid was amazed. As the paper was going to bed Saturday night, Reid exclaimed, "Grant, you're making the *Tribune*
more of a sports paper than anything else! At this rate, we're
becoming ALL sports, and damn the rest of the world!"

"You could do worse," I replied, trying to manage a straight
face.

Matter of fact, that week end was one of the greatest in
sports. George Von Elm defeated Bobby Jones for the Amateur
golf crown at Baltusrol. Rene Lacoste defeated Big Bill Tilden
in the National tennis final at Forest Hills. The crush on Philadelphia was under way, with 25-dollar tickets being gobbled up
at anywhere from 100 to 175 dollars each—and Rickard threatening to call the fight off, so great were Dempsey's legal com-
plications. Down in Miami, a tornado was all but knocking
Florida's glittering Gold Coast off the face of the earth—leaving
untold death and destruction. I had steered clear of Miami,
thank goodness, but I was spinning in all the other directions
like a roulette ball on a galloping wheel.

That brings up another matter. I'd been fighting a cold all
that week with hard deadlines, no sleep and too much prohibi-

tion whiskey. McGeehan and I landed in Philadelphia the evening of September 22nd to make sure we'd get plenty of sleep and be fresh for the big fight on the 23rd.

We'd eaten and were headed back to the hotel when one of us recalled a roulette wheel less than two blocks from City Hall. We decided we'd drop by for just a few innocent whirls of the wheel. Along about 2:00 A.M. I was 1,200 dollars ahead; McGeehan was 800 behind.

"Let's get out of here," I said, "and get some sleep."

"Like hell!" replied McGeehan. "I'm going to get even!"

At 5:00 A.M. we had enough, between us, for taxi fare to the hotel. I was ready to curl up with a pint of whiskey and a revolver.

When I awakened about noon, I was still 48 years old— and felt 88. Following a breakfast of bicarb and coffee we managed to struggle into our clothes and head downstairs. On the sidewalk in front of the Bellevue-Stratford stood Rickard and his famed malacca cane. He was conversing with Gibson, Tunney's manager, and a few sports writers. The day was foggy and Rickard was worrying about rain and the possibility of postponement. Suddenly a writer came swinging through the door.

"Heard the latest, Tex?" he said. "We just got word that Tunney's flying into town for the weigh-in. . . ."

(Don't forget, this was a year before Lindbergh made the world airplane-conscious.)

"Flying into what?" stammered Rickard, nearly swallowing his cigar.

"He's flying in . . . Gene's in the air now!"

Rickard turned to a dumbfounded Gibson, who had left everything in readiness back at Stroudsburg for Tunney to travel into town by automobile.

"Goddamn that son of a bitch!" exploded Rickard, whacking

his cane on the pavement. "What's that Tunney trying to do to me?"

"What's he trying to do to you?" countered McGeehan. "What about himself?"

I couldn't blame Rickard. This is what happened. Casey Jones, the airplane stunt flier and instructor, had flown his little biplane up to Stroudsburg and landed it on the golf course the morning of the fight—after Gibson had left.

Casey could smell out a promotion stunt quicker than the next man. Gene had never been in a plane. Jones convinced him that it would be far easier and quicker, too, to fly down the Delaware River to Philly, a distance of only 70 or 80 miles, than it would be to drive. To prove his point, Casey would take Gene for a 5-minute trial hop. Tunney, in fine mental fettle, agreed, climbed aboard and they were off into the wild blue yonder. Once they were airborne, however, the golf course and all surrounding terrain were immediately socked in. Jones couldn't land. He took a compass heading for Philadelphia and drilled into a fog bank.

"I could have reached over that open cockpit and touched the Delaware Water Gap with either hand," said Tunney later. "It was that close! It took us about an hour and twenty minutes to cover eighty miles. I think we came by way of California."

Tunney had been air sick. After the weigh-in, he hid out in a friend's apartment, ordered a steak and went to sleep. The steak burned up. "We had a spare," said Gene. "I stayed awake till that one was on the platter . . . ate . . . and then dozed off for several hours. I felt O.K."

With a crowd of 135,000 contributing to the first two-million-dollar gate, Gene Tunney, a superbly cool and efficient boxer, marched out of his corner at the opening bell and hit Dempsey, the fighter, with a high, hard right hand. That blow sealed Dempsey's doom. It started to rain in the fourth round and

by the tenth and final round it was a deluge. At the end, Dempsey's face was a bloody, horribly beaten mask that Tunney had
torn up like a ploughed field.

Speed of foot, a sharp jab and a right cross that ripped
Dempsey's face like a can opener were going for Tunney that
night against a man who, despite a rocky training period, had
been installed at 4– and 5–1 favorite. Tunney, at 29, had arrived
on his toes. Dempsey, at 31, departed—flat footed. Dempsey had
never been knocked out, but had the fight gone 15 rounds, the
referee would have had to stop it. Blind by the final bell, Dempsey grabbed one of his seconds and said, "Take me to him . . .
I want to shake his hand."

It's fine to help build a champion. But when his time comes
to step down, as it always will, it's unpleasant to tear him down
and bury him. I intended to give Tunney a fitting tribute in my
overnight story that historical night. And I intended to go as
easy on Dempsey as I could. I did neither.

Due to the rain it was impossible to use a typewriter. I
dictated the description of the fight to my wire man. With me
that night were Lardner and Benny Leonard, the lightweight
champ from 1917–1925. Back at the hotel a raging sore throat
and a hangover had me in bad shape.

"Take a slug of bourbon and lie down," said Lardner. "I'll
file your overnight." Leonard, a Dempsey man, told Lardner
that he suspected the fix had been in for Tunney to win. The
story appearing next day under my byline blistered the hide off
both Tunney and Dempsey. Neither spoke to me for several
months. I couldn't blame either, but I couldn't open my mouth.
I had a ghost.

Incidentally, where did the Ghost Writer in sport first show
on the scene? According to George Ade this type of story was
first used in this country at the Fitzsimmons–Maher fight in
Texas in the early 1890's.

George was quite fond of John L. Sullivan. He covered the Corbett–Sullivan fight in New Orleans in 1892.

"Did you ever see Sullivan after that fight?" I asked him.

"Oh, yes," George said. "I saw him at the Fitzsimmons–Maher fight, staged just across that muddy creek, the Rio Grande, on Mexican soil opposite the Texas town of Langtry. When I ran into John L., he told me he had been sent down by a Boston paper to cover the fight and added, 'I've a young fella from Harvard with me who is doin' the writin'.'

"The fight lasted two punches worth," continued Ade. "Maher knocked Fitz down with the first punch and Fitz knocked Maher out with the second. . . . Here was John L's lead as written by his Harvard ghost, the first ghost writer I ever heard of:

E'en as the mantle of the dewey eve settled over the silvery Rio Grande tonight—

It was signed by John Lawrence Sullivan.

The second Dempsey–Tunney fight, in Chicago, exactly one year later, was pretty much a repetition of the first—except for that long count.

There's an old saying that "champions never come back." They all but had to bury that old truism that night at Soldiers Field before 104,943, who had paid 2,658,660 dollars to see the bomb go off. It was Tunney's first defense of his crown. As for Dempsey, he'd chipped a lot of rust off his plates two months earlier against Jack Sharkey. His seven-round KO of Sharkey had been Jack's hardest victory.

There was never a more popular underdog than ex-champ Dempsey going into the second Tunney fight. With old-timers, whether it be baseball players or fighters, the ability to hit goes last. And Dempsey could still hit—as proved in the Sharkey debacle.

At Chicago, it seemed that everybody and anybody short of President Coolidge was calling the shots, and throwing coal on the fires of intrigue. The fight was made to order for Chicago, a boom city that was busting its breeches with prosperity and the honkytonk that goes with it.

In 1927, the sports world wore seven-league boots as Babe Ruth boomed, "It's great to be alive . . . and a Yankee." And The Babe was spearheading the greatest of all Yankee teams to the American League pennant and a clean sweep over Pittsburgh in the World Series. That year Ruth blasted his Homeric mark of 60 home runs. Tommy Armour, the Silver Scot with the deadly long irons, won the U.S. Open and Bob Jones reclaimed the Amateur title. Lindbergh took his big hop to Paris and the French won the Davis Cup from us—and the U.S.A. didn't get it back for ten more years.

Tunney did his training at Lake Villa, Illinois, while Dempsey pitched camp at Lincoln Fields race track outside of town. Meanwhile, the whole world started to descend upon Chicago. Even Al Capone seemed lost in the crush.

On the afternoon of September 22nd George Whiteside, Tunney's lawyer, and Leo Flynn, Dempsey's legal mind, met at the Illinois Boxing Commission offices to clear up the knockdown rule—"once and for all." It was firmly agreed to by both parties "that the fighter scoring a knockdown shall immediately go to the farthest neutral corner and wait there until signalled by the referee to resume hammering his man," or words to that specific effect.

That night, every name sports writer in the United States plus a huge assemblage of foreign newspaper men were at ringside—along with 104,943 other paying guests. Never again will I witness the mass of seething humanity that jammed Soldiers Field. Typewriters snarled their keys endeavoring to outdo the next machine with bombastic descriptives and double superlatives.

As clean shaven as Tunney in that first fight at Philadelphia, Jack reverted to his old custom of entering the ring with three days' growth of black beard. He was tan as a month of work under a hot sun could bake him. Tunney, by contrast, was pink and white . . . with white trunks. Dempsey wore black trunks. The betting was even money.

The first six rounds were a repetition of the Philadelphia fight. Tunney boxed beautifully, his straight left jab and combinations jarring Dempsey but not hurting him particularly. I was thinking of my overnight lead in the seventh—when, lo and behold—Dempsey landed a right cross over Tunney's left lead. It landed like a bomb on the left side of Tunney's jaw. The lights in Tunney's mind flickered as a second right to the jaw knocked him into the ropes. As Tunney came off the ropes, clearly dazed, Jack caught him with a short and crucifying left hook . . . then a right . . . a left and a right. Tunney was down on the canvas, his left hand clutching the middle rope near one corner.

Dempsey landed six or seven punches. Had Tunney enjoyed anything less than 100 per cent physical condition, he would have been "out" at the count of 20 . . . or 30. In the space of two seconds, Soldiers Field became a braying bedlam. As Tunney hit the deck, Referee Dave Barry signalled Dempsey to "that farthest neutral corner." His mind set on just one thing, the final and utter destruction of Tunney, Jack moved straight ahead to the corner where the battered Tunney lay and stood behind him, his arms on the top rope. Barry charged Jack, grabbed him around the waist and pointed to the opposite corner. Then Jack moved. How many seconds elapsed between the time that Tunney fell and Dempsey reached that far corner I'll never know. I do know that when Barry started his count

and reached seven, Tunney was on one knee, listening atten-
tively, and was up at nine. A tiger flew at Tunney. But Gene,
already in almost complete command of his faculties, back
pedalled and circled out of range until his head had completely
cleared.

That was Dempsey's last chance—the only round of the
ten I could score for him.

Tunney never saw that first punch, the right cross that
landed over his left lead.

"I had injured my right eye in training about a week before," said Gene in recapping the fight for me. "The retina had
become partly detached and there was just a spot of astigma-
tism in it. I caught that punch "blind"—from nowhere—but it
was dead on the target.

"I had never seen Barry in my life until he called us together
at center ring," continued Gene. "I recall he explained the knockdown rule, slowly and clearly to us. After he finished he said,
'Do you understand, Champ?' I had never before been called
'Champ.' It felt good. Then he said, 'Do you understand, Jack?'
We both said, 'Yes.' He then said, 'In the event the man scoring
the knockdown does not go to the farthest neutral corner, *I will
not* start counting until he does reach it. . . . Do you understand that, Champ? . . . Jack?'

"We both answered, 'Yes.' "

Tunney defended his title once more, in New York, against
a tough but inept Tom Heeney, whose arms that night didn't
seem any longer than a seal's flippers. I felt the natural follow-up
would have been Sharkey "The Sailor" against Tunney "The
Marine," but that's water over the dam. Directly following the
Heeney pushover, Gene retired to the life of a country squire
. . . with a beautiful bride, Polly Lauder, daughter of a steel
family.

Tunney today, at 55, is a fine figure of a man enjoying robust middle age. He is a director of several corporations with offices on Vanderbilt Avenue near Grand Central Station, and we frequently have a cocktail and lunch together.

Looking over the Tunney of today as compared with the Tunney of '26 and '27, I can read the figure of a man who dedicated himself to a task as no other athlete, with the exception of Ben Hogan, ever dedicated himself. For at least six years the Tunney of Philadelphia fame trained for that first big chance as perfectly as a man can train: no drinking—no smoking—proper food—proper exercise—no deviation from the straight and narrow—all harnessed to a tremendous power of concentration.

We were discussing those Golden Twenties one day recently over luncheon at the Chatham Hotel.

"Life's been good . . . awfully good to me, Grant," said Gene. "In my trade at the time—prize fighting—there will never be another period like those Twenties. . . . There were a lot of first rate competitors . . . also, there were millionaire sportsmen around who had a genuine interest in all sports. If you thought you could make your point, those were the days to prove it."

They sure were.

CHAPTER TWELVE

Big Bill Tilden

Launched on the flood tide of the Dempsey–Willard fight, the Golden Age—from 1919 to 1930—was under way. And the biggest gold nugget of them all, at least with a tennis racquet in his huge right paw, was William Tatem Tilden II, in my opinion the greatest player who ever stepped on the court.

I had gone out to Forest Hills to cover the National Tennis Championships. It was September, 1919. I was after a column on the singles final between Tilden and Bill Johnston. That day I had lunch with "Little Bill" in the dining room of the clubhouse. No bigger than a sack of Harry M. Stevens' peanuts, Johnston weighed 121 pounds—after a long match he weighed as little as 112! His right arm, the one that propelled his famed forehand, was no bigger around than a billiard cue. The little guy ate calmly, talking objectively of the coming match. He seemed in a grand frame of mind.

Tilden was cagewalking like a tiger around the clubhouse. Finally, as Johnston was toying with a glass of iced tea, Tilden lunged over.

"Come on, Bill! . . . Let's get this over," he said.

"I'm ready, Bill," replied Johnston, sipping his tea.

The following match went down as one of those David and Goliath things. Because, if ever an adversary seemed outmanned for sheer size, and outgunned in stroking ammunition, it had to be "Little Bill" Johnston, the California half-pint who never knew when he was licked.

That afternoon Johnston whipped Tilden three sets to one. His forehand was devastating—an attacking weapon that swept Tilden before it. That marked the first and last time Johnston defeated Tilden in a title match. Big Bill won the cup from 1920 straight through 1925 and again in 1929.

As an all-time champion, Tilden emerged from the strangest surroundings imaginable. Particularly in sport, champs, as a rule, have fought and clubbed their way up from comparative poverty. Dempsey often knew the gnaw of hunger as a railroading roustabout in the switchyards of the Rockies where he fought for survival. Cobb was no pampered youngster! Tunney came off the sidewalks of Greenwich Village, and Ruth had only the haziest recollection of parents and home. Bob Jones came from comparatively plush circumstances, but Hagen and Ben Hogan weren't raised with a silver niblick.

Tilden was born at Germantown, a suburb of Philadelphia, in February, 1893. His father was a giant, physically—a robust swashbuckler—enormously successful in business, leader of the Republican machine in Philadelphia and president of the Union League Club of Philadelphia. His mother was beautiful, tall, refined . . . a completely artistic woman whose voice had been trained for opera. His elder brother Herbert was as much like his father as young Bill was like his mother. When Mrs. Tilden died Bill was but 18. Four years later both his father and his brother died. As a boy who had been babied by his mother, Bill, despite early schooling at Germantown Academy, spent most

of his formative years under the guardianship of women—
particularly his aunt. Buster Brown collars, velvet suits—young
Bill wore them all. Instead of bats and baseballs at Christmas
he received dolls and other girlish gifts.

I learned about Tilden, from Tilden, only in shreds and
patches of informal conversation. I learned much more from
Vincent Richards, Bill's amateur and professional sidekick
through the early and late years. Bill and young Vinnie first
teamed together in 1919 to win the National Doubles crown
at the Longwood Cricket Club in Boston. In 1944, a quarter
century later, Old Bill and not-so-young Vinnie again teamed to
win the National Professional Doubles title at Forest Hills.

Whatever Tilden's shortcomings as a member of society,
I'm convinced that his abnormal upbringing gave him a complex. Bill was stand-offish and show-offish. Proud, sensitive, he
craved affection and respect from mature people—just as any
man—but received it from few.

But let him climb into those long white flannels and march
to center court with a bundle of racquets under his long arm
and it was, Silence! Master at Work.

Tilden won his first National Singles Championship in
1920, at the age of 27—considered late for an athlete to make
his big move. (At 28, Jones had declared himself out of competitive golf.) But when he finally arrived—with both big feet
firmly planted on Forest Hill's center court in 1920—the fans
knew that this fellow Tilden was about to become a second Rock
of Gibraltar.

Ty Cobb and I watched Tilden practicing one spring day in
1930 in Augusta, Georgia. Following the geese, the amateurs
were threading their way back north—including a stopover
tournament at the Augusta Country Club. Tilden, it seems, had
been having trouble with his cut shot and went out to practice.

Cobb watched Big Bill work over that shot for one solid hour
. . . hitting ball after ball. Ty admired what he saw, "He's quite
something," remarked Cobb. "He's not afraid of work."

Bill knew he was so much better than the rest. He had the
physical equipment—the tools for the game. Tennis was 100
per cent Bill's life—whenever he strayed from the court he was
pathetic.

I recall the year—it must have been '23 or '24—when Bill
had his little adversary, Bill Johnston, two sets to one at Forest
Hills in the National Singles final. The big guy was winging along
in the fourth set—towards match game. Thunder clouds, black
and ominous, suddenly started swirling in. Bill took one look at
the weather, turned to Johnston and ripped across four service
aces . . . to close out match and title just before the down-
pour.

In 1930 I was with Tilden while he dressed for his semi-
final match against John Doeg, the cannonballing California
southpaw. I remarked on a big strawberry bruise on the point
of Bill's right hipbone.

"It's not much. . . . I got it from a spill. It catches me
whenever I push off the right foot," remarked Bill. "But Grant,
I've won enough on two good legs. I want to see what I can do
with just one."

Doeg beat him that day in a match that went 80-odd
games. Once under way, Bill moved into the ball as fluently as
ever. But he just wasn't up to those sudden starts that had him
flinching.

That particular "experiment" failed . . . not to take anything away from Johnny, whose service that day was truly magnificent. But the point is, Tilden never stopped experimenting
even during championship matches.

"At times I've got to practice, but I don't really care anything about it except to erase some mechanical stroking error I've slopped into," said Bill. "I like to see how a particular stroke . . . or any new tactic I'm thinking about shapes up under pressure."

Ellsworth Vines, an extraordinary player and later a respected if not altogether successful circuit touring golfer, was amazed at Tilden's stamina . . . particularly after Vines joined Tilden's touring band of pros in the 1930's.

I ran across Vines while he was on tour with the Tilden troop.

"Why, Bill's an old man!" remarked Vines. "But his stamina would kill a horse. A few weeks ago we were playing in Buffalo. It was Bill's birthday—up towards his fortieth—and he beat me with his finest tennis, with one set going to seventeen–fifteen.

"Dammit, Granny, I'm much younger than Bill but at the end of that match I was whipped. I stumbled to our hotel . . . flopped down on my bed and just lay there. For twenty minutes I couldn't move.

"In bursts Bill, looking like he just stepped out of the barber's chair. He's had his shower . . . is all decked out in that long polo coat with a bushel of racquets under his arm. He's pulling out for Cincinnati—right then at one A.M.—with an eight-hour drive staring him in the face. His only admonition was, 'Be there . . . on time, boy! We should do well in Cincinnati!' . . . and he was gone."

Tilden was the true artist . . . and like artists, he was subject to those black moods when melancholia owned him.

I recall the night I had a phone call from Vines.

"Bill told me he's committing suicide this afternoon," barked Vines. "We gotta stop him!"

"What do you mean . . . *we* gotta stop him," I said. "If Tilden has decided to commit suicide, neither you nor I nor the Fire Department is going to stop him. Don't worry about him."

"Don't worry, hell!" replied Vines. . . . "I don't want him to kill our tour!" Such was the 'my brother's keeper' aspect of those old barnstorming tours—with each stop a potential jackpot or blown fuse.

As long as I knew Tilden—from 1919 until his death in June 1953—he was always in debt. He was like Babe Ruth in his heyday. They both knew how to spend the green stuff but neither knew anything about conserving it.

In 1925, when Tilden was kingpin of the court world, a panel was called at the old Waldorf to discuss "amateurism and bylines." Gathered together were Judge John K. Tener, Devereux Milburn, the polo star, Tilden, several others, and myself.

Milburn had been offered 5,000 dollars to write up the International Polo Matches the preceding year. As a member of the United States team, he had finally decided he couldn't take it. Tilden, on the other hand, had been writing tennis pieces— for magazines particularly—about the rank and file of the tournaments he was then playing. And no mistake about it, Bill—to the tune of 25,000 dollars one year with the Philadelphia *Public Ledger Syndicate*—could write tennis! A simon-pure amateur—with several fortunes in the bank—Milburn, along with Tener and others, wanted the question cleared up.

"I would *like* to have accepted that money to write about my particular sport," said Milburn. "But I simply felt that as an amateur, I couldn't accept it."

"It's a matter of taste, not amateurism!" retorted Tilden.

To my mind, that reply of Bill's remains one of the great answers—on sport or any other subject.

It was finally agreed upon that an amateur could write about a match he witnessed but *not* as a competitor.

Tilden kicked away the principal of two solid family fortunes before he died with less than ten dollars in his pocket. It was simply a case of "having and spending," and when Bill had it, first class wasn't good enough.

I studied Tilden against the best of his age during an era when those adversaries were at the top of their game. There are some fine tennis players making the rounds today, but honestly, I don't think they compare with those of Tilden's time. Looking at the names who came and went during Bill's long tenure, I'm convinced of it: Norris Williams, on Tilden's '26 Davis Cup team; Vinnie Richards; Bill Johnston; Rene Lacoste; Henri Cochet; Jean Borotra; the two Franks, Hunter and Shields; Gerald Patterson. Bill dominated the crowd of them when they were at their peaks. And looking back through the records, I'm still astounded when I recheck the fact that Bill was 37 in 1929, defeated Frank Hunter for the title at Forest Hills and was 38 when he became champion at Wimbledon for the third time—in 1930!

Like Tommy Hitchcock in polo, Willie Hoppe in billards, Cobb in baseball, and perhaps Pudge Heffelfinger in football, Bill was a notable exception to the adage that time and tide wait for no man.

Vinnie Richards, who played Tilden more than 1,000 singles matches over their tremendous span, was reminiscing about Tilden recently.

"Granny," he said, "we know that many scientists, writers and other creative persons reach the peak of their productivity between thirty-five and forty-five. Statesmen, political leaders and top professional people frequently come into their own much later—between fifty and sixty. But the headliners in the physical skills ordinarily are at their best at about twenty-seven or thereabouts—but rarely past thirty—and from there on the process of their bodily decline takes its toll.

"By this reckoning, Tilden was nearly a quarter century

'past due' in his field when he died. Yet he persisted in meeting any challenge up to the very end. After winning every tennis title of importance, national and international, at home and abroad, he maintained in the twilight of his days a standard of play, for at least one set, that thrilled fans and experts alike."

Tilden depended more on body action for his power than perhaps any athlete I've known. Tennis is a "wristy" game, but unlike many players who use a heavy racquet to make up for a lack of force, Tilden favored a very light bat—lighter than most women do! But his cannonball service attested to its effectiveness for him. The strength of his entire physique went into those serves.

Competitive guts? Big Bill had his share, plus. Few knew that long before he became a tennis headliner, Bill won his spurs in a bodily contact sport as one of the best hockey players ever to represent the University of Pennsylvania. But, to me, the big fellow never showed more intestinal fortitude than in the Davis Cup matches at Forest Hills in 1921 when the United States singles tandem of Big and Little Bill—Tilden and Johnston—whipped Japan 5–0 in the Challenge Round.

I covered those matches. Zenzo Shimizu, greatest of the Japanese, had Big Bill down two sets to love and was within 2 points of taking set, game and match when Tilden put on one of his historic rallies.

The crowd thought—along with most of the press, including Grant Rice—that Tilden deliberately let the Jap push him to the wall so he might make the most out of a dramatic comeback. And frankly, that's the impression I still retained when Richards straightened me out some 30 years later.

"Bill was in agonizing pain during those first three sets," said Richards. "He'd gone into action that afternoon with a boil as big as a walnut on his right instep and it had burst during that third set.

"As Tilden left the court at the intermission, he spied a doctor he knew in the stands and signalled him to follow him into the locker room," continued Richards. "Overhearing Tilden's few words, I followed the doc. The physician decided the infection had gone so deep he would have to lance the foot from the under side.

"Bill submitted to the painful incision without flinching and then insisted, against the doc's advice, on resuming play. With the foot tightly bandaged and wincing at every step, he limped back to the court and crushed Shimizu in the next two sets while losing but three games.

"That, Granny, took guts!"

In 1942 he could and did go out there and give Don Budge a rough time of it—for one or two sets. It was in August 1942—at the Eastern Grass Court Championships at the Westchester Country Club in Rye, New York. I don't recall who won that tournament—either Bobby Riggs or Don McNeil—but I do recall Tilden's exhibition match with Budge—best of three sets.

Then fiftyish, Bill defeated Budge 7–5 in the first set; but Don walloped the pants off Bill in the next two. I wandered into the locker room with Tilden, the vain has-been who wouldn't admit or submit to anything as prosaic as old age.

We were upstairs, and Bill, skinning off his flannels, was heartsick, fuming but saying little. As he turned to head for the shower he spotted a tall, well-built young fellow about 27, with a towel wrapped around his midriff, headed for the spray.

Bill took one look at the young man. "Dammit!" he cried. "Just give me your legs . . . no, to hell with your legs . . . just give me your feet and I'll go right back there and whip the daylights out of that Budge! The legs can still carry me. But the feet are heavier than lead."

There was nothing left to say. I patted Bill on the shoulder, told him he was magnificent, still, and left.

Tilden was 61 when he died. But he'd played in the professional championships the previous year . . . and defeated Wayne Sabin in an early round and had Frank Kovacs battling to whip him in the next round. That's quite a span of tennis— from the finals at Forest Hills in 1919 to the round of four at Cleveland in 1952—about 35 years of continuous championship play in a particularly strenuous game. For my money, at 59, Tilden—for one set—was still the best.

It's small wonder that the pros looked up to Bill for leadership when they were trying to get their sea legs as an organization in the mid 1940's. But Tilden was never cut out to be an administrator. Completely egotistical, theatrical, Bill was too impatient and arrogant to handle others.

Bill took a great, if sometimes foolish, pride in being well informed about things other than tennis. One year during the French championships in Paris Bill ran into an old friend, Mary Garden, the opera star, who was giving a concert there. She mentioned that our ambassador Myron T. Herrick had requested her to sing "The Star Spangled Banner" as a prelude to her regular routine . . . and that she was stumped for the words. She asked Bill to write them down for her. Bill, although equally rusty on the lyrics, was unwilling to admit his ignorance. So he promised to deliver them to her hotel that evening.

Our hero spent a miserable morning visiting Parisian music stores in a vain attempt to nail down the verses of the American national anthem. While brooding over his embarrassing plight at the Roland Garros Stadium that afternoon, he explained the situation to the French ace, Rene Lacoste.

Rene burst out laughing and promptly sang the words in English while Bill jotted them down. Thus he was saved from making a humiliating confession to Mary Garden.

One final reflection on Tilden the racquet wielder. Like Dempsey, he was always the attacker.

"Granny," he said, "I've found that the best way to break down the other person's morale is to attack his best shot. That's why, instead of being content to retrieve his best shot I attack it. Whenever the score is close, when the pressure's on, I attack harder than ever. No, I never discussed or worked out that court philosophy with anyone else. I discovered it for myself." Again, the mark of the champion.

As a "brain," Tilden was colossal on court. His change of pace, his mix-up shots were terrific. One of his best was a shot that looked like a heavy return—only to be a very soft shot. It fooled 'em for years.

Vincent Richards, Tilden's doubles partner and one of the game's great volleyers, still shakes his head at the mention of Tilden.

"I could beat that long drink of water—or at least I used to *think* I could beat him in title competition—if I could figure his next move. He was so damned unpredictable. My best payoff shot against Bill was a hard return right at his feet. . . ."

Where others had tennis elbow, Tilden, throughout most of his career, had a chronic tennis knee, I think his right one. It was shaky . . . at times gave him hell. But he never allowed it to interfere with his wrecking an opponent, either by slow, dramatic buildup or by sheer explosive force.

The last time I saw Tilden he didn't see me. It was in January, 1953, and Kit and I were spending a few weeks at the Beverly Wilshire in Beverly Hills. Our fifth-floor rooms over-looked the tennis courts. Down on the court below, Tilden, a gaunt, bespectacled figure in shorts, would work out with Frank Feltrop, the professional. For one set, he'd give Feltrop a rough time. At 60, right to the end, Tilden remained the complete stylist.

One morning while I was watching Bill work out, Kit stood by my shoulder. "Granny," she reflected, "somehow it's a tug . . . watching Bill down there, isn't it? He's still magnif-icent—in spurts. But compared to the Bill we knew, it's like watching a scarecrow go through the motions. You once wrote some verse entitled 'To Any Athlete.' It fits Bill. It fits us all . . . I guess."

To Any Athlete

Why is it each is the last to find
That his legs are gone—that his eyes are bad,
That the quicker reflexes have left his mind,
That he hasn't the stuff that he one day had,
That lost youth mocks, and he doesn't see
The ghost of the fellow that used to be?

How can they slip from the heights so far
And never know that the day has gone
When their eyes were fixed on a rising star
With a firm foundation to stand upon?
How can they slip as the comets fall
And read no writing upon the wall?

Caught by a stride which they used to beat—
Nailed by a punch that they used to block—
Trailing the flurry of flying feet,
But dreaming still of the peaks that mock—
Each is the last to learn from fate
That his story is finished—and out of date.

The reverential crowds of the Golden Twenties and the Turbulent Thirties had long departed, but enough of the Old Bill remained to capture the attention and the imagination of a 16- or 17-year-old youngster who watched Tilden play each morning. The boy's name is Mike Franks. According to Feltrop, he's about ready to be launched on the circuit. Well Mike, if you become half the tennis player Tilden was you'll be plenty good.

You wonder why I didn't go down and say hello to Bill?

The reason is sound. I've known many artists—some great ones. Whether they're musicians, actors, brush or pen-and-ink artists —or sports headliners—they're all high on vanity . . . pride . . . which is what got them to the top in the first place. But I seldom enjoy seeing the shell of a person who once was the complete headline. That's how I felt about Bill Tilden. That's how I know Bill, a tragic artist at the end, felt about himself.

CHAPTER THIRTEEN

The Two Horsemen, Hitchcock and Milburn

Back in the gloaming, I wrote a piece of verse entitled, "Alumnus Football" which closed with these two lines.

For when the One Great Scorer comes to mark against your name,
He writes—not that you won or lost—but how you played the Game.

I can't imagine two competitors who lived these lines with fiercer abandon than two friends of mine, now dead. They were polo players, both all-time ten-goalers. Their names were Tommy Hitchcock, Jr. and Devereux Milburn.

Of the two, Dev Milburn was only a trifle more conservative. I believe Hitchcock would charge headlong into a two-pronged, raging rhinoceros if the critter blocked his path. Milburn would first ask it to move.

I met Milburn and Hitchcock for the first time at Hurlingham, England, in 1921 when I was covering polo, golf and tennis

for the New York *Tribune*. They were playing on the U.S. Polo
Team with Watson Webb and Louis Stoddard. Hitchcock and
Milburn were fresh out of active war service. Tommy had been
shot down at the age of 18 as a flyer with the Lafayette Esca-
drille, but had later escaped. Milburn had been a major on staff
duty.

At that time I felt Milburn, roughly my age, was an old
friend. I knew Hitchcock less well—he seemed very quiet and
extremely reserved. Milburn was more loquacious. Later, at
the age of 57, he was still playing high-class polo although he
had any number of stitches holding him together as well as
several mended bone fractures. Like an old bull moose, he'd
been through the wars.

We played a lot of golf together and when he was my
partner I used to caution him not to swing too hard or he'd
start falling apart. I always feared a bone or a ligament would
drop out. But you couldn't stop him.

There was one thing in particular about Dev Milburn I
always agreed with. It was his philosophy of competitive sport.
The philosophy of many coaches is that winning is all that
counts—"The will to win" all that matters.

"That is a lot of nonsense," Milburn used to say. "It is the
battle—the contest—that counts, not the score. If two meet,
one must win and one must lose. But they can both have a great
afternoon!"

We were sitting in the clubhouse at Meadowbrook one day
when he explained his stand in further detail.

"We have just finished a match against the British team,"
he said. "We won easily—seventeen to two. I was bored to
death. No fight. Nothing but sitting on a horse. Years ago I
remember we met the British here. Cheape was riding for them.
What a fight! Hard, rough, knockdown battle all the way. We

lost. I never got such a kick out of a game. Who won wasn't important. It was the scrap. That's all—all!

"Take it this way," Dev continued. "In playing golf, I'd rather Bobby Jones beat me eight and seven than for me to beat some duffer nine and eight. I never got any fun out of beating second-rate opponents." That is a pretty fair line and Dev meant every word of it. He wanted to battle with his superiors or at least his equals.

Milburn and Hitchcock were the forerunners of modern polo. In the older days when Harry Payne Whitney was the U.S. captain, polo was largely a matter of finesse. The ball was hit for someone else to handle. It was worked forward towards the opposing goal in short takes. Harry Payne Whitney was a master at this art. He would help stickhandle the ball 5 or 60 yards down the field.

But when Tommy Hitchcock came along, his idea was "To hell with all this. We'll get the fifty yards with one wallop."

Milburn was always tough—at polo, golf or anything else.

I was playing with him as a partner one day when the match was all even at the final hole. Our opponents both got off fine drives; I was badly bunkered. Milburn sliced his drive into the middle of a bramble forest.

"Any chance?" he said.

"I'm buried," I said. "I'm out of it."

So Milburn disappeared into the thicket. Lost, I couldn't see him. One of our opponents stood and watched grimly.

"That's just what Milburn wants," he said, "a completely impossible shot."

There was a crash and the ball came sailing out some 200 yards and stopped eight feet from the cup. He had used a wood where I thought a niblick was impossible. That was Milburn. Nothing was impossible.

One Saturday I visited Meadowbrook to play golf with him.
It was snowing hard—midwinter. No one else showed up. Dev
was beaming. "Ever see a finer day?" he asked. "We'll have a
picnic."

"We can't play golf today," I said.

"Oh yes we can," he said. "We are all fixed." At which point
he brought out ten red-painted balls. We played until all the
balls were lost in the snowdrifts.

No game was quite tough enough for him. He wanted a
handicap on the side. Dev always wanted to face odds. If he
ever had the best of it he wouldn't play. That was the competitive philosophy of Dev Milburn—only the game and the contest
count—never the score.

I don't think anyone ever knew Tommy very well. My
friend Teddy Roosevelt, Jr. used to arrange softball matches for
various charities near Oyster Bay. Present would be Babe Ruth,
Tommy Hitchcock, Lowell Thomas and many more. We had a
lot of fun.

I recall the time I met Hitchcock again in Chicago at the
East-West polo matches around 1933. He was the head of the
eastern outfit—210-pound Cecil Smith led the westerners. Hitchcock always played furiously. Several times he was knocked off
his pony. Knocked unconscious, he suffered a bad concussion.
Told not to play again, he returned for the next match.

I don't remember many conversations with Hitchcock. Years
later, we'd often sit together and say little, but we were always
comfortable in each other's company. In some ways he reminded
me of a piece of rock. There was one conversation, however, I
won't forget.

In 1941, after war had broken out, I saw a piece in the paper
that Tommy Hitchcock was soon leaving to enlist as a flier. He
was then 43 years old. I made a date to call on him at his office
in downtown New York. There was no particular reason for my

doing so except my admiration and affection for a man I thought was going off to die needlessly.

"Well," Hitchcock said, "I'm glad to see you. But what's the story?"

"I understand," I said, "you are going back in the flying corps."

"That's right," he said. "What's wrong with that?"

"Nothing," I said, "except you've done your part and you're forty-three years old. I just happen to like you. I don't want to see you commit suicide."

Hitchcock smiled. "I'm only forty-three," he said. "That is still young. I feel sure I am as young as a man of twenty-four. I am in fine condition. My reflexes are perfect. I can play polo as well as I could ten or twelve-years ago—or twenty years ago!"

"You broke in as a kid," I said. "This is something else again. Don't you think you've done enough for your country?"

He looked at me a long time. Finally he said, "Can you ever do enough for your country?"

"Yes," I said, "when you have passed the peak of usefulness."

"I haven't even reached that peak," he said rather violently. "I'm just coming to my peak." He looked it. Young looking and strong, a 43 that looked 25. We shook hands, said "So long," and the rest of it. As I turned to leave he said, "What difference does it make—now or a little later on? I'm not worrying . . . don't you." His was a genuine smile as I left.

> Cowards die many times before their deaths;
> The valiant never taste of death but once.
> —Shakespeare

> Whether it's Heaven or whether it's Hell—
> Or whether it's merely sleep;

Or whether it's Something in Between
Where ghosts of the half-gods creep—

Since it comes but once—and it comes to all—
On the one fixed, certain date—
Why drink of the dregs till the Cup arrives
On the gray date set by Fate?

One by one till the line has passed—
The gutter-born—and the crown—
So what is a day—or a year or two—
Since the answer's written down?

What is a day to a million years?
When the last winds sound their call?
So here's to the days that rest between—
And here's to the last of all.

I realized Tommy Hitchcock truly didn't care. In April '43
I read that a P-51 Mustang he had been testing suddenly hurtled
high from the heavens to the earth below. A very game and
gallant gentleman had left our circle—one of many others, but
not any other Tommy Hitchcocks. Or Devereux Milburns. Polo
players? They had all the gameness and courage of Dempsey
and Tunney, Cobb and Hagen, Tilden, Nagurski and Thorpe.
They fought for the love of fighting, for the clash of battle, for
the give and take of the competition—not for the puny bauble
that goes to the victor, but for the thrill of the actual game.
Death to them was just an incident.

CHAPTER FOURTEEN

Knute Rockne
and the Four Horsemen

Coach Jesse Harper of Notre Dame took the real forward pass east in 1913. He brought it to West Point where Army and Notre Dame met that year for the first time. Harper gave the ball to quarterback Gus Dorais, who threw it to his broken-nosed roommate, Knute Rockne. Rockne caught it and Army was slaughtered 35–13. I didn't meet Rockne on that trip. I met him some years later when I returned to the Point after he became head coach at Notre Dame.

Ring Lardner, a keen Notre Dame and midwestern rooter, went with me on that trip to the Point in the fall of 1920. We ran into John J. McEwan, the big Army assistant coach. John J. was loaded with confidence. One of Army's all-time centers, John coached the Cadet line. Army's strong squad was headed by the flying Walter French, who earned his spurs—and an appointment to West Point—at Rutgers.

"I understand," said Lardner, "that Rockne is coming in again with that kid named Gipp."

"Who the hell is Gipp?" snorted McEwan.

"You'll find out at ten minutes to two tomorrow," replied Lardner.

McEwan did. With Army and the irrepressible French leading 17–14 at half time, Gipp put on a second half one-man rodeo as the Irish pulled out the game 27–17.

"How'd you like Gipp as a football player?" I asked McEwan after the game.

"Gipp is no football player," retorted McEwan. "He's a runaway son of a bitch!" One of the more volatile English instructors in West Point's long history, McEwan's descriptives remain as pungent as they are concise.

Self-reliant as a wild mustang, George Gipp came out of the iron-ore country near Calumet, Michigan, on Lake Superior's Keweenaw peninsula. He came up the hard way, but at making his point on a football field, Gipp could open with sevens and keep rolling 'em. He had more than his share of speed, power, daring and deception. At times he even baffled Rock. The following, told to me by a former Notre Dame star and assistant coach, occurred during the intermission of the historic 1920 Army game.

"Being behind by three points, Rock was really laying into the boys," he said. "He had about finished and Gipp, standing nearby, asked me for a drag of my cigarette. Rock looked up and spotted Gipp leaning against the door, his helmet on the back of his head, puffing the cigarette.

"Rock exploded, 'As for you, Gipp,' he crackled, 'I suppose you haven't any interest in this game. . . ?'

" 'Listen, Rock,' replied Gipp, 'I've got five hundred dollars bet on this game; I don't aim to blow any five hundred!' "

Rock was younger then. Later, not even Gipp would have got away with it.

In his own quiet way I rate DiMaggio, Joe, up near the very top. A marvelously graceful outfielder, Joe had a great throwing arm and a line-drive bat.

Sam Andre

NBC

Just before Ruth made radio history, or set it back a decade, in '28. By the time our interlocutor, Graham McNamee (center) got Babe back on the track, Ruth had blown fuses all over the NBC network and had rewritten the history books.

Pop Warner, perhaps football's greatest inventor.

Rockne's magnetism helped put Notre Dame into big type.

Sam Andre

Earl Blaik seldom speaks in public but when he does, Red's as dynamic as his Army teams. Blaik's coaching "precision" reminded me of Haughton.

"Point a Minute" Yost in a fairly formal mood. He was the "mostest" zealot.

With Duke's Wallace Wade at Durham (N. C.) in the mid '30's. With Ace Parker sparking Wade's attack the Blue Devils really rolled.

Introducing Lonnie Stagg at Rose Bowl lunch in '46, I mentioned…"the snows of winter may be on your head but the sunshine of eternal spring is in your heart." It fits Stagg.

Kit and me...I don't know where we're going...or coming, but we're on our way.

Two of my favorite children—Mr. and Mrs. Fred Butler.

Alex J. Morrison

Nothing more to say.

Walking the Atlantic with Bob Jones aboard the Europa route to the '36 Olympics.

Wide World Photo

Do you recognize this pair? The photograph was snapped in May, 1945, when Tilden and Richards won the National Professional doubles title 27 years after they had teamed to win the Amateur doubles crown.

Orating at orphans breakfast in LA in '42. Among the enthralled are Babe, Bob Meusel, McLemore and Hyland.

Hal McAlpin

With Jock Sutherland (at my right) at a golf match. Jock enjoyed good golf. Look closer and you'll spot Tommy Armour and Bud Kelland.

With Archie Reed and John Jackson, ex-USGA presidents, at Baltusrol in '36, when Tony Manero came out of nowhere to win the Open.

Alex J. Morrison

"Fishing" during Artists & Writers outing at Miami Beach in '29. I had hooked a 400 lb. shark but, feeling thirsty, I handed him over to the party's photog who handed him to someone else who finally cut loose the monster. Meanwhile, I was no longer interested. As a big game fisherman, I never saw a sailfish that didn't look better in the ocean than on somebody's line—or wall.

Notre Dame's Cyclone Beats Army, 13 to 7

Fleet, Powerful Western Backs and Hard Charging Line March Down Field for 2 Touchdowns

Cadet Score Comes On Brilliant Fake

55,000 at Polo Grounds See West Point Lose Gamely to Better Team

By Grantland Rice

Outlined against a blue-gray October sky, the Four Horsemen rode again. In dramatic lore they are known as Famine, Pestilence, Destruction and Death. These are only aliases. Their real names are Stuhldreher, Miller, Crowley and Layden. They formed the crest of the South Bend cyclone before which another fighting Army football team was swept over the precipice at the Polo Grounds yesterday afternoon as 55,000 spectators peered down on the bewildering panorama spread on the green plain below.

A cyclone can't be snared. It may be surrounded, but somewhere it breaks through to keep on going. When the cyclone starts from South Bend, where the candle lights still gleam through the Indiana sycamores, those in the way must take to storm cellars at top speed. Yesterday the cyclone struck again, as Notre Dame beat the Army, 13 to 7, with a set of backfield stars that ripped and crashed through a strong Army defense with more speed and power than the warring cadets could meet.

Marvelous Backfield

Notre Dame won its ninth game in twelve Army starts through the driving power of one of the greatest backfields that ever churned up the turf of any gridiron in any football age. Brilliant backfields may come and go, but in Stuhldreher, Miller, Crowley and Layden, covered by a fast and charging line, Notre Dame can take its place in front of the field.

Coach McEwan sent one of his finest teams into action, an aggressive organization that fought to the last play around the first rim of darkness, but when Rockne rushed his Four Horsemen to the track they rode down everything in sight. It was in vain that 1,400 gray-clad cadets pleaded for the Army line to hold. The Army line was giving all it had, but when a tank tears in with the speed of a motorcycle, what chance has flesh and blood to hold? The Army had its share of stars in action, such stars as Garbisch, Farwick, Willson, Wood, Ellinger and many others, but they were up against four whirlwind backs who picked up top speed from the first step as they swept through scant openings to slip on by the secondary defense. The Army had great backs in Willson and Wood, but the Army had no such quartet, who seemed to carry the mixed blood of the tiger and the antelope.

Cyclone Starts Like Zephyr

Rockne's light and tottering line was just about as tottering as the Rock of

One of Rock's greatest gangs was his 1924 team that featured a veteran array of backs functioning behind a powerful, combative line.

In the fall of 1923, Army met Notre Dame at Ebbets Field because the World Series between the Yankees and the Giants was taking place at the Polo Grounds. I preferred the football game. That afternoon I took along "Brink" Thorne, Yale's great 1895 captain. We had only sideline passes so Brink and I watched from the rim of the playing field. In one wild end run, the Irish backfield of Harry Stuhldreher, Jim Crowley, Don Miller and Elmer Layden, swept off the field over the sideline. At least two of them jumped over me, down on my knees.

"It's worse than a cavalry charge," I said to Brink. "They're like a wild horse stampede."

That thought occurred to me a year later at the Polo Grounds when that same backfield beat Army 13–7 en route to an undefeated year, and the "Four Horsemen" emerged on my copy paper. I'm afraid it was those four football players who averaged only 157 pounds and the glory they won that made the phrase stick.

They were an amazing four men. Fullback Elmer Layden, better than a 10-second sprinter, weighed 164 and was the heaviest of the lot. Quarterback Stuhldreher, at 154 pounds, was the lightest; and the halfbacks Miller and Crowley were in between. Layden could run, block, kick and handle a forward pass. Fast and shifty, the Four Horsemen had a brand of rhythm that was beautiful to watch. They were a hardy lot and were seldom hurt. They could all block and tackle and carry the ball —the memory of them made me scoff a little during the days of platoon football, with offensive and defensive specialists cluttering up the premises each Saturday afternoon.

All were keen and smart. Rockne liked players on his squad like these four—all individualists who did their own thinking.

Jimmy Crowley was one of the wittiest men I ever knew. In practice one day, Rock said to Jimmy after he had muffed some play, "What's dumber than a dumb Irishman?"

"A smart Swede," Jimmy replied. No further conversation.

They were and are a great bunch. I'm proud to list them among my closest friends, and that's been true for a quarter of a century and more.

What circumstance brought The Four Horsemen together under Rock? I asked Don Miller that question one day recently at Toots Shor's. With Miller were Layden and Crowley, three of the original four. It was a nice reunion.

"Actually," said Miller, "I didn't have much choice in the matter. My mother had sons at Notre Dame all the way from 1905 through 1925. My brother Harry made Walter Camp's Third Team as a halfback in 1909. Another brother, Walter, played in the same backfield as George Gipp in '19. I met Elmer, Jimmy and Harry for the first time when we were thrown together during our freshman year. How did you "happen" at South Bend, Jimmy?"

"Curley Lambeau was my coach back at Green Bay High," said Crowley. "He played with Gipp at Notre Dame in '18. We were State champs and when Curley mentioned Gipp and Notre Dame . . . well, I was on my way."

"I matriculated at the University of Iowa first," smiled Layden. "I'd played football and basketball at Davenport (Iowa) High. But I picked up a knee in basketball. The next fall at the University, they examined the danged knee and decided it wasn't worth the gamble. My high-school coach, Walter Halas, George (Chicago Bears) Halas' older brother, contacted Rockne. Rock was never too sure of that knee . . . but it never bothered me" . . . (I recalled the Yankees took a gamble on a rookie named Joe DiMaggio, knee and all, after he'd been turned down by scouts from several other teams.)

Stuhldreher played high-school ball at Massilon, Ohio, the long-time hotbed of early professional football, and then finished off at Kiski Prep. Harry's older brother, Walter, was a senior at Notre Dame when Harry entered.

And that's how four midwest kids happened to matriculate at Notre Dame. Compared to today's hunt for high-school heroes, it doesn't sound like much, does it?

Crowley currently manages a television station in Scranton, Pennsylvania; Stuhldreher handles public-relations work for United States Steel; Layden is a top salesman for the General American Transportation Company in Chicago; and Miller has his own law firm, Miller and Kennedy, in Cleveland.

Compared to many of the high-speed horses galloping around big college backfields today, the Four Horsemen were pony-sized.

"If we stepped on a scale today, I don't know who'd be more embarrassed—the scale or us," cracked Crowley. "But in those days our playing weight was legit. Before the Princeton game, at Princeton in '24, Rock invited the press to our dressing room. Then he called us out. 'You've been questioning the program weight of my backfield,' he snapped. 'Here's your chance to find out . . . exactly.' Rock then signalled us on the scales— one by one. Elmer then weighed one hundred and sixty-one . . . Miller and I were about the same, at one hundred and fifty-seven, and Stuhldreher was a few ounces under one hundred and fifty-two."

"We weren't very big—then," said Miller, "just big enough. After all, Rock's entire attack was based on speed and deception —scientific football. We breathed and lived Rock's rhythm and cadence and then play execution followed. Also, we all had to block on rotating plays. No prima donnas . . . Rock saw to that."

"Another thing," added Layden, "Rock used to load us down with extra-heavy practice gear. On Saturday, when we climbed into game suits we felt like four Lady Godivas. Actually we were four pounds lighter on Saturday than on weekdays."

"That's right," chuckled Crowley. "We might not have been any faster but we sure felt faster. . . . Psychologically, it was great."

It's been years since The Four Horsemen last shone as four satellites in what was perhaps Rock's greatest football constellation. I'd written countless leads before they arrived—I've written thousands more since.

"Granny," said Miller. "Rock put us together in the same backfield but the day you wrote us up as The Four Horsemen, you conferred an immortality on us that gold could never buy. Let's face it. We were good, sure. But we'd have been just as dead two years after graduation as any other backfield if you hadn't painted that tag line on us. It's twenty-nine years since we played. Each year we run faster, block better, score more TD's than ever! The older we are, the younger we become—in legend. Another thing. In business, that tag line has opened more doors . . . has meant more to each of us in associations, warmth, friendship and revenue, than you'll ever know."

That's as nice a compliment as a fellow can receive.

Rock had another remarkable character in his assistant, "Hunk" Anderson, tougher than saddle leather at 170 pounds. A bulwark up front on the '19, '20 and '21 teams, Hunk took over the coaching reins at Notre Dame from 1931 through 1933, immediately following Rock's death.

I never saw Hunk in trouble but once, in '35 or '36. He was then head coach at North Carolina State. He was expecting a big year but his team lost steadily.

"What's your trouble down there?" I asked Hunk.

"I don't read enough American history," he said. "I thought the Civil War was over. I have an all-southern line—good, big and fast. All my backs are from the North. My southern line is cutting down my northern backfield before any of them can start."

Rockne was the star between-halves orator. After one of his exhortations, Notre Dame was likely to rush out and sweep the grandstand away. One of his best was but one line: "So this is Notre Dame"—he'd say after a comparatively sloppy first half, and then leave the room. The explosive result carried the day.

Rockne's "Let's win this one for the Gipper," is ancient history. It's the kind of history, however, that American sports thrived on during an age when school spirit, college try, or what-you-will, added up to a great deal more than cynicism—which has no place in collegiate football.

In 1928, the Irish had perhaps the least successful of Rock's teams. Army was loaded with talent, depth, and most of all, a red-headed back named Christian Keener (Red) Cagle, who could handle a halfback slot on anybody's all-time eleven. The Army coach, "Biff" Jones, a solid organizer, brought the Cadets down to the Yankee Stadium loaded for Irish.

Friday night before the game, Rock called me at our flat at 1158 Fifth Avenue, where Kit and I still make our New York home.

"Grant," he said, "the boys are tucked in for the night. How about coming down and sitting around with Hunk and me here at the hotel?"

"Better still," I replied. "Hop in a cab and come up here. Kit wants to see you. We can warm our sides by an open fire, have a spot of Tennessee 'milk' and watch the rest of the world go to hell."

That evening, sitting by the fire, Rock said he expected to be up against it—but good, next day.

"You recall Gipp," said Rock. "He died—practically in my arms—eight years ago next month. He's been gone a long time but I may have to use him again tomorrow.

"You saw Gipp on one of his better days—against Army in 1920," continued Rock—not in that staccato voice but in a quiet, hushed tone. "He fell sick later that same season. In our final against Northwestern, at Evanston, he climbed out of bed to make the trip. I used him very little that day. We were away and winging—the final was thirty-three to seven. But in the last quarter the stands chanted Gipp's name so loud and long that I finally sent him in for a few plays—on that ice-covered field with the wind off Lake Michigan cutting us all to the bone. I got him out of there, quick; but after returning to school with a raging fever, Gipp went back to his sick bed. He never got up. Pneumonia had him backed to his own goal line. He lived barely two weeks. Shortly before he went, Father Pat Haggerty baptized him into the church. After the little ceremony, I sat with him on his bed. His face seemed thinner than the Communion wafer he'd just taken—and just as white . . . but his forehead was strangely cool.

"Gipp looked up at me and after a moment, he said, 'Rock, I know I'm going . . . but I'd like one last request. . . . Some day, Rock, some time—when the going isn't so easy, when the odds are against us, ask a Notre Dame team to win a game for me—for the Gipper. I don't know where I'll be then, Rock, but I'll know about it and I'll be happy.'

"A moment later Gipp was gone.

"Grant, I've never asked the boys to pull one out for Gipp. Tomorrow I might have to."

The following day that '28 Army–Notre Dame game played, as always, to an overflow sellout. At the half it was 0-0. The rest is history.

A sobbing band of fighting Irish raced out for the 3rd quarter. When Notre Dame lined up for the kickoff, I knew they were playing with a 12th man—George Gipp.

But Red Cagle didn't see any ghost as he circled deep behind his own line, reversed his field and galloped for great chunks of terrain. Cagle's runs and passes carried Army to Notre Dame's two. There, I recall, a cadet named Murrell plunged over. Bud Sprague, Army's burly tackle, missed the conversion. Notre Dame fired right back, smashing and clawing 80 yards, and Jack Chevigny rammed into the end zone crying, "Here's one of them, Gipper!" The point after was missed, and after getting the ball the Irish started another march. Rock sent in Johnny O'Brien, a pass-catching, one-play demon. O'Brien, juggling the ball as he fell, held on to Johnny Niemiec's long pass into the end zone to put Notre Dame ahead, 12-6.

Cagle wasn't through. With little more than a minute left, the Army flash gathered in the kickoff on his 10 and, circling to his own goal line, started moving. He covered 65 yards before being thrown out of bounds on Notre Dame's 35. After an incomplete pass, Cagle swept 21 yards to the 14. That was Cagle's last shot. He'd played himself off his feet and had to be helped from the field. His replacement, Johnny Hutchinson, attempted two passes, the second connecting on the 4. Hutchinson smashed to the 1-yard line but before the Cadets could fire again, the game was over.

Notre Dame carried that day, 12-6. Somewhere, George Gipp must have been very happy.

My friend Jack Lavelle, one-time Notre Dame guard, recalls his freshman year at South Bend.

"Under Rockne," said Jack, "there was a saying, 'Freshmen get nothing but abuse . . . but plenty of that.' How true. Some of us waited in line for three days just to get a uniform. Shoes? No matter how beat up they were, they always told you, 'Here you are, freshman. Gipp wore these!' It was a toss-up as to who wore more cleats or slept in the most inns, Gipp or George Washington. The pair I got had nails as big as shark gaffs sticking clear through the insoles. I tried to change 'em. They told me the *South Bend Times* was plenty thick . . . to make my own inner soles."

Notre Dame has long featured agile, keen, faking quarterbacks. That brings up Rock's meeting with Nate Leipsic, in my opinion one of the world's greatest magicians.

It was early in Rockne's career. He was in New York when I suggested we go to an afternoon cocktail party given by Mr. Vincent Bendix, the airplane builder, at his apartment in the Fifties. Never overly keen about parties, Rock wanted to know why we should go.

"Nate Leipsic is going to entertain," I replied. "You'll see him do some great tricks—proving again how much faster the hand is than the eye. This ought to fit into handling a football . . . especially in the quarterback's faking."

We went to the party. Rockne was astonished at Nate's skill. There was one trick where Rockne was given two rubber balls to handle, one in each hand. "Keep your grip tight," said Leipsic. Rock did. Then Nate waved a hand and said, "Open them up." When Rock did, he had two balls in one hand, none in the other. Rock got Leipsic to repeat this trick five or six times.

He also had other mysterious tricks repeated. "I've learned a lot today about deception in handling a ball," Rock said. "One thing I'm going to do is to send my quarterbacks to a magician. This matter of handling and faking with the ball is one of the biggest things in football. . . . I aim to make it bigger." I can't recall a Notre Dame quarterback who wasn't a good faker. Nate Leipsic himself would have faked an opposing team out of the park.

Rockne was a man of great force, deep charm and an amazing personality. I have never known anyone quite his equal in this respect. Coaches who have been my friends include: Percy Haughton of Harvard, an exceptional coach; "Hurry Up" Fielding Yost of Michigan; Bob Zuppke of Illinois; Fritz Crisler of

Michigan; Lou Little of Columbia; Jess Hawley of Dartmouth; Dan McGugin of Vanderbilt; Bernie Bierman of Tulane and Minnesota; Alonzo Stagg of Chicago; Pop Warner of Cornell, Pittsburgh and Stanford; John McEwan and Biff Jones of Army; Tad Jones of Yale; Tad's brother, Howard Jones of Southern California; John Heisman and Bill Alexander of Georgia Tech; Bob Neyland of Tennessee; Red Blaik of Dartmouth and Army; Tom Hamilton of Navy; Frank Thomas of Alabama; Frank Cavanaugh of Fordham; Jock Sutherland of Pittsburgh; Frank Leahy of Notre Dame; and too many others to mention.

But whenever there was a gathering of coaches in any city, there was usually just one question, "Where's Rock staying?" That's where they all gathered.

There have been so many fine coaches, such great inventors as Pop Warner, Lonnie Stagg and Bob Zuppke, that no one can pick the greatest. But Rockne was the greatest of all in the way of human appeal.

I consider Warner, Stagg and Yost the advance guard of the football inventors. I think that Rockne and Percy Haughton were two of the greatest coaches, with Rockne's personality and rare human touch lifting him to the front. The man had an incisive manner of speech that electrified those around him. His manner of raising the pitch of his voice rather than lowering it at the end of a sentence was as spontaneous as it was effective. You never could misunderstand Rockne.

No, you could never misunderstand Rockne—and there's a little story behind that, too. Gus Dorais, Rock's college roommate and later his assistant, told me why.

"From the start, Rock's mind traveled quicker than his tongue," said Dorais one night in New York. Rock had been dead some ten years but to Gus, much of Rockne will never die. "Don't forget, Rock was about four years older than the rest of us when we were in school. He was always threatening to quit, but of course he never got around to it. Anyhow, in those days and some years later when he became head coach, he was a stammerer. In 1918, his first year as head coach, Rock attended an alumni dinner at which he was called upon to speak . . . and he stammered pretty badly. He was ashamed of himself and next day he told the Father who was toastmaster that he'd made a mess of himself. Father told Rock he had done nothing of the sort and passed it off.

"One month later Rockne had become a terrific public speaker," continued Dorais. "But there was a reason for that strange, machine-gun stacatto of his. His thoughts tumbled out in bursts . . . but he had to give his tongue a breather between those thoughts."

I've sat through a lot of dinners through a lot of years. In my mind Jimmy Walker was the paragon of after dinner entertainers, but Rock was the only man who could follow Jimmy Walker. Rockne had a colossal memory. I've been with him at clambakes in some big towns where clusters of strange faces would congregate around him. He'd pick out a face in the crowd and go over and shake the fellow's hand.

"I saw you . . . last spring . . . in Atlanta. . . . Now don't tell me. . . . It's Smith . . . Bob Smith. . . . How are you, Bob?"

And Bob Smith, or whoever, would leave walking on clouds. That's one prime reason why as many as 21 special trains were needed in the Chicago railyards when Notre Dame travelled to Los Angeles to play Southern Cal. Those trains were loaded "with Rock's friends."

He was the greatest personal salesman I've known. It was small wonder that at the time of his death, Rockne was slated to take over the presidency of the Studebaker Corporation. He would have been the Eddie Rickenbacker of the automotive industry. However, where Rick is the prototype of the accepted

picture of dynamic big business brass—Rock was just the opposite. His dress—a gray or blue suit—was neat but seldom
pressed. His hats—brim turned up, capping a kewpie-doll skull
and a bashed, pixy nose—made him an incongruous picture the
first time you saw him.

I recall I was with Westbrook Pegler—who didn't meet him
until Rock was famous. Peg was amazed.

"He looks like a beaten up tin can," wrote Peg.

Rockne never forgave him.

The Vanderbilt Hotel was Rock's home in New York. And
whenever he was in town, his suite looked like a roadhouse. Because Rock—and Notre Dame—were on the road so much during those years, there was always a lot of baggage about. One
of Rock's little tricks was to scatter rocks indiscriminately
through everybody's bags. He liked to see them lug rather than
carry their suitcases. He'd point to any bag and ask one of his
aides to pick it up. If the fellow didn't practically lose his arm,
Rock knew the bag wasn't loaded and would then take it himself.

I've been at gatherings, particularly coaches' conventions,
when the noise erupting from a main room sounded like a reunion of bellowing steers. Rock, with his flair for the dramatic,
usually made it a point to arrive perhaps ten minutes late. When
he did enter the room the noise would throttle to a whisper.
You could hear a pin drop. They'd just stand there and stare at
him. Like Ruth and Dempsey, Rockne was a man of the crowd
. . . and whatever the crowd, he was its leader.

"Whenever Rock opened his kisser," commented Harry
Grayson, "the throng became silent as a tomb."

The Rockne coaching clinics—at the opening of his spring
practice—had to be witnessed to be appreciated. High-school
coaches from all over the map would descend on South Bend
thirsting for a morsel of the Rockne wisdom. I came through
there in '29 and took in the first day of the clinic. Between six and

seven hundred coaches were on hand. From twirling the baton to
blowing the tuba, Rock was the whole show. Standing on an
elevated coaching platform with his hundreds of disciples seated
around him—and the Irish varsity on a nearby playing field—
Rock would go into his spiel.

"Now we'll run the pass play. . . . Marchmont (Schwartz),
run that pass play." He'd point to the team and the coaches
would stampede over to the sidelines . . . and Marchmont
would run that pass play.

"Now is it perfectly clear . . . perfectly clear?" he would
say. "Don't be bashful . . . This play is for you coaches. . . .
You men . . . Marchmont, run that pass play again!"—And
Schwartz would run it, faking to this man . . . throwing to that
one. Small wonder that practically every high-school coach in
the midwest sought the personal accolade of sending a future
star to Notre Dame.

The soul of propriety at various alumni gatherings throughout the country, Rock, nevertheless, wasn't against imbibing a
bit. During such off-the-cuff evenings—with "practical" and
important alumni making a fuss over him—Rock would at times
get carried away and sign contracts to coach at Columbia, University of Southern California and I don't know where. Then
he'd have to bail himself out, telling them that while his football belonged to America, his soul belonged to Notre Dame.

Saturday evenings during football season, we used to have
"open house" at our apartment—with food and drink for any
and all coaches who happened to be in the neighborhood. (I
remember Yost used to sit there with his ear cocked to the
radio trying to catch the scores despite the noise of the crowd.)
Those Kaffee klatches were great fun, and many times were
responsible for some pretty fair columns. Also, whenever he
was in town for the Army game, Rock would come up for a late
"brunch" on Sunday. In '23 and '24, he brought along his little

quarterback, Harry Stuhldreher, for bacon, eggs and coffee. The recollection of Rockne's "brain" Stuhldreher, sitting there all slicked up, his feet not even reaching the floor, is a picture that Kit and I treasure.

During Rock's dozen years as head coach—from 1918 to 1930—years when Notre Dame picked up followers by the millions, the Rockne System became the great vogue, from Yale to St. Mary's. The more the Irish won, the greater became Rockne's vision of not only giving Notre Dame spectacular seasons but of giving his alma mater the Number 1 place in the football world.

Rockne took his teams far and wide, seeking the intersectional powerhouses of the country. At West Point; Atlanta, Georgia; Princeton; Lincoln, Nebraska; Palo Alto; Chicago—wherever Rockne went—he was a Pied Piper picking up followers by droves. In that way the teams of Notre Dame became the teams of the people, and Rockne became football's personal trademark for some 30,000,000 fans throughout America.

I saw Rockne at New York's Polo Grounds in December, 1930. Phlebitis had claimed his once swift legs. Muffled in a blue blanket, he was wheeled into place beside the bench of the Notre Dame All-Stars, who were playing the New York Giants in Mayor Jimmy Walker's answer to the depression. The game, played for the relief of the unemployed, was a pushover for the Giants. Benny Friedman had a field day with his passes and the Owen brothers, Steve and Bill, had a huge barn party in the line. Several of Rock's old stars, Jack Cannon at guard and Adam Walsh at center, along with graduating Frank Carideo at quarterback, played some great football. However, brought together from the four points of the compass at the last moment, they simply were no match for the Giants.

The following day Rock and I had lunch together at the Park Lane Hotel. Despite the condition of his legs, he moved pretty well and seemed in good spirits. Hollywood wanted his technical direction for a football picture, and he wanted me to write the script. I agreed.

"We ought to make it next spring or early summer. It'll take only three or four weeks. I'll go out there sometime this winter to get things in order."

"All right, Rock," I said . . . "and good luck."

I believe that's where Rock was heading when his plane, carrying a half dozen other passengers, crashed in a Kansas cornfield on March 31, 1931.

On the afternoon of Saturday, April 4, a vast assemblage of people from every walk of life gathered at Notre Dame to pay their last respects. They were all there, from the butcher's boy down on Main Street to the personal representative of the King of Norway.

Rock's last team carried him to his grave, near his beloved university, beneath the great branches of a gigantic oak. Knute Kenneth Rockne, an Olympic personality in American football, had barked his last command.

CHAPTER FIFTEEN

Colorful Coaches

Asa Bushnell, guiding hand of the National Collegiate Athletic Association, a federation which includes all colleges with a registration of more than 25 football players, recently asked me to rate the top 15 or 20 coaches I've known through the years.

I couldn't do it. There are too many friends I'd have to leave out. However, for about 25 years—from 1904 through the late 1920's—I kept running into a group of the most colorful coaches football has ever known. Warner . . . Yost . . . Zuppke . . . Stagg . . . McGugin, Heisman . . . Haughton—most of them were great coaches because they were strong personalities. Their won and lost records had little to do with my affection and respect for them. I've learned more from a coach talking with him after a losing game than I ever did in discussing the play that won for him. Lou Little remarked on this one evening after Columbia had been dumped by a midseason foe. I wandered into the Columbia dressing room after this particular game and found Lou practically alone.

192

"Granny," he chuckled, "why is it that you always show up after we lose, but I seldom see you when we win one?"

"It's this way, Lou," I said. "After you've won, I've got to buck a subway rush even to get a glimpse of you. But on afternoons like this . . . well, it gives us a chance to get together for a nice chat. That I like."

Those pioneers were the zealots. Then there followed such men as Knute Rockne, Little, Earl Blaik, Fritz Crisler, Howard and Tad Jones, Bob Neyland, Chick Meehan, Bernie Bierman, Biff Jones and John McEwan, Bill Alexander, Frank Cavanaugh —and many others who were just as able but lacked the flaming color of the earlier group. For example, after an Illinois-Michigan game, Yost and Zuppke were discovered still on the field in a violent argument at 10 o'clock that night! It was Zuppke who invented and first used the huddle. It was Stagg who used the direct pass from center to the ball carrier with the quarterback eliminated. I can't find out who invented the "T", but it was used as early as 1908.

Yost never listened to anyone in an argument. Once I met him and another coach in a violent debate in the lobby of a New York hotel around 5:00 P.M. I was going to a football party. They were supposed to be there. When I left for home around 2:00 A.M. they were still involved in the same wordy argument. I asked the other coach, name forgotten, why he had hung around seven hours. "I was trying to get in a word," he said, "just one word."

Yost was the most serious man I ever knew. I was hunting wild turkey and quail with him in the East Tennessee mountains one year—I think it was 1908. We started home after dark. We had to ford a shallow, swift-running river. About halfway across I slipped on a rock and was dumped into the river. I kept yelling but he never heard me. He was clear across, driving for home, when he first missed me, still unable to make headway against the rocks and the current. He came back, picked me up, and then went on talking as if nothing had ever happened.

Yost and his brother-in-law, Dan McGugin of Vanderbilt, were exact opposites. Dan had a keen sense of humor. A great coach, he refused to criticize his men on the field in any way. He waited until after the game. Yet he had deep respect for Yost's football judgment. For Yost knew football. I asked Pop Warner once, in Yost's presence, who invented the spiral pass.

"Yost," Warner said, looking directly at him. "He also invented everything else in the game—including the football." Yost seriously thanked Pop for the admission.

Yost had a fire in his gaunt system that he passed on to his team. He came to Michigan in 1901 and was undefeated in 56 games before being beaten 2 to 0 by Stagg and Chicago in 1905.

Ring Lardner was travelling with Yost in the early 1920's when some argument came up about the Michigan-Pennsylvania game of 1906.

"Penn won that one, 17–0," Ring said.

"No, Michigan won it," Yost said. "That was the year we had Garrels, a great fullback."

"Penn won it," Ring repeated. "That was the year they had Scarlett and Greene."

Finally Yost bet Ring five dollars, a tremendous bet for Yost. They looked it up in a record book. Score: Pennsylvania 17—— Michigan 0.

"I told you Pennsylvania won," Yost said.

"You are right," Lardner, who had named Penn, said.

Yost refused to take any money, but he beamed in the thought that he was "right."

"The reason I knew he was wrong," Ring said, "was a verse I remembered from F.P.A. following that '06 game.

> "O east is east and west is west
> And when the twain shall meet,

The Red and Blue is the real who's who
In the land of the Flying Feet."

Franklin P. Adams, being the best writer of light verse this
country ever knew, registered more with Ring than Yost did.

Those earlier coaches were brilliant. I recall Illinois and
Zuppke in 1916. Illinois was playing Minnesota. Minnesota, that
year, had an all-powerful team. They were beating Big Ten
teams 50 to 0, teams that had whipped Illinois badly. I know
Lardner, in the *Chicago Tribune,* had picked Minnesota 50 or
60 to 0 over Illinois. No experts figured Illinois better than a 40
to 0 defeat. The day of the game came on. Zuppke called his
Illinois squad, headed by 139-pound Ed Sternaman, together.
His address to his team remains a classic.

"I am Louis the Fourteenth," he said, "and you are my court.
After us the deluge." The team didn't exactly know what Zup
was talking about, but they cheered.

"Today," Zup said, "I want you to have some fun. Get
beaten one hundred to nothing if you want to, but have fun. But
I want to tell you something. I've had this great team scouted.
On the first play 'Galloping' Sprafka will take the ball. I want
eleven of my men to tackle Sprafka. On the next play big Anderson will take the ball. I want all eleven of you guys to tackle
Anderson."

"But suppose," one of his men said, "somebody else takes
the ball. What then?"

"I'll tackle him," Zuppke said.

According to rumor, Minnesota had built a special box for
Walter Camp, the famous All-America picker. "Camp is sup-
posed to pick seven All Americas from Minnesota today,"
Zuppke said.

Just then a loud cheer was heard. Zuppke took young
Sternaman aside to watch the Gophers run onto the field to
warm up. "As Minnesota came on the field," continued Zuppke,

"Anderson threw a fifty-yard pass that practically stuck in Baston's right ear."

"I don't see an elephant on that squad," said Sternaman.

Illinois stopped Minnesota dead in three plays. Illinois got the ball and scored on the first play, one of Zuppke's weird inventions.

"And those big Swedes stood and hung their heads below the goal after the touchdown," Zup recalled. "They were so ashamed."

Illinois beat Minnesota that day 14 to 9 for one of the greatest upsets in football history.

I recall the trip Frank Craven, the actor, and I made to Illinois to see Red Grange at work. It was 1925, Grange's last year, and the Illini were opening against Nebraska. When we arrived, Zup looked at us and said, "I'm sorry you came to see this game."

"Why?" asked Craven.

"I'll tell you," replied Zuppke. "My team has got away from me. They think they're unbeatable, even before their first game. I can't wake them up. So I've given them only four plays against Nebraska. Grange won't make a first down."

Nebraska won 14–0. And Grange didn't make a first down. For all that, I got to know Zuppke in a different and deeper light so it was all worth while. It was during that trip that Zup remarked to me, "Grant, all I ask is for my team and myself to be respected. Nothing more." Both Zuppke and Illinois were always respected, you can gamble on that.

But Zuppke was the toughest of all coaches to beat when he pointed for a certain game—especially if he could find some psychological wedge to use against the enemy.

For example, Fritz Crisler, Michigan's able coach once made an important mistake. It was when Tom Harmon was at the height of a brilliant career and Michigan, with Evashevski blocking for Harmon, was all-powerful. Crisler made few mistakes in his coaching career. He was one of the ablest of them all—especially as an offensive coach. His mistake was in giving out an interview before the '39 game with Illinois, stating that Harmon was a better back than Red Grange. Zuppke saw his chance.

"So Harmon is better than Grange," Zuppke said to everyone he could reach. That is about all he told his team that week —"Crisler says Harmon is better than Grange." His war cry ran around the Illinois campus—"Crisler says Harmon is better than Grange—Crisler says Harmon is better than Grange." He even got the professor of psychology interested. "Yes," Zup told me, "and he was the professor of pragmatic psychology."

When Illinois, an inferior team with a far inferior record, met mighty Michigan, Tommy Harmon thought he was playing against 20 or 30 tartars. Every time he took the ball he was tackled by eight or nine men. He was hit so hard and so often by so many wearers of the Orange and Blue that he practically gained no ground at all. He no longer made long runs—or even first downs. Illinois won 16–7 and Zuppke went back to his study of philosophy and painting which he liked as much as football.

Zuppke admired Howard Jones, especially that Southern California coach's thoroughness. One of the best, Howard was a very serious man. He never took a drink of liquor in his life. One day in January of '35, while I was on the Coast, both Zuppke and Jones dropped in together to say hello. Zuppke finally turned to Jones and said, "You are a great coach, Howard, but you'd be an even greater one if you'd take a drink once in a while. You'd have more imagination."

Jones replied. "I never heard of a drink yet figuring out a play."

"You never did?" Zuppke asked. "Well, I've just had two drinks and I've figured out three new plays. They are the Flea

Flicker, the Whoa Back and the Double Jump. Here they are—
I'll diagram them for you. I am going to use them next fall when
Illinois meets Southern California out here."

All three were new plays. Zuppke used each of them the
next fall and beat Southern California 19 to 0. He scored with
each play.

Percy Haughton, Harvard's famous coach from 1908–16,
was one of the best in football's long history. It was Haughton
who first developed the hidden ball perfectly. He worked his
team to the limit in this deception where everyone had to be an
actor. He developed the "Mouse Trap" fully. I asked him before
one Yale game if he could stop Yale's big line.

"I'm not going to try," he said. "I'll let them break through
and then cut them down from the side."

Harvard won that 1914 game 36 to 0.

Haughton had another odd slant. In contrast to the practice
at Yale, he wanted no old stars haunting his practice field. I sat
there with him one afternoon before practice as Charley Brickley
and one or two other famous wearers of the Crimson came in.
As he left for the field they started with him. "I'll see you fellows back here," Haughton said. "There's no room on the practice field."

I recall one day before a Harvard-Michigan game when I
was standing with Yost. Haughton spotted some Boston newspaper men at the edge of the field. He had them all chased out
of the park. Yost sighed heavily. "Gee," he said, "I wish I could
get away with that out West. If I did that they'd run me out of
football."

As far as Haughton was concerned, one of his most pleasant
victories occurred the day he persuaded President Lowell
that part of the "over interest" in the game was due to the presence of football writers at the daily practice. So he persuaded
Harvard's president to have them barred.

At times Haughton was a hard man to work for. One Saturday, Sam Felton, the famous end and star left-footed kicker, booted the ball 60 yards. Haughton jerked him out of the game. "I told you to kick forty yards," Haughton said. "The ends can cover at that distance. Forty yards doesn't mean thirty-nine yards or forty-one yards. It means forty yards."

When next Saturday's game arrived he sent Felton out of the Stadium to warm up. "You might want to show this crowd you can kick sixty yards again," he said to Sam.

"I'll tell you about Haughton," Tack Hardwick, one of Harvard's all-time competitors, said to me one day. "If he told us to jump off a cliff one hundred feet high, all fifty of us thought he'd catch us. And every man would take the jump. He is a hard man, but a great one. He's all iron."

It might be mentioned that Haughton was the most systematic coach in football. He would sit up until 2 A.M. or later each night developing the next day's work. It was five minutes for this—ten minutes for something else, until the two hours were planned. And there was an extra rule—no Harvard player could walk on the field. He had to be running. He used the touch-tag system during practice. "We were all so fresh and keen by Saturday that we wanted to murder somebody," Hardwick said. "Harvard teams were never battered up in practice. They were always fresh."

The days and nights I spent with Yost, Zuppke, Rockne and Pop Warner will never be forgotten. Neither will the many hours I spent with Jock Sutherland, one of the greatest when he had full control at Pittsburgh. Jock was never quite sold on the forward pass. He was a master at the running game and he didn't like to turn the ball loose in the air. He liked to feature ball carriers and blockers.

In certain ways, Jock wanted the center to be the best man on his team. "The running game," he said, "which is, or should be, the better part of football, depends on split-second accuracy and timing from center. If the ball gets to the runner a tenth of a second too soon—or too late—the running play may be spoiled. So in looking over my talent I pick a man for center who is never rattled or hurried or upset by anything."

I know that if I was in doubt in picking All-America talent, I was dead sure to get a good center from Pittsburgh when Jock ruled the Panthers.

Jock's great Pitt teams rumbled and blasted out their yardage on the single wing, unbalanced-line attack. When Jock had the horses, which was his custom, the Golden Panthers' attack was something to behold. Broken in spirit by the attacks on him by a clique of his own fellow alumni who disapproved of his taciturnity, dictatorial methods, and his habit of "too much winning," Sutherland left Pitt in 1938 and turned to the pros. On April 11, 1948. he died following a brain operation.

In his passing I lost a friend. a comrade. The following day I wrote the following lines in memory of "The Scotchman."

There's a fog now over Scotland, and a mist on Pittsburgh's field;
There's no valiant hand to flash the sword or hold the guiding shield,
There's a big, braw fellow missing from the golden land of fame
—For Jock Sutherland has left us—and the game is not the same.

We hear the roaring chorus—and we get the age-old thrill;
But when a pal has left us, there's a gap that none can fill,
There's a shadow on the thistle and the Panther's growl is low
—As the bagpipes send their message to the friend we used to know.

The laurel fades—the olive dies—the cheers are silent now,
No more the chaplet from lost years adorns the master's brow.
But here's to Jock, through fog and mist, beyond the final score,
—As we turn down an empty glass to one we'll see no more.

Sutherland, in certain ways, was something like Gil Dobie of Washington, Navy and Cornell. One year, 1925, Dartmouth beat Cornell 62 to 13. Dartmouth passed; Cornell ran.

"Well, we won," Dobie said, "thirteen to nothing."

"What about Dartmouth's sixty-two points?" I asked.

"I don't count those scores made by passing," Dobie said. "That isn't football."

Lonnie (Alonzo) Stagg illustrated the great difference that has come to football. In 1890 he both coached and played. Chicago was to play Illinois. Stagg was hurt in practice, so Illinois asked him to referee—which he did. Could you imagine Army asking Navy's Eddie Erdelatz to referee the Army–Navy game? There was no complaint about Stagg's work as an official.

Another thing about Stagg was that he wouldn't allow any rough language by his players. He demanded clean play and clean language.

Eddie Cochems, at St. Louis University, was the first coach to get real mileage from the forward pass in 1906, the year it was made legal. However, Stagg was working with the pass at Chicago and winning games with it—seven years before Harper and Notre Dame wrecked the Army team with Dorais to Rockne. It was a dozen years before Harvard, Yale and Princeton gave it any attention.

Bo McMillin used to cry a lot over his "pore little boys."

"They're too little to play against these giants," he'd tell me. I was sitting with him one day when his players came in to dress. The first man was 6 feet 3 and weighed 230 pounds. I looked at Bo. He looked away. The next one was around 235. The third was about 219. "Is that one of 'the pore little fellers'?" I asked. Bo grinned, but didn't answer.

Speaking of colorful coaches, I want to say a word about

another friend of mine, Herman Hickman, a lot of coach . . .
and today a lot of television character, all 300 pounds of him.
I saw Herman play guard for Tennessee and picked him for my
All-America team in 1932.

For years, after Earl Blaik returned to Army from Dartmouth in 1941, I would usually return from the Pennsylvania–
Army game at Philadelphia with Blaik and the Army team. Once
Pete Dolan, of the old *New York Sun,* and I found ourselves
alone with Hickman, then Army's line coach, in the private
diner before the call for dinner. This was around 1946, the year
that Dale Hall and Max Minor were in Army's backfield. We
proceeded to "replay" the Penn game. (Army had made its customary slow start at Franklin Field but had won handily.)

Then I asked Hickman about the Navy game two weeks
hence. Army had lost Kenna and some ranking players and the
Navy game figured to be close. In the midst of the discussion,
Hickman suddenly laughed—his 300 pounds almost shaking the
car off the tracks—and said, "Granny, the best way I can put it is
this"—and he immediately broke into a string of verse, delivered with meticulous inflection in a trained, vibrant voice.
On and on he went, building up to the climax:

> "Though much is taken, much abides; and though
> We are not that strength which in old days
> Moved earth and heaven, that which we are, we are—
> One equal temper of heroic hearts,
> Made weak by time and fate, but strong in will
> To strive, to seek, to find, and not to yield."

Estimate the number of persons in the world who, without
a moment of warning or preparation, could deliver letter perfect, and fitting the moment and discussion, the last 16 lines of
Tennyson's "Ulysses."

I told that story in my column in newspapers throughout

the land. A world of sports that had known Herman Hickman only as a collegiate and professional football player, a professional wrestler and an assistant coach, has since come to know "The Poet Laureate of the Great Smokies" for the Phi Beta Kappa and elocutionist that he is.

Herman Hickman had had his screen and television test before that audience of two on the Army diner.

CHAPTER SIXTEEN

Football's All-Timers

We met an old grad who didn't care whether you roasted or boosted his college football team . . . or whether you even mentioned it. It was the first funeral we had attended in years. —Grantland Rice Sportlight, October 17, 1924.

The fellow who brought the word "All-America" into prominence was, of course, Walter Camp.

I had known Camp only casually prior to the first World War and it was not until October, 1920, that I got to know him well. An executive of a New Haven clock concern, Camp looked every inch the administrative type. Handsome, with rather a narrow face, he was somewhat less than 6 feet tall and around 170 pounds. He always took good care of himself but wasn't averse to a friendly drink.

Pop Warner's Pittsburgh team was rolling with the Warner power and Camp wanted to get a look at the Panthers. He and I traveled to Syracuse to see Pittsburgh play Chick Meehan's rough Syracuse team which, I recall, featured Joe Alexander, a great rock and sock artist, at center. We had breakfast on Saturday morning with Pop and Chick at the Onondaga Hotel.

"I didn't get a chance to scout you this season," said the precocious Chick over the ham and eggs. "You have anything new . . . anything I don't know about?"

"Not a thing, lad," replied Pop. "We'll use about five plays . . . two reverses, an off tackle, a trap play or two and perhaps a pass. I promise not to use anything else, but I won't tell you in what order I'll use 'em."

"That's O.K. with me," replied Chick.

Pop stuck to his promise as Pitt and Syracuse fought to a 7–7 standoff.

That morning Camp and I slipped out to the Onondaga Country Club for a round of golf. I recall Camp had numerous golf theories; so had I. But I don't think either of us ever won an Open.

A star halfback on the Yale teams of 1879, 1880—the year I was born—1881 and 1882, Camp returned in 1888 as Yale's first head coach and remained through 1892. Prior to that, the Elis were "coached" by their current captain. Camp's teams were meat eaters. His great '88 team, which followed in the wake of the Blizzard of '88, scored 704 points to the opponents' zero— with Harvard, the 14th and final foe, forfeiting 6–0. I asked Camp the secret of "The Camp System," as famed in its day as the Warner or Rockne systems years later.

"It was very simple and very sound," he replied. "At the end of the season I'd call a meeting at which we'd determine who was graduating and who wasn't. Then we'd screen the returnees. Were they fast? Did they pack power? The type material we would have pretty much determined our mode of offense.

"We moved the ball with more authority because, as a team, we worked much harder on signals than our adversaries,"

continued Camp. "As far as I know we also had the distinction
of being the first team to develop the cutback—where a back
starts at one point in the rival line and hits at another. This got
us many, many yards. Remember, however, that everything and
anything we tried in those days was new. Also, we had the
players! We had men like Bill (Pudge) Heffelfinger, Lonnie
Stagg, Frank Hinkey, Brink Thorne, Chad Brown, Lee Mc-
Clung . . . yes, and Edgar Glass, the most powerful tackle I
ever saw."

I mentioned that I never saw the great Frank Hinkey play
end for Yale.

"You didn't?" exclaimed Camp.

"No, I didn't," I replied. "When he was starring for Yale in
'91, '92, '93 and '94, I was still in prep school back in Nashville."

"Grant," said Camp, stopping on the fairway and seeming to
relive for the moment the sight of Hinkey, "you and I have seen
a lot of football players . . . some really top ones. However,
pound for pound, I believe that Hinkey had more explosive
football in his one-hundred-and-fifty-pound system than any
athlete I ever saw. When Frank tackled the ball carrier it was
like an exploding bomb! I called him The Disembodied Spirit.
He moved like a ghost."

Years later, in 1929, Hinkey, living at Pinehurst, North
Carolina, was a very ill man. His old teammate, George Adee,
quarterback on the '94 team, and I decided to visit him. Adee
wired Hinkey the time of our expected arrival. Several hours
later, Adee received a wire which read: "Too late, Charon is at
the crossroads—Frank."

Hinkey died that night.

Prior to 1925 I'd never attempted to name any mythical
national eleven. I felt then and now that it's completely impossible for one man to name the eleven best players in the country
—after scouting a handful of games through one pair of eyes.

Back in the dim past I attempted to select an all-southern team with John (Jack) Heisman. However, in March, 1925, Camp suddenly passed away. Since 1889 Camp had made his annual selections of the great players he'd seen. Because in its early stages football was largely an eastern game, players from Yale, Harvard, Princeton and Penn dominated Camp's selections. *Collier's Weekly* picked up Camp's annual "picks," made usually with an informal group of friends and given heavy publicity each fall. Following Camp's death, Lee Maxwell, president of the Crowell-Collier publications, asked me to take over the job for the 1925 season. I squawked loudly. I didn't want any part of the job. I had been writing a page of copy for *Collier's* each week for nearly ten years without missing an issue. However, in 1924 *Collier's* had experienced rather a poor promotional junket with Camp's All-America, and Maxwell pointed out to me that it was too much of a discrepancy having one man picking the All-America and another writing the sports page. I agreed to try it for a year. At the end of the year I brought in a flock of experts, including H. G. Salsinger of the *Detroit News,* Clyde McBride of the *Kansas City Star,* Braven Dyer of the *Los Angeles Times,* O. B. Keeler of the *Atlanta Journal* and others, to help out. This body was known as the Collier's Board. We picked the team for the next 21 years.

If it was the "eleven best" the fans wanted, we tried to give them just that without any particular favoring of "geographical distribution" of players to fit the national scope of readership. In 1929 Dink Templeton, my West Coast operative, told me, "There's nobody out here worth a damn!" That year the team went no farther west than Minnesota. I placed Bronko Nagurski, a great fullback in '29, back into his former tackle slot alongside Pitt's scrappy end, Joe Donchess. My West Coast mail was both terrific and terrible. However, I respected Templeton's judgment then and I still do.

In 1947 *Look* magazine, in conjunction with the Football Writers Association—made up of some 500 accredited football writers throughout the country—took over the Grantland Rice selections as an annual promotion under the guidance of Tim Cohane. As a salute to the American athlete, a mythical team or teams can't hurt. I've yet to see where an All-America flunked his exams in any test regarding his country.

I've been asked to rank my all-time collegiate and professional elevens. This side of a house full of ghosts, nothing could be more mythical, but I'll give it a whirl. Ranking some of the greatest games I've covered, however, isn't quite so difficult.

As a starter I give you the 1935 game between Notre Dame and Ohio State, a brawl in which the Irish were rated the underdog. But between the passing of Notre Dame's Bill Shakespeare and the running of Andy Pilney, the Irish pulled it out in the last seconds, 18–13. That was a great battle. So was the Sugar Bowl game in 1944 when Duke defeated Alabama 29–26 in a seesaw battle that knew no odds.

And as long as football remains a game of heart, as well as speed and muscle, I'll not forget the Pennsylvania–Michigan game of 1908. It was a scoreless tie until Michigan's great center, Germany Schultz, a one-man gang in himself, had to be dragged from the field. Then Penn stormed all over the Wolverine, 29–0.

Back to the modern era, Yale's 1934 team—comprising eleven 60-minute Bulldogs led by the irrepressible Larry Kelley —whacked favored Princeton, 7–0. It was Kelley who grabbed a pass to touch off one of his spectacular marathon rambles, all but faking Princeton's last two defenders out of their cleats en route to the end zone.

The Notre Dame–Oklahoma games of '52 and '53 were other thrillers. Alabama's 29–13 victory over Stanford in the '34

Rose Bowl game was a corker—with that deadeye combination Dixie Howell to Don Hutson renting Stanford's battle flags. There was the Georgetown–Boston College game in 1940 in which I not only saw football played; I could hear it. Others? A host of them.

There's something about the sight of a top-flight football player that's just a little different from any other athlete—with the possible exception of a fighter or a thoroughbred. And because college football, as long as it's worth the name, will be played by young undergraduates . . . so will it be supported in the stands by the old grad. Here's to him!

The Old Grad

He hears the echoes calling him from long and long ago;
Where ghostly shadows beckon him from days he used to know;
And after backs had flunked the charge, or stricken forwards reeled,
The mocking memory of youth has blurred the open field.

The old thrill leaps to life again, and through the roaring cheers
He sees the youth that used to be, beyond the drifting years;
He feels the old stir in his breast; where Time has galloped back
To place his slashing speed again in front of the attack.

Why, it was only yesterday, he heard the whistles blow
And fought his way for thirty yards against a reeling foe;
The sum of spring is in his heart, and yet with mantle spread
He knows the snows of wintertime are thick upon his head.

Sometimes I wonder if the years that slip beyond recall
Are marked upon the Book of Time as week-ends after all?
We hit the line with unchecked youth—and as a vision gleams
We find that we are gray and old along the road of dreams.

It may be that we kid ourselves with what we used to be,
Forgetting that the calendar rolls on by land and sea;
But why not follow some brave dream, wherever it may call,
In place of bowing to the years—the clock upon the wall?

We hear the plaudits of the crowd—in some off-tackle play.
We throw our speed into the charge amid the golden fray;
And as we turn to look again, upon the selfsame sod,
We see forgotten youth walk by without a careless nod.

Great youth—that flaunts its years at us with still unharried soul,
Poor youth—that still has yet to learn what waits beyond the goal.
Youth should give its soul to know the way to Journey's End—
And we—who'd give our hearts for years that youth has still to spend.

I was talking a short while ago with a fellow named Harold
(Red) Grange. I have known Grange over 25 years, since his
days as the Galloping Ghost with Bob Zuppke and Illinois.

"I am trying to pick the four greatest backs in football
history," I said to Red.

Red is a very modest fellow. "Well," he replied, "I know you
haven't picked me. But, anyway, I'd say it couldn't be done. I
don't believe anybody could pick the eight greatest backs—
much less the four greatest. Do you realize how many great
backs football has produced?"

"All right," I said, "we'll leave you out. But I want you to
help me." So we went to work.

Who are the greatest backs in football? Who are the next
four best? I have called on many others to help out. I have
asked at least 50 of the best-known coaches for their ratings and
opinions. Then I have done the best I could. In lining up the four
stars there are two categories that must be considered: the four
best who played both professional and college football and the
top four who played only college ball.

Who were the best men I have looked at who played both
games? The lot must include Jim Thorpe, Red Grange, Bronko
Nagurski, Ernie Nevers, Ken Strong, Bennie Friedman, Steve
Van Buren, Cliff Battles, Dutch Clark, Bill Dudley, Norm Stand-
lee, and such great passing quarterbacks as Sammy Baugh,
John Lujack, Sid Luckman, Otto Graham and Frankie Albert.

This does not include the star collegians who never played pro football. They will be handled in a different group.

There are three names that leap out at me through the years They are Jim Thorpe, Red Grange and Bronko Nagurski. They were great collegians and great pro stars for many years. Their imprint upon the game was deeper than any running and kicking backs, or tackling and blocking backs, or whatever else made up football greatness. All three had that indefinable quality known as color.

It seems a shame to leave out such backs as Ernie Nevers; Cliff Battles, who ran over and around all opponents; and Ken Strong, the magnificent runner, passer, blocker and kicker. Any decision is tough since these were all good friends of mine who played long and brilliantly.

Getting back to Thorpe, Grange and Nagurski—one of Thorpe's high points was his kicking. He was a great punter, a deadly man at place kicking, and a fine drop kicker. He had accuracy and long range to work with.

Grange was not only a baffling runner—the type that once broke away for four long runs to touchdowns in the first period against Michigan. He could also block, tackle and handle passes expertly.

A great many coaches, including his own Doc Spears, name Bronko Nagurski as the greatest player of all time. He was a star end, a star tackle and a crushing fullback who could pass. I believe 11 Nagurskis could beat 11 Granges or 11 Thorpes. Bronko weighed 228 pounds and he was fast and quick.

Now we come to the toughest assignment of them all—the selection of the greatest passing quarterback to go with Thorpe, Grange and Nagurski. Here is the leading list: Baugh, Graham, Luckman and Albert, with Bobby Layne coming up in a hurry and Bob Waterfield in close consideration. These men are something more than mere stars. They are accomplished artists, well above the average. Of course, there will be others later who may prove to be as great or even greater.

I first saw Sammy Baugh in a battle with Southern Methodist at Fort Worth in 1935. He was playing for Texas Christian. The second TCU got the ball on its own 15-yard line, Baugh fell back and began passing. TCU had good runners, but its attack was Baugh's passing. The period between 1934 and 1952 is a long time—18 years. Yet Slingin' Sam faced the savageness and the drive of college and pro football for 18 years where, as the passer, he was knocked down more times than a machine could register.

When you throw Baugh, Graham and Luckman together, there is a very slim margin left in favor of Number 1. But Baugh is picked for 18 brilliant years and also for his able kicking most of the time.

This leaves the backfield as follows:

> Quarterback—Sammy Baugh
> Halfback—Jim Thorpe
> Halfback—Red Grange
> Fullback—Bronko Nagurski

Selecting the greatest all-time college backfield is simpler. We have a fine group to pick from: Gipp of Notre Dame, Oliphant of Army, Frank of Yale, Mahan of Harvard, Coy of Yale, Eckersall of Chicago, Heston of Michigan, Pfann of Cornell. Unfortunately, Willie Heston played before the day of the forward pass in a different game. He was probably the finest running back of the lot.

Most of the more famous college stars have gone out for pro football in recent years. So those stars who made their reputations on college teams without the aid of the pro game make up a much briefer list. The four college backs finally selected include Gipp of Notre Dame, Frank of Yale, Mahan of Harvard, and Eckersall of Chicago.

There is no doubting George Gipp's standing. He and Frank were perhaps the best college backs I ever saw. Gipp could crash through a line or sweep an end. He was a fine kicker. He was also a fine passer. Over 6 feet, weighing around 190 pounds, he had speed and power combined.

Earle (Greasy) Neale, who has been as close to the college game as anyone else, says Clint Frank of Yale is not only the best college back but the best all-around back he ever saw.

"Frank was a very fine offensive back, but in addition to that he was a real miracle on defense," says Neale. "I've seen him play back to break up passes and still make his tackles at the line of scrimmage. He was all over the field—knocking down passes and smashing line plays, often tackling back of the line for heavy losses. Despite poor eyesight, Frank could do everything and do everything brilliantly."

Eddie Mahan was a star running back, a good kicker and passer, and an all-around worker. When asked how he ran so well, how he side-stepped so many tacklers, he merely said, "I give them one of my big toes, right or left, then I take it away." He was one of the few star football backs who didn't care too much for an interferer. Unlike Nagurski, who ran his own interference, Mahan liked to pick his own way up or down the field. He was Harvard's main star in the big years of Haughton's dominance.

Walter Eckersall was a brilliant quarterback on Stagg's Chicago teams around 1904, 1905 and 1906. He was extremely fast and slippery, a sensational kicker—punt or drop—and he ran his teams with fine judgment. He was also one of the best of all safety men.

When you've looked at so many hundreds of college backs for 50 years, the picture is bound to become confused. But

George Pfann also belongs high on any list. This Cornell star was a brilliant, hard-fighting back who went all-out on every play. Elmer Oliphant also rates high. A bull for both Purdue and Army in all sports, Oliphant ranked with Harvard's Charley Brickley and Thorpe as a field-goal kicker.

I don't feel qualified to pick a complete all-time pro team. Men are shifted back and forth too often and there are stars for offense and stars for defense. You would have to keep naming them for a week. However, there is a much better shot at an all-time college team. Here is our choice:

> Center—Germany Schultz, Michigan, '06
> Guard—Pudge Heffelfinger, Yale, '92
> Guard—Herman Hickman, Tennessee, '32
> Tackle—Joe Stydahar, West Virginia, '35
> Tackle—Bill Henry, Washington and Jefferson, '20
> End—Don Hutson, Alabama, '35
> End—Bennie Oosterbaan, Michigan, '28
> Quarterback—Sammy Baugh, TCU, '37
> Halfback—Jim Thorpe, Carlisle, '15
> Halfback—Red Grange, Illinois, '25
> Fullback—Bronko Nagurski, Minnesota, '30

This team will do until another comes along. It seems a crime to leave out such men as Sid Luckman, Otto Graham, Walter Eckersall, Elmer Oliphant, Eddie Mahan, Cliff Battles, Bull Dog Turner, Bill Dudley, Bill Hewitt, Danny Fortman, George McAfee, Bob Waterfield and so many more who have starred brilliantly so long. But as the big pack has passed before us for 50 years, this is the best picture our memory can recall.

The East is at a low ebb lately, but there were other years.

I think I can name an All-East backfield squad that would more than match any section today. How about Jim Thorpe, Eddie Mahan, Ken Strong, Clint Frank, Ted Coy, and Cliff Battles? Name me six backs any greater than these. There are more . . . Oberlander, Dooley, Marsters and MacLeod of Dartmouth . . . Pfann, Kaw and Barrett of Cornell . . . Blanchard and Davis of Army . . . Tack Hardwick and Barry Wood of Harvard. . . . Koppisch and Ralph Hewitt of Columbia. Only lately, Princeton had Kazmaier but I well recall that '35 backfield of Sandbach, LeVan, Pauk and Constable.

I recall a conversation I had with Judge Steffens, coach of Carnegie Tech, after Ken Strong, the New York University marvel, had murdered his team, 27–13, in 1928.

"I've seen Heston," he said. "I've seen Eckersall. But here is the greatest football player I ever saw. It is the first time I have seen one football player run over my team. We beat Notre Dame twenty-seven to seven last Saturday. We were undefeated. But Strong runs, passes and kicks us into the ground."

Speaking of great backs, I can't forget little Albie Booth. Yale can step forward and lay proud claim to this 148-pound phenom, a spectacular runner and a tremendous inspirational force.

Few states can equal the talent that comes from Pennsylvania and New Jersey. It was from Pennsylvania that Jock Sutherland gathered in so many stars . . . hard-rock kids with anthracite in their legs. It was from these same diggings that Jimmy Crowley built his famed Fordham teams that challenged the nation and handcuffed Pitt in the mid-1930's.

The South and the Midwest were the first to move in on the Eastern supremacy. Then the Far West and the Southwest came with a rush. These teams, coached by men like Dan McGugin, Yost, Stagg and Zuppke led the way.

Gil Dobie and Howard Jones were two of the first to bring

the Pacific Coast into the spotlight. Jones won eight Rose Bowl
games in succession. The part played by Eastern colleges is
mentioned here because, in recent years, a large part of the
East has had its earlier ambitions checked with a wrench that
I am not at all sure is entirely wise. You can't laugh off school
spirit, college presidents notwithstanding. And as sure as the
Ivies, one-time kingpins of the game, shrivel and decline, something far more important than athletic scholarships will go out
the window. I've never seen it fail. The more abject a "name"
school's football team, the more virulent becomes the cynicism
and sophistry of its undergraduates. Likewise its alumni. I well
recall the crowds of 70,000 that poured into the Yale Bowl for
the Dartmouth games of the 1930's. Tell me, if you can, what
was wrong with those crowds as compared to the 25,000 and
30,000 that trickled into the Bowl when the Green Indians hit
the warpath for New Haven in recent years. Lo, the poor Indian
. . . and lo to the rest of his Ivied brethren. You can't emascu-
late a spirited youngster's desire to play winning football in college and still retain the basic kernel of Spartan good in that
youngster. Bowl games, as a form of post-season madness, have
been over-commercialized in some respects. But tell me, if you
will, you Ivy college presidents, what good have you legislated
by outlawing the East-West Shrine game for crippled children
as a worthy goal for the star or stars of your teams?

It isn't the all-time all-timers, however, who have made
football live for me down these many years. I may not be around,
but there will be others who will move up to take their places
on any all-time list. They'll be great, sure. But the youngster,
the collegian, the boy, the scrub—who all but bursts his lungs
and breaks his gut trying to put *his* team across instead of on
ice—to me he is football's eternal answer to those who would
put it down as an all too commercialized sport.

Football's Answer

They reform me each new season
As they point to each new fault.
And their hands are turned against me
As they crowd me to the vault.
But amid the growing clamor,
They still know around the clan,
I'm the soul of college spirit
And the maker of a man.

O, I know I'm far from perfect
When the autumn leaves turn red,
When the tackle's neck is furrowed
By the half-back's heavy tread;
But you hear them still admitting
As they put me on the pan,
"He's the soul of college spirit,
And the maker of a man."

Perhaps I'm overfeatured
In the headline's stirring plea.
Perhaps I'm more important
Than a mere game ought to be;
But with all the sins they speak of,
And the list is quite a span,
I'm the soul of college spirit,
And the maker of a man.

CHAPTER SEVENTEEN

This Game of Football, an Appraisal

I saw my first game of football on Thanksgiving Day, 1892, before I had reached the dignity of long trousers. Vanderbilt met her staunch rival Sewanee that day and won 12–0. I have been playing, refereeing and covering football ever since. In many respects, I grew up with the game.

I wasn't conscious of football back in '82, when Yale's Walter Camp worked out team signals; but I was knocking heads as a ten-year-old when Camp had his big guard, Pudge Heffelfinger, pulling out and leading interference in 1890, the same year that Eli's McClung perfected the cutback on wide breaking plays. I was conscious of "Watch the Ball!"—a Camp byword for his crushing defensive lines.

In 1900 when cross checking, the first mousetrap, became fashionable, I was a senior at Vanderbilt. I saw the Flying Wedge as dreamed up by Yale's George Woodruff in 1893 become a murderous mass weapon that had to be outlawed. Why hell's bells, I was a pea-green freshman when the six-man line, with the center dropped out, started the scrambling of defenses!

Bob Zuppke's short spiral snap from center was newsworthy in 1906 as was the legalization of the forward pass. Zup was the first to drop back his guards to protect against passes in 1910, the same year John Heisman divided the game into quarters.

In 1910 I thrilled to the power Pop Warner achieved from his single wing attack, and a year later to the deception of Pop's double wing. Prior to World War I, Percy Haughton explained to me his conception of floating defensive tackles covering crashing ends and vice versa. That was when Haughton first baffled 'em with his cycle of deceptive plays. I wrote about his "will to win," applied psychology with which Haughton primed and rolled his Harvard teams. Rockne's "shock troops" were another psychological wrinkle. Amazing pass patterns and the unending search for speed on the line were other Rockne moves . . . but we're now into the modern era.

The point I'm stressing is that after centering much of my life around football, much of the game still leaves me bewildered.

Due to the ingredients . . . courage, mental and physical condition, spirit and its terrific body contact which tends to sort the men from the boys . . . football remains one of the great games of all time.

But football has one glaring weakness. The game is built largely upon constant rule breaking such as holding, off-side, backs illegally in motion, pass interference and other factors that play a big if illegal part in results.

The game has four officials who can't see or follow one-third of the rule infractions.

"It is football's big weakness," Fielding Yost told me. "I am certain that there is a penalty that could be called on every play. Most of the infractions that take place are not seen or called . . . but the big point is, they shouldn't be made in the first place!"

How many times have you heard, "There's a horn on the play," that age-old bleat that slows the average game. Perhaps it slows the game for the spectator, but I've seen at least 50 important games lost—or won—because the officials failed to call fouls that were easily detected from the press box high above the field. I've found out that I could see what was happening from the press box much better than from any vantage point on the field as an official. The official, looking from level ground, is too often cut off by one of the 22 players.

The forward pass brought in another official headache on "pass interference"—one of the toughest of decisions to call correctly. Football is loaded with fouls which coaches invent, such as the "fainting act," when time is running out. The big excuse that these violations are used by more than 80 per cent of the coaches is probably true. It is also completely fallacious. Most coaches, in their frenzied desire to win at any cost, employ any known or possible act to win the game, regardless of its legality. For this I blame the majority of coaches—not all of them. They may all be decent, honest people—and most of them are—but too many are split or schizophrenic maniacs . . . Jekylls during the week, Hydes when Saturday's kickoff whistle blows.

Pressure from alumni and students and criticism from football writers, which doesn't happen too often, crowds them into an untenable spot. They're all supposed to win when only half of them can. They forget that, entirely! Nothing makes me sorer than to have a coach say, "Sure I did it. I broke the rule. But so does every coach in the country."

It is like a murderer's defense—"Sure I killed him. But there are ten thousand killers who do just as bad."

It has been the idea of too many coaches that the main offense or penalty in breaking a rule was to be caught. "If you can get away with it, fine . . . just don't get caught."

I don't know of any coach who spends any amount of time in teaching his squad *not* to hold . . . *not* to be off-side . . . *not* to consciously break any rule. A golfer who sees his ball move, but who doesn't call the penalty is a cheater. The player who does the same in football, holds or lunges off-side and gets away with it, is a hero. Can you imagine a big tackle saying, "That gain doesn't count. I held on the play"?

Years ago I ran across a fine young tackle playing on a glamour professional team. "Good work," I said after a particular game.

"Not yet," he said. "I don't know enough."

"What do you mean?" I said.

"About holding. All the older fellows know all the tricks. They'll grab you by the pants for just a split second. This throws you off balance but they never get caught. It takes only a split second."

"Do all linemen hold?" I asked.

"Every good one I've played against," he said. "They are trained that way. I'm not too good, yet. I've been caught three times this season and the coach didn't like that forty-five yards it cost us."

Coaches forget that a holding penalty, an off-side or some other penalty may offset an 80-yard run or a touchdown effort. They should be the most ethical sport directors we have. They are playing a game full of dynamite on the side of fouls. Players should be thoroughly trained in *not* breaking the rules.

While many coaches may be ethical, a great many still follow the old slogan of "Winning at any cost," no matter what rules are involved. When a coach has a bad team he will say jokingly, "I'm building character this year." There is no place for a joke in this situation. A coach that isn't building character should be fired. No matter if he wins every game, he is doing far more harm than good. If football isn't character-building it is no game to be played.

Football is a peculiar game featuring 22 contestants on the same field unusually keyed up and ready for mayhem. It is a tough game to control. We have no especial quarrel with the over-anxious player who is off-side or who holds an opponent. But there are entirely too many foul moves that are deliberate. There are too many foul actions that lead to injuries.

Any number of leading stars have told me there is no excuse for excessive roughness, for the deliberate foul tactics so often employed. This goes for both college and pro. Especially pro. "I can't see any reason for so much illegal and unnecessary roughness," Otto Graham, one of the game's best, told Tim Cohane, one of the game's soundest critics.

Football, one of the greatest games, can be made greater only if it is cleaned up and protected. It has taken more punishment than boxing has—and boxing, on the average, doesn't deserve to be mentioned with any decent sport. Comparatively speaking, football is in an entirely different setting. It has practically none of the thugs, crooks, cheaters, bums and chiselers that boxing knows to a large degree.

Most of the people connected with football—college and pro—are decent citizens. Their mistakes are not connected with boxing's knavery. They are merely connected with football's frenzy to win, regardless of hiring players, recruiting stars, even regardless of the rules they play by. Football must change its ways in this respect.

Did you ever hear of any scandal connected with Knute

Rockne and the Four Horsemen? With Red Grange, the Galloping Ghost?

I will stand for the fierce and continued spirit of Notre Dame teams. They have led the list through the years. Spirit is the most vital of all football factors. They got this from the Fathers at Notre Dame and from Knute Rockne. It can't and should not be destroyed.

But such teams as Notre Dame, Michigan, Yale, Princeton, Southern California, Tennessee, Georgia Tech, Oklahoma, Duke, Texas and the others must see to it that football is played in the spirit of the rules—that it is kept clean from hypocrisy and dirt and placed on a high level of decency in every way.

The keenness to win—the will to win—is important. But the desire to win, even illegally, is too great. I'll admit I have hammered on these points for over 40 years without making much of a dent. But if big changes, critical changes, are not made soon, football will die through its unwillingness to face up to its greatest mistake.

IV

Who Stand and Fight Amid a Bitter Brood . . .

CHAPTER EIGHTEEN

Jim Thorpe,
the American Indian

The Indian is a great natural athlete. Given the same chance, he has the white man lashed to the post. His heritage is all out-doors. His reflexes are sharp. He takes the game—in fact every form of life—as it comes to him. He rarely gets excited or off balance.

An example was Chief Albert Bender, a Chippewa. A pal of mine, the Chief was a great pitcher, a fine shot and an able golfer. He strong-armed Connie Mack's pitching staffs from 1903–1914. Mack told me he was once undecided whether he should pick Mathewson or Bender to pitch a game that meant a million dollars to him.

When Bender pitched for the Athletics against the Giants in the 1911 World Series, I noticed that he often quarreled with Eddie Collins at second or Stuffy McInnis at first. "What was the fuss all about?" I asked the Chief.

"Well," he said, "they're young. In assists to firsts or second

I was throwing them curves. I just wanted to let 'em know the World Series was just another ball game."

I played a lot of golf with Bender from 1911 through 1914. Whatever the game, he was a great competitor. Nothing ever bothered him.

Bender brings up another, even greater Indian. His name is Jim Thorpe. In many ways, Thorpe was like Bender. Nothing ever bothered or upset him. Both Bender and Thorpe had the philosophy of the ages. At football Jim was a brilliant ball carrier, a fine passer, a good pass receiver, a place kicker, a drop kicker and a punter—and also a murderous blocker. Undoubtedly the game's greatest all-around kicker, he rated Camp's 1911 and 1912 teams as a halfback.

Old-timers may tell you Thorpe couldn't hit a curve . . . but he was a big league ball player. He was also a fine shot. And in 1912 he was a decathlon and a pentathlon winner at the Olympics in Stockholm. That was long before the long grind of training improved so many others who, as natural athletes, couldn't fan Jim's brow.

Thorpe did little training. Francis Albertanti, who covered the 1912 Games for the old *Evening Mail,* told me that going over on the old Red Star liner *Finland* Thorpe would sit alone while the rest of the track squad pounded a stretch of cork laid down on one of the decks.

"What are you doing, Jim," asked Albertanti one day, "thinking of your Uncle Sitting Bull?"

"No . . . I'm practicing the broad jump," replied Thorpe. "I've just jumped twenty-three feet eight inches. I think that can win it." He did win, at five inches less.

John J. Hayes, the 1908 Olympic marathoner who helped train our 1912 team, tells of another anecdote concerning Thorpe and his Olympic "chaperone," Warner. Pop, of course, had Thorpe at Carlisle.

"Mike Murphy, who coached the Yale and later the Penn track teams for so many years, trained our boys along with Lawson Robertson and several others," said Hayes. "Mike was a martinet—at least for those days. One hot morning out on the track Mike missed Thorpe for the third consecutive day. He blew his top and hunted him out. He found Thorpe asleep in a hammock behind the living quarters of our marathon team. Seated nearby and soaking up the Swedish sun was Warner.

" 'Glenn,' said Mike, 'I've seen some queer birds in my day but your Indian beats all! I don't see him do anything . . . except sleep!'

"Pop eyed Mike benignly," added Hayes. "Then he said: 'Mike, don't worry. All those two-for-a-nickel events you've got lined up for Thorpe won't bother him. He's in shape . . . what with football, lacrosse, baseball and track back at school, how could he be out of shape? This sleeping is the best training ever —for Jim.' "

Hayes reflected that the few times Thorpe appeared for work he'd simply study the broad jump take-off or the high-jump pit, place a handkerchief out well past 23 feet—or on something higher than six feet—and then sit under a tree and study his marks. Jim's practice was 90 per cent concentration.

As Warner had prophesied, Thorpe shambled his opposition, the pick of the world's best. He won four of the five firsts in the pentathlon and four of the ten firsts in the decathlon. These included a winning 4:40.1 in the 1,500 meters . . . after he had competed in the dash, hurdle and other field events.

When King Gustav, a sincere sport fan, presented the gold medal following one of Thorpe's victories, the King uttered the accolade which Jim never forgot: "Sir, you are the greatest athlete in the world."

During his later and bitter years, Jim used to brood on that appellation whenever the subject was broached concerning the return of his Olympic trophies because of charges that he had violated his amateurism by playing semi-pro baseball prior to the Games. "At least they couldn't strip me of the King's words," Jim told me. "I played a little summer baseball while I was at Carlisle, for eating money. But whatever the competition, I played with the heart of an amateur—for the pure hell of it."

Dan Ferris, who was James E. Sullivan's personal secretary for those Games, sets the record straight as to why Thorpe failed to show when King Gustav of Sweden asked that he appear at the castle for the King's personal accolade at the close of the Games.

"The decathlon events took place on the last day," recalled Ferris. "Immediately following Jim's victory, he and a few of his cronies went on a well-deserved spree. It was a case of too much Swedish punch . . . at least for Thorpe. Our ship was anchored in Stockholm harbor; and when the tender finally poured Thorpe's party aboard, Jim proceeded to leap about the deck, jumping and kicking in cabin doors. I remember he kept yelling, 'I'm a horse! . . . I'm a horse!' In the midst of all this confusion a delegate came to our ship to request Thorpe to visit the King . . . to receive Gustav's personal homage. We had to inform him that Thorpe wasn't aboard."

When Thorpe was running wild for Carlisle, the Indians played few games at home. Aptly called The Nomads of the Gridiron, they roved east, west and into the southwest. "Carlisle's entire student body comprised no more than two hundred and fifty boys," recalled Warner years later. "And bear this in mind . . . they were all youngsters—including Thorpe. None were more than sixteen or seventeen. They were really high-school boys playing against college men . . . but my God, how they could play!"

"Yes, Pop," commented Gene Fowler, "they may have been kids when they started playing for you at Carlisle, but they were old men when they stopped. Those Redskins played for years and years . . . with Carlisle as their home reservation."

Warner's only reply was a chuckle.

It was around 1914 that I asked Thorpe, then out of college for a year or more, if he'd ever been hurt in football.

"Who in hell can get hurt playing football?" scoffed Jim. "I never needed to call time out during any college game."

Thorpe liked to wrestle with anybody who would roughhouse. He and Jack Dempsey would have made a wonderful team for about 15 hours a day. Both carried an enormous excess of energy, and Dempsey also has Indian blood in his veins.

McGraw had an iron-clad rule on the Giants that none of his ball players were to wrestle or "play" with Thorpe. Down at spring training in 1916—it was while the Giants were at Marlin, Texas—Jim went on a happy rampage one day and practically clobbered the whole team. All in play, he was as gentle as a wild African water buffalo.

Elmer Oliphant, one of West Point's all-time immortals and today a vice-president with Metropolitan Life in New York, appreciated Jim's ability to hit the long ball. This I can vouch for and you can check it with a fellow named Omar Bradley, one of West Point's best outfielders.

"It was 1916," said Oliphant. "As a yearling, I was batting fourth and blasting drives all over the Plains. First-classman Bradley was batting third. I held what I considered the Academy's long distance clouting mark—hitting a ball so far it hit in the road in front of Cullum Hall and bounced against the building. That day the Giants played Army in an exhibition game at the Academy, a gesture they still carry out each spring. Bradley and I were watching the Giant batters in practice. They could hit, sure . . . but I was telling Omar what I intended to do with the Giant pitching.

"Bradley looked me over a moment, then said, 'Ollie, you

can hit 'em pretty good. But last year, when the Giants played up here with Jim Thorpe, he parked three balls ON TOP of Cullum Hall, not against it.' "

You had to like Jim. He was a very decent human being. He rose to great fame in a hurry and then sank. He was a gentleman, but there were times when firewater got the better of their long feud. Years ago I went out to the ball park in Rocky Mount, North Carolina, one day with a local writer. On our way out he showed me a big iron can about five feet high. "This," said the writer, "is where Thorpe stood our sheriff on his head one day—just picked him up and dumped him in, upside down. The sheriff was trying to arrest Jim."

The one man Jim was leery of trying to handle, however, was Warner. When Carlisle played Brown on Thanksgiving of 1912, Thorpe and Pop got into a heated argument over a drink Jim had taken that morning to celebrate the pact between the Indians and white men in the Massachusetts Bay Colony. Pop gave Jim a hard riding. Late that afternoon I ran into the referee who worked that game.

"I've just officiated at a game in which I've seen the greatest football player————ever," he said. "Jim Thorpe defeated Brown thirty-two to nothing—all by himself. Runs of fifty and sixty yards were nothing . . . the Indian was a tornado. He wrecked the entire Brown team." The referee's name was Mike Thompson, one of the best.

In the 1912 game against a strong Army team, Carlisle was on their own 10-yard line. Thorpe dropped back to kick. Bill Langford, the well-known referee, dropped back with him. "They think I'm going to kick, both us and Army," Thorpe muttered to Langford. "But I ain't." After faking a kick Thorpe ran 90 yards and the Indians broke open the game and won 27–6.

"He was an unbelievable competitor," reflected Langford. "The game has never seen his like."

It was during Jim's junior or senior year at Carlisle that Lafayette was playing host to the Indians in a track meet. It had been well publicized and a welcoming committee, headed by Lafayette's coach Harold Bruce, met the train. All were stunned when a party of two alighted at Easton—Warner and Thorpe.

"What's this?" demanded Bruce. "We expected the Carlisle track team."

"Here it is," replied Warner, casually pointing to Thorpe. Jim racked up practically every blue ribbon on the field in a rout for Carlisle.

In street dress Thorpe, like Dempsey, wasn't particularly imposing. Both were so perfectly proportioned that nothing seemed unusual about either man—both scaled around 183 pounds at their respective peaks.

"In addition to having every needed physical asset, Thorpe had a rare spirit," reflected Warner in later years. "Nothing bothered Jim. When he was 'right' the sheer joy of playing carried him through. When he wasn't, he showed it. For that reason I used to call him 'a lazy Indian' to his face. I'll admit, though, it didn't bother him. But when he was right, he was the best. The reason I picked Ernie Nevers over Thorpe as my all-time football player was because Ernie gave one-hundred per cent of himself—always. In that respect, he was a coach's ideal. Thorpe gave it only on certain occasions. It was difficult to know if Jim was laughing with or at you."

Down the last 15 years, when Thorpe was up but mostly down, the Circus Saints and Sinners in New York took an interest in him. Fred Benham, a New York publicist, who handled the "Fall Guy" at those luncheons, was close to Jim.

"We were talking one night," said Benham, "and I asked Jim if there was any material about him that hadn't been done to death in the papers."

"Yes . . . one thing," grunted Thorpe. "I'm a twin. My twin brother died when we were five . . . or six."

"How did it happen?" I asked.

"We were raised on canned condensed milk," replied Jim seriously, "and we ran out of cans."

No matter what the sport, Thorpe was the complete natural. He could play tennis, he was a whiz at billiards or pool, and he was adept at these games long after his pro football days were over. Thorpe was a cornerstone, badly used, but nevertheless a cornerstone of professional football from 1920 through 1926. His pro days started nearly eight years after he finished at Carlisle: the Canton Bulldogs in 1920; the Cleveland Indians, in '23; with Rock Island in '24 and '25, the year he came to the New York Giants; and back to Canton for the '26 season—his last. With the exception of the Giants those names may strike a weird note with neophytes, but pro football was built around those early franchises. In this respect, Thorpe was born at least 30 years too soon. In '20, when the League was formed, Jim was already a veteran, an old man in the strict competitive sense—slowing down for that last painful grind through the homestretch of his career. By '26 he was barely getting by on a pair of scarred and weary legs, legs that had carried him through more competitive miles than all the campaigns of the French and Indian wars.

Lacrosse may be the pure Indian game; but football, by its very nature, carries heavy Indian appeal. Witness Thorpe, Calac, Guyon, Exendine, Houser, Mt. Pleasant, Little Twig, Long Time Sleep (Nokolas Lassa), Newashe, Tomahawk and others including Wheelock and Metoxen and all the Big and Little Bears they had in tow. I believe an All-America, All-Indian team could beat the All-Time Notre Dame, All-Time Michigan or All-Time anything else. And Thorpe would have been the big reason . . . an unleashed Thorpe giving his best. Take a look at that backfield—Thorpe, Guyon, Calac, Mt. Pleasant.

I can still see Thorpe as Pop Warner described Jim when he first came to Carlisle from the plain country of Oklahoma: a skinny Indian youngster weighing around 130 pounds . . . but moving like a breeze—no strain. He grew into 185 pounds of muscle, blue-steel ligaments, split-second reflexes and a keen competitive brain that gave him a supremacy in football and track and a high ranking in almost every sport he tried.

I seldom go out on limbs to crusade for individuals, much less a sport, my attitude towards public projects of this sort being with the "sink or swim" school. However, if ever an individual was pilloried by the shabby treatment he received from most of the press and the public, Jim Thorpe is that man. As a symbol of the greatest athlete of his day, if not all time, Thorpe should have been utilized by the Department of the Interior where he could have helped his own people . . . not after he had become a broken down caricature but while he was a young man. Instead, he was allowed to live on the five dollars a day he received as a movie extra—when and if.

The act that barred Thorpe could never be justified. Baseball and track and field are totally apart. Thorpe was truthful when he maintained that all he got from summer baseball at Rocky Mount, while he was at Carlisle, was barely enough to pay expenses. In those days—in fact until recently—college ball players from all over the map and particularly the Ivy schools, played on summer teams, including various hotel nines for far more cash than accrued to Thorpe and were still held as clean, pure amateurs and passed for football, track and other college sports.

What right did the AAU have to Thorpe's private gifts, fairly won in those 1912 Olympics? They merely robbed the Indian in a cold-blooded fashion. They have never known where those trophies were sent and have never offered to help retrieve them. I wrote several letters, in later years, to Avery Brundage, the Chicago contractor and keystone of our Olympic organization, stating the case for Thorpe. Brundage's replies were weak and implied a "so what . . . it's dead and forgotten" attitude. The treatment accorded Thorpe, in my opinion, is one of the cruel turns of all American sport.

Since his death, Thorpe's body has been more in demand than it ever was during the last 20 years of his life. Civic do-gooders and chamber of commerce people, both in Oklahoma and in Pennsylvania, want his burial mound for a tourist shrine. Looking down on it all, old Jim must be chuckling an ironic chuckle.

It would be fitting that an effigy of the American Indian should stand prominently in the entry to the Indian wing at the Museum of Natural History in New York. That effigy should be a red copper, life-size, detailed likeness of Jim Thorpe—this country's, if not the world's greatest all-around natural athlete.

CHAPTER NINETEEN

The Other Babe
and Women in Sports

For more than 50 years I have watched a great sport story gather tidal-wave force. This is the story of women in competition, a story practically unknown at the turn of the century. Who were the women golf and tennis stars of 1900? I'll have to admit I don't recall, although there must have been a faint flutter of interest in certain games at that time.

However, in my opinion, the two girls who did most to turn the world spotlight on their sex—with the possible exception of Cleopatra—were Elenora Sears and Babe Didrikson Zaharias, a Boston society girl and a solid Texas miss. I didn't glimpse the Sears girl in the early 1900's when she was blazing a trail by kicking holes in all feminine concepts of competitive sports. She played "a man's game" in tennis. An excellent player with a smashing game, she was also a powerful swimmer, a golfer who could "punch" her shots, a fine horsewoman and a

237

squash rackets champion for many years. I read where this wonderful girl played in the national championships during the winter of '54—at 70 years young.

"Anything You Can Do I Can Do Better" was a hit when Ethel Merman sang it. Elenora Sears was "living" that concept in her attitude towards sports competition with men back in the early 1900's. She won her cause and was the prime liberator of women from steel and whalebone corsets to the shorts and T-shirted gals of today.

The successor to Miss Sears was and remains my old girl-friend "Babe." It is an odd turn that perhaps the two flashiest figures in sport—two of its immortals—were called "Babe." Babe Ruth and Babe Didrikson. They stand above the mobs and the multitudes. They will still be alone and above the others when you and I are dust.

I heard something about Babe Didrikson in 1931 when this clerk-typist of the Employers Casualty Company of Dallas, Texas, came east to enter the Women's National Track and Field championships at Newark, New Jersey. As I recall, she won six firsts, jumping and running off with the meet.

I first met the Babe a year later just before the Olympic Games opened at Los Angeles. The officials would allow her to enter only three events. Babe was upset. She wanted to enter six or seven. She won the javelin and the 80-meter low hurdles, but was disqualified in the high jump and had to settle for second place when her record leap was disallowed. The day after the Games, Paul Gallico and I made a golf date with Babe and took her out to Brentwood. The Babe was then a tallish, slender young kid of 17. In legs, arms and body she was constructed to be a champion. She had powerful hands, legs like a halfback and, above all, complete confidence in herself. She had held a golf club several times but had played no golf.

Watching the Babe that day in early August, 1932, I

thought I saw the makings of a champion—not in track and field where she already had proved her gold medal rating—but in golf, a sport where a girl might compete with men on their own terms. In my mind, she had all the physical attributes . . . wonderful legs, slender enough but strong . . . long-muscled arms . . . nice height and above all, a pair of fine strong hands and wrists.

Westbrook Pegler and Paul Gallico were pounding away on their own stories when I mentioned that we might be looking at the greatest future woman golfer of all time.

"She tells me she's never played golf but that she'd like to try it," I said. "How would you like to go out early tomorrow to Brentwood? I'll bring the Babe along and we'll see what she can do."

Next morning we picked Babe up and drove out to Brentwood. Braven Dyer, sports columnist of the *Los Angeles Times*, was along and on this, Babe's baptismal round of golf, we must have been as clubby a fivesome as ever cluttered up a fairway. Babe and I stood the other three.

Recalling that round recently, I thought Babe had done pretty well. Olin Dutra, the club pro, a former Open champ, watched her make one long carry. All he said was, "I saw it, but I still don't believe it."

"That was the only shot I hit all day, Grantland, and you know it," snorted Babe when I mentioned that baptism. "I was all over the course! I hit a few pretty good shots, but I never got a drive out there two hundred and fifty yards as you 'recall.' I recall I seldom got the ball off the ground. You tried to look out for me so you couldn't play your own game. I remember we came to the short seventeenth hole and you said, 'Babe, we're all even. We've got to do something.' Gallico drove the green; you and I were trapped. You said, 'That makes it tough.' Remember?"

I sure do. Babe whispered, "Don't worry, Grant. I'll handle this." Then she turned to Gallico. "Paul," she said, "I'll race you to the green." Paul takes no challenge from any woman and few from men. It was downhill; then uphill. Babe was in Olympic condition. Gallico, a one-time Columbia oarsman, was not. Babe kept two feet ahead of him all the way—like Rusty the electric rabbit at a dog track. As they reached the green, Gallico collapsed . . . all out and all in. When it came his time to putt, Paul four-putted. We won the hole and the match.

Since watching her break an Olympic javelin record at her first heave several days before, I had been moving towards Babe's corner. But after that match I was in it—completely. Boosting the Babe was one of the most pleasant and satisfying jobs in sport. She so rarely let me down on any competitive assignment. "Grant's girl," they called her. It was all right by me.

I tried to find something she couldn't do. Frankly, I failed. But I was certain, one day, I had the stopper. "How is your sewing?" I asked. "I frequently make my own clothes," she replied. "And if it interests you, I'm a pretty good cook." I forgot to ask how her archery was. I knew it was excellent. In 1933, when Babe was barnstorming around the country playing basketball, our Sportlight film company made a moving picture of her in 12 sports. The film was shot mostly in and around Dallas. Perhaps the sequences of her playing football with Ray Morrison's Southern Methodist team were gagged a little, but the important point is that she was adept at running and handling a football. She threw a baseball 296 feet, an Olympic mark. Her points in diving were close to perfection and her 100-yard swim test was but a fifth second off. Babe's reflexes were instantaneous. She was strong where strength was needed—quick where the premium was on speed and deftness.

In 1935 Babe took up golf seriously. By the end of 1935 she

was playing championship golf and 19 years later, at the age of 39—none of my gals ever quite reaches 40—she was still at the top of her game! In between, her game survived an attack of cancer with a serious operation. Following that long period of hospitalization, Babe went up to George May's big Chicago Tournament of Champions and played brilliantly. Soon her game had returned to rounds of 70 and 71.

Several years prior to that dread operation in 1953, Babe —in poor health—dropped out of championship play for a time. Her husband, George Zaharias, a one-time seal in the wrestling racket but one of the more intelligent and most gentle men I know, took Babe to a little home in Denver where she quickly became a housewife with the most beautiful rose garden in town. But before very long, she returned to competition.

"Why did you come back?" I asked.

"I'll tell you," she replied. "You wrote a piece in which you picked champions for the coming year and you selected Louise Suggs at the top of the girls' list. That sorta took the slack up in my game. I worked just that much harder to prove you wrong."

During the war the two Babes—Ruth and Zaharias—played a War Bond match against Mrs. Sylvia Annenberg and Mysterious John Montague, the strong man who plays par golf with hoes, rakes and shovels. The match was played at the White Marsh Country Club on Long Island, since gone the way of all turf as a housing development. Promoted by the Hearst papers and Bill Corum, the show drew between 25,000 and 30,000 people, who stampeded the course like great herds of sheep. Off the first tee around 1:00 P.M., it was near 6:00 P.M. when the foursome reached the ninth green. Ruth, trying to keep his shots on a string to prevent his ball from skulling a tourist with a hook, had a rough journey. As for Babe, she needed a putt of less than six feet for a 32 when the crowd swallowed balls on contestants on the ninth green.

While Babe was winning the British Women's Amateur in 1947 over the gale-swept course at Gullane, Scotland—the first American to win it—I was fighting a battle of my own with pneumonia. The morning she arrived back in New York I had hoped to be there to help greet her when she came down the bay. A suite had been reserved at the New Yorker Hotel. When I called, Babe and George wanted to come up to see me! But Babe had come through a far more spectacular victory than I. I spent a short half hour at their hotel quietly celebrating with Babe and George Zaharias—two wonderful kids, who I feel constitute an unusually warm and wonderful American love story.

Babe not only has the speed, strength, co-ordination and competitive temperament but a quality of stamina that, until recently, has been unlimited. I doubt that anyone except Ben Hogan has played more rounds of golf during the past 18 years than has Babe. I asked her in March of '54 if she had any idea how many rounds she'd played since starting her relentless attack on par in 1935.

"I haven't given it too much thought," she replied. "But figure it this way. For the best part of eighteen years I've averaged a round a day. That's three hundred and sixty-five rounds of golf times eighteen, or six thousand, five hundred and seventy rounds . . . a lot of walking . . . a lot of shots. I've worked, Grantland; I've worked like hell.

"I want you to know something else," Babe continued. "Since I've been playing serious golf, I've seen you many times . . . at many clubs. But mostly it's been just a greeting en route to the first tee. 'Hello, Babe . . . how's your game?,' you'll say and I reply, 'Fine, Grantland . . . just fine!' But that's not enough! We play big matches on tour these days. When more of the public realizes we're no carnival act, they'll be bigger!

"Your best columns have been gotten from the men's locker

room following a big match. That's where a gal's at a disadvantage. We have no one to talk to but ourselves. Somehow, the locker room's the best place to discuss what shots won or lost a match . . . and what's going on, with you or me. Looking back a little, I wish I'd known you in there, Grantland."

A star in 1932, she was a greater golfing star in 1954. More than 20 years have gone by but the famed Babe has remained at a remarkable peak. In her day and time she had been the finest woman athlete of all time. She remains one of the great golfers in the one sport she has selected for a sporting and a competitive career.

A large part of my interest on the female side of the case has been centered in Helen Wills and Glenna Collett at tennis and golf, largely because they were the first two young stars I followed and watched develop almost from childhood to world fame. In tennis I've studied them from Helen Wills to Maureen Connolly.

Helen Wills came east to prove her place in the shining sun of fame when she was only 12 or 13 years old. She was a serious faced youngster, earning the name of Little Miss Poker Face. Even then she had fine power for a kid, perfect concentration and the will to win. From the start she was a fine competitor. Helen never quite had the deft-footed action and amazing hand wizardry of Suzanne Lenglen, the French wonder. In their only meeting Lenglen—before the Wills girl had reached her peak—was the victor. Helen was a stouter competitor than Mlle. Lenglen and she had more power. I doubt, however, that any woman tennis player ever had Lenglen's rare skill or artistry. She was lightning fast on the court.

First as Mrs. Helen Wills Moody and later as Mrs. Aidan Roark, the original Helen Wills continued to play fine baseline tennis many years after she retired from competition. She was never in the least afraid to meet any opponent. She had great faith in her mental and physical make-up. She was not in any way slow footed—she merely lacked the swifter foot action of a Lenglen.

Glenna Collett, since 1931 Mrs. Edwin H. Vare of Philadelphia, remains one of my favorites. Like Helen Wills, Glenna was worth looking at; like Helen, she was on the quiet side. When she was only 15 or 16 years old, Glenna was my partner in many matches we played against Dorothy Campbell Hurd and others at Belleair on the Florida West Coast.

Glenna Collett Vare won six U.S. National Amateur championships. Excellent with both woods and irons, her most famous golf match was with Joyce Wethered, the English champion, at St. Andrews, Scotland, in 1929. This match was really for the world championship, as both were recognized as the two greatest at the time. Shooting a 41 for the opening 11 holes, Glenna set a whirlwind pace for the first 18 to lead with a brilliant 73. But in the afternoon test, Joyce finally wore her American opponent down. Miss Wethered was undoubtedly the finest woman golfer in history.

Marion Hollins was another fine woman athlete, being not only a champion golfer but the best of the women polo players. She had a bad automobile accident one day, but she insisted on playing a golf match she had the next afternoon. She had to quit at the 16th hole. A later examination brought out the painful fact that the accident had cost her two broken ribs!

I can't elucidate on the finer points of Gretchen Fraser's or Andrea Mead's maneuvers with the skiis, but I do know the Fraser girl scored in the 1948 winter Olympics and then the slender Miss Mead knocked the skiing world on its ear by winning two gold medals in the '52 Games. What's more, both looked awfully pretty on or off a pair of skiis. Also, I don't have to tell you what Sonja Henie did to the United States mint when she laced up her skates and started to hula all over the center ice at Madison Square Garden.

Concerning the gal swimmers, they're fine . . . only more so. The Australian girl, Annette Kellerman, made a handsome looking mermaid encased in her fish scales of the early 1920's; but she'd be alone on a barnacled rock compared to Esther Williams in her silk and sequin suits. The female swimmers and divers will always have appeal and most of them are the best sort of competitors. In this list I remain partial to Gertrude Ederle, the first of her sex to conquer the Channel, Aileen Riggin and Eleanor Holm—three stars of the earlier years. They and their sisters were all fine competitors, champions of high rating.

Returning to golf for a moment, two other favorites of mine were Helen Hicks, first girl to turn professional, and Virginia Van Wie. I have watched both play in the low 70's—many times to my financial disadvantage. The Van Wie girl, a lovely creature, was also a three-time champion, taking the Amateur crown in '32, '33 and '34.

I ran into Helen Hicks one day at Exmoor, Chicago. I came up with her at the tenth tee. "How do you stand?" I asked.

She was playing with a good looking kid of 17 or 18. "I've got to get to work," Helen said. "I've caught one of these damn Jones pupils and I'm lucky to be all even. We are both out in thirty-seven."

Ernest Jones was the girls' and women's favorite teacher then. He still is. "I'd rather teach women," Ernest told me one day. "They are much better listeners. The average man will listen to instruction for a few minutes and then decide he knows all the answers and won't listen any longer." Jones was and still is an advocate of simply swinging the clubhead—a pretty good idea!

The improvement in women's scoring has been phenomenal. In the old days, from 1910 to 1925, few women ever broke

80. Now they get into the 70's. Most of the good ones play in the low 70's.

It remained for Freddie Corcoran to assemble many of the women leaders in a roving professional band of good looks and talent. This enterprise was never dreamed of even ten years ago, but is proving itself as one of the smartest moves in sport. The men, with the happy exception of Jimmy Demaret, can be awfully grim; but the gals, bless 'em, can grin and still hit their shots with the authentic crispness of their brothers.

CHAPTER TWENTY

The Negro Race

When I began fooling around with sport in 1900, there was a vast discrimination that has since vanished. There were no Negroes in any white competition. Big time sport was almost entirely a white man's playground.

Oh, there might have been an occasional player like Lewis, the fine center on a distant Harvard team, Robeson of Rutgers, Pollard of Brown or Slater who played tackle on Iowa's undefeated 1921 team. Slater was the only man that ever matched Notre Dame's fiery Hunk Anderson. Long after Iowa defeated Notre Dame 10–7 that year, Hunk admitted it. The only difference was that Hunk weighed 170 and Slater scaled 220.

But as a general rule, when I first came along the Negro was all but shut out—except in boxing. In the ring game the Negro race produced such early terrors as Joe Gans, Jack Johnson, Joe Walcott (The Barbadoes Demon), George Dixon and some others but in other sports they were excluded. No one can say how many Negro champions were barred from practically all fields.

Next to Abraham Lincoln, the biggest white benefactor of the Negro has been Branch Rickey. Branch and I have had our squabbles but in the case of the Negro, he did right. Since Rickey brought in Jackie Robinson, the big leagues have been dotted with colored skins, many of them high up in the game.

Strangely enough, the first Negro to reach any real pinnacle on the sporting map was Jack Johnson who won the heavyweight boxing crown in 1908. Never a great fighter, Johnson had the fastest pair of hands I've seen in a big man. Nobody has come close to him as a defensive master and counter puncher. A bad actor socially, Johnson was a poor representative for his race. He certainly didn't help the cause of the Negro.

In this respect, no one in the sporting world has helped his people to advance with such speed as Joe Louis. In the first place, Louis was a great heavyweight. Aside from defending his title 25 times, more than all modern heavyweights combined, Joe was a clean, fair sportsman—above most white men in his own game. He was completely honest in a game where honesty is not the watchword. Louis was a beacon, a glowing example also for the white race to follow.

I value Louis as a friend. What I admired most about him, however, was Joe himself; not his fighting equipment. Sportsmanship should be the very mortar of an athlete but never an entity in itself for conscious display. Nobody better exemplified this quality than Joe. During the 1940's and for a time following the war, Louis and I often sat together at ringside. We rarely talked fights . . . golf was the subject.

"Mr. Rice," he said one night, "I'm havin' trouble with my midiron."

"Joe," I replied, "you're not alone. Bobby Jones and Gene Sarazen had trouble with that club. After the nineteen thirty-four Open at Merion, Gene stayed away from the Number two iron."

"How come?" said Joe, a good listener who enjoys hearing about championship golf.

I described the 11th hole at Merion and how a Y-shaped brook bisects the fairway with the bottom of the Y continuing down the fairway and trailing off to the right of the elevated green. In the third round, Sarazen played his tee shot with his midiron, then pounded his long approach across the brook and onto the rising green for a sound par 4. In his fourth and final round, however, when Sarazen tried to repeat this tactic, he hooked his tee shot into the brook, had to lift out and then pushed his third shot into the bend of the brook where it guards the green. He finished with a 7.

"That hole cost Sarazen the Open," I reflected. "Olin Dutra won it by one shot. Walking off the 18th green, Gene said, 'Granny, today you saw me lose three shots with this midiron. I hate it because I can't trust it. I've stuck it into my bag for the last time.'"

"What did Sarazen use instead?" asked Louis.

"His Number four wood," I replied. "That's the club he used when he holed out a two hundred and thirty-five yard shot for his double-eagle in winning the Masters Tournament at Augusta the next spring, in 1935. The midiron is an extremely dangerous club, Joe. You ought to forget it and use your Number four wood. It's easier, safer and will get you there most every time."

"You're probably right," said Joe. "But it's just that I like to use the club the distance calls for. . . ."

With Joe, it was simply a case of right being right.

Another evening at ringside I mentioned to Joe that I was going up to Lou Nova's camp. This was before the Louis–Nova fight. Did Joe have any message for Lou?

"Just tell Nova that I'm changin' my style for this fight," he said. "In my last two fights I fought flat-footed. Tell Nova for this one I aim to be on the balls of my feet. . . . I'm comin' to him."

Nova wasn't happy. "That's not the way I wanted it," he said. Nevertheless, Joe did come to Lou in that fight as Lou's "cosmic stance" was shattered in the sixth round.

Since the advent of Louis, rings everywhere, from Minneapolis to Miami, from New York to Los Angeles, are filled with Negro fighters. Many of them, particularly the heavies, have been much better than the whites—at least until the arrival of Rocky Marciano.

Who were the main leaders that paved the big advance? Joe Louis, Jesse Owens, Ray and Jackie Robinson, Larry Doby, Roy Campanella, Willie Mays, Monte Irvin, Luke Easter, and many others scattered over the map. Certainly the leaders were Louis, Owens, Jackie and Ray Robinson, and Campanella. And in his own ageless, effortless manner, who is to say that Satchel Paige, had he been given access to the major leagues 20 years ago, wouldn't have stood all the record books on their heads . . . including the one that Methuselah cherishes?

Who, in my book, is the all-time "tops" of the Negro athletes? For the sport he chose and for the way he mastered it— Jesse Owens. Joe Louis may have been a bit of a sucker for a right hand, but there was no visible chink in Owens' track armor. I've been looking at track and field stars since my days at Vanderbilt—before 1900. I've covered AAU championships, Penn Relays and various other championships including three Olympic Games; in 1924 at Paris, at Los Angeles in 1932 and at Berlin in 1936. Of these select world athletes, no one made the impression on me that Jesse Owens did.

When the rest of the so-called civilized world—athletes and tourists—congregated at Berlin for the 1936 Olympic Games, a feeling of acrimony already existed between Germany and the

United States. An elephant could have sensed it. Hitler had apparently already dismissed Great Britain as lacking a "backbone." France, torn with six kinds of socialism, her working masses putting in about one hour a day—with six more for lunch —was a sitting duck. As for Italy—no matter what role she chose —Hitler knew he had Mussolini's deranged Fascists in his pocket. Concerning the United States, Adolph didn't quite know what to make of us. He was probably hoping, even then, that Uncle Sam would play Uncle Sap at the poker table of nations where the blustering German bluff might drive off a pair of wired aces.

I'll not forget the sight of those German storm troopers, in their severely cut black uniforms . . . looking every inch the super race. You would see them in the streets, out at the jam-packed Reich Sportsfeld, at the Hofbraus. They didn't stroll; they marched . . . and gutturalized with the quiet, confident bearing that betokened their Cheshire cat scorn of "less endowed" mortals.

Overhead, great Junkers transports—with bomb racks exposed like wolf fangs—droned along in flying wedges at less than 2,500 feet. Yes, Germany in 1936 was a living, throbbing world poster—painted in the garish hues of a nation well primed for war.

Into this arena of nations and nationalisms, crystallized on the competitive field, stepped a tan, taut-skinned thunderbolt from Ohio State University. He was Jesse Owens, one of America's "African Auxiliaries" as Hitler so condescendingly phrased it. In the vast Berlin bowl—teeming with 100,000 souls of which at least 90,000 were Germans—Jesse Owens was ready.

"Owens? Who in hell is Owens?" they asked. After all, hadn't Max Schmeling, a true, loyal and proud *Deutscher*, knocked out another American "superman" named Joe Louis . . . barely a month before? No matter what the sport—boxing or track and field—"class" would tell. Reactivated Germany under Hitler possessed that class . . . *had* to!

During that first week of August, 1936, the Berlin weather was cold and rainy . . . hardly the weather that Owens would have chosen, for Negroes generally function best in intense heat. The answer was inside Owens himself. In four straight days, he made 14 consecutive appearances, running four heats each in the 100 and 200 meters and jumping six times. He broke Olympic records a total of nine times and equalled them twice.

In the 100 meters, he ran 0:10.3, 0:10.2, 0:10.4 and 0:10.3 against a world record of 0:10.3. In the 200-meter final, he returned 0:21.1 twice, 0:21.3 and 0:21.7 against the Olympic record of 0:21.2. He bettered Olympic records in all five of his measured leaps. The world, including Adolph Hitler, was willing to concede that it had never seen a sprinter-jumper like Jesse Owens.

In the qualifying trials, Owens, failing to get off properly, had twice fouled. With his third and final chance to qualify coming up, I watched Jesse from the press box with a pair of powerful glasses. I was searching for some telltale sign of emotion. Calmly he walked the sprint path in to the take-off board, then retraced his steps. Studying the situation a moment, the American athlete anteloped down that runway and took off at least a foot behind the required mark—but qualified!

In the final of the broad jump competition, a German jumper was leading the pack at a mark approaching 26 feet, a mark, incidentally, that no white man has yet surpassed. Owens or no Owens, the Reich was doing all right. Hitler, watching from the "royal" box, was preening his tailfeathers. Poised for his next attempt, Owens shot down the runway. As he hurled himself through space, the Negro collegian seemed to be jumping clear out of Germany. The American cheering started while Jesse was airborne. Hitler must have had his answer right then, for he started leaving his box immediately and was not around for the presentation of the laurel to the American who had just jumped 26 feet 5⁵⁄₁₆ inches for another Olympic mark that still stands.

When I encountered Owens after that jump, back at his quarters, he was the same modest person he had always been. He seemed to consider it all in a day's work. He had no feeling whatever about what Hitler had or had not done.

"I haven't even thought about it," he said. "I suppose Mr. Hitler is much too busy a man to stay out there forever. After all, he'd been there most of the day. Anyway, he did wave in my direction as he left the field and I sort of felt he was waving at me. I didn't bother about it one way or another."

The story of Owens isn't all told in his vivid Olympics showing. At Ferry Field, Ann Arbor, Michigan—home of the Wolverines—on a warm spring day in 1935, Jesse Owens had proved his greatness. In little more than an hour he had demonstrated his speed as a foot runner and jumper, and his uncanny stamina. The young Buckeye opened that particular Western Conference meet by winning the 100-yard dash in 0:09.4, tying the world record set by Frank Wykoff in 1930. Just 30 minutes later, he won the 220-yard dash in 0:20.3, three-tenths of a second off Roland Locke's 1926 mark. He then ran the 220-yard low hurdles in 0:22.6, four-tenths of a second off C. R. Brookins and Norman Paul's mark of 23.0. Here, then, were three competitive trials with two world records smashed, and a third equalled.

Then Owens came to the broad jump. The first American to have beaten 26 feet, on this afternoon he raced the runway knowing his "hot" form would be vital in shooting for a new mark. Exploding from the take-off board, he soared 26 feet 8¼ inches. All in all, he was rather a handy bloke to have around a year later at Berlin.

Watching Jesse run and jump that day at Berlin, I began

wondering if there was a set of limitations to any human's speed. Charley Paddock, labelled "the fastest human," thought there was. "We had a track meet coming up on the Coast," he told me one day, "and I determined to use this as a final test of my speed. I started working for this one sprint weeks ahead and I concentrated all my thinking towards it. The day finally arrived and every detail was perfect for the test. I was in top shape . . . the track was very fast . . . and the day was warm and windless.

"At the starter's gun I was away perfectly. By the time I had reached the eighty-yard mark I could see nine seconds flat . . . I was running at that rate, I knew. Then the muscles in the calves of both legs began to strain and quiver . . . and I have big, strong calves. In a flash I knew I was going to be crippled. I had to ease up—which I did. I still ran that hundred in nine and six-tenths after easing up the last twenty yards. I never tried to run the hundred in nine flat again. I knew my legs wouldn't stand the pace."

Will anyone ever run 100 yards in nine seconds? I doubt it . . . if Jesse Owens couldn't. He had great power in his legs . . . he had blinding speed . . . and his style was flawless— with no sign of extra effort. Jesse was as smooth as the west wind. Yet no one can tell for as I write this two men have smashed the supposedly unbreakable four-minute mile barrier, Roger Bannister and John Landy.

I've yet to hear of a great Negro pole vaulter but since 1930, the greatest sprinters and jumpers have been Negroes. All but invincible at distances from 60 to 300 yards, and in the high and broad jumping pits, such running gazelles as John Woodruff have walloped all comers up through a half mile. Now Mal Whitfield, a great Olympic middle distance star, has set his sights on the mile.

V

I Hear Them Tramping to Oblivion

V

CHAPTER TWENTY-ONE

Sportlight Films, Television and Sport

For one who doesn't drive an auto, who hates planes and avoids the melee of the mob, I believe that I have an unusual affinity for the fearless in heart. Reptiles and dangerous beasts and their human handlers fascinate me. Tales of the Everglades, the Amazon, Africa and other danger spots of the globe keep me spellbound for long periods after their disclosure. And for more than 30 years now, my association with the Grantland Rice Sportlight films has afforded me the opportunity of seeing and participating in a way of life I otherwise would have missed.

Whatever identity I've enjoyed from my byline, the Sportlight title board on movie shorts has given me contact with countless movie goers who may not know an inning from a goal post—and care less. Women, particularly, have been entertained by sporting action on the screen and I believe these experiences they have shared have given them a keener appreciation of sport in general.

257

It was back in 1920 that I ran into Jack Eaton in New York. Jack was a motion picture man with ideas; I was a sportswriter with a solid 20 years of background in my field. Jack suggested we make a series of one-reel sport motion pictures with John Hawkinson, a fine cameraman and a hard worker. The films would be called *The Sportlight* after the column I had been syndicating since 1913.

We picked various distributors for our product, making a picture a week, a pace that had all of us mumbling, and after a year we called off the attempt. Then in 1925 Hawkinson returned to the scene. Eaton, meanwhile, was running a theatre in Denver so after talking things over Hawkinson and I decided to have another go at it. I made the deal with Pathe. We were to make three pictures on a trial basis and if they liked them, we'd sign a contract.

The financing was my headache, including buying such new equipment as we needed for the job. I had nearly reached the bottom of the barrel when we delivered the three films. They were accepted and the contract was signed.

Later on we decided to join forces with Amadee Van Buren, who was making Aesop's Fables and other one reelers. Van Buren and I fell out. Then Hawkinson decided to quit the film racket and return home to Hartford, Connecticut and get married. I persuaded Eaton to return as a full partner.

Right here I want to say we were fortunate in that we could count on the friendship of Bob Jones, Jack Dempsey, Bill Tilden and other famous members of the Golden Age. The films had the authentic flavor. We were moving along full steam ahead when the first sound picture, The Jazz Singer with Al Jolson, hit the country. However, the transition to sound didn't take place over night and by 1932, when we joined Paramount Pictures on a contract of one picture per month—we were geared for most anything. Graham McNamee, a good friend, handled our first sound commentary. Ted Husing followed; then Bill Slater and a flock of others.

The core of our *Sportlight* team evolved around cameramen Russ Ervin and Ernest Corts—with Rod Warren, who joined us after graduating from Penn State in '29, as our advance man. Corts, now a Californian, handles much of our shooting in the West. Erwin and Warren with Eton at the helm, constituted a team that pretty much ran itself. As a sometimes unnecessary adjunct my relationship has always been one of deep interest, often excitement in the motion picture side of sport.

Our next *Sportlight* location may be in Canada, Florida, California, Australia, South America, England, Scotland, Mexico, Spain, the western desert—in fact anywhere in the world with the exception of the Iron Curtain countries. There is no limit on what our cameras may attempt to capture. Month after month, we have a one-reeler in the can. Incidentally, Paramount is the friendliest company I've worked with in any line. We have moved along without an argument.

Our field was and remains the world of sports, particularly participant rather than spectator sports: Salmon fishing in Canada . . . quail shooting in Georgia and the Carolinas . . . puma and crocodile hunting in Florida, as well as under-water action, and salt-water game fishing . . . grouse shooting in Scotland . . . lion hunting . . . or the koala bear and the kangaroo in Australia.

Our first talking picture, in 1929, was a film called *Four Aces*, in which Tex Rickard introduced four champions—Dempsey, Jones, Tilden and Hitchcock. Since then we've run a gamut that includes 123 activities under the classification of sport. From marbles to pushball—we have shot the human interest and competitive side of them all. We discovered that spectator sports don't make particularly good subjects. We needed novelties. Women, we were quick to learn, are heavy movie goers and the novel side of a sport seems to have the greater appeal for them.

In addition to playing in 7 or 8 thousand American theaters, *Sportlight* films appear in some 1,000 theatres in the British Isles alone. From there the trail leads all over the civilized world—except the Russian orbit. People want to see our top athletes in action, but they don't want to be force-fed the value of the American way. We try to keep all flag waving to a minimum.

We've built action around Ty Cobb, Red Grange, The Four Horsemen, Babe Didrikson, and such famed horses as Man o' War, Twenty Grand and Greyhound, the trotting marvel. Johnny Weissmuller gave our cameras excitement during the boomtime 1920's—in Miami and then at Silver Springs, Florida, where we made *Crystal Champions*, a great grosser.

The four Olympians, Helen Meany, Martha Norelius, Pete Desjardins and Weissmuller, plus Stubby Kruger, the diving clown, helped put Silver Springs on the map with that picture. During that trip Weissmuller and Kruger went on a spree in Miami and turned on a fleet of fire alarms. Steve Hannagan, rest his brilliant promotional soul, bailed them out of the hoosegow.

We were also the first people to film Cypress Gardens, Florida, when we worked with water skier Dick Pope and his Aquacade on skis.

I recall especially well two escapades our *Sportlight* crew undertook. In 1926 we made the one-reeler *The Call of the Wild* in New Brunswick, Canada, with my old *Tribune* boss, Bill McGeehan, in the role of the "heavy." Bill was supposed to be tracking a giant moose through the tundra, muskeg and blueberry bushes. The combination of Bill's bad heart and non-co-operative moose made it tough sledding. However, the agile minds of Eaton and Warren jackpotted. They "rented" a particularly noble, if dead, moose from a native guide and propped him up in the densest bush with stilts, baling wire and ropes. Then

Bill banged away with his muzzle loader at the defunct critter. That moose should have shared equal billing with McGeehan.

The *Sportlight*, like other short subjects, was hit hard by the double-feature blight which eliminated short features from thousands of theaters. However, these ten-minute reels are still being produced on a one-per-month basis. We are proud of the fact that despite five other competitive reels, throughout the years *Sportlight* has always led its particular field. We have been nominated for the Academy Award six times and have managed to win two Oscars for the Best Single Reel.

Due to my interest in animals, particularly wild animals of all types, I've long been partial to our films dealing with them. In this connection, two of my closest friends have been Ross Allen, a feature contributor, who heads the Florida Reptile Institute; and the late Raymond Ditmars, curator of the Bronx Zoo.

Allen has not only captured alive several thousands of rattlesnakes but wrestles with live alligators . . . and knows thoroughly the secrets of the famous Everglades. A very handy man to have around, Allen takes his chances. Not too long ago Ross deposited a seven-foot diamond back rattler in the corner of his work-room. Then he started for a bush in the room to look after a coral snake hanging there.

"It was the first time," he wrote me, "that I ever saw it happen. But the rattler uncoiled and followed me. I had on heavy boots up to my knees. From several feet away he dived at me and struck just above the boot top." As a result, Allen was near death for several weeks and was terribly ill for three months.

Perhaps you saw the film, "Killing the Killer," made in the mid-1920's, of a fight to the death between a cobra and a mongoose, an Indian mammal the size of a weasel. The mongoose, a great in-fighter, circled his foe for a moment—like Dempsey stalking a bum—then stabbed in and finished off the cobra with dispatch. Van Beuren had a chance to buy the American rights to this German film for 3,000 dollars, but decided to wait down the price to 2,500. Somebody else stepped in and purchased the short and grossed a fortune with it. I decided to film my own death struggle between the mongoose and our American diamond back. The plan fell through, however, when we were unable to import a mongoose to this country. I feel certain it would have been no contest. The rattler—so much quicker than a cobra—would have flattened the mongoose in five seconds.

I was discussing the subject of snakes with Raymond Ditmars, the curator of the Bronx Zoo over a cocktail at the Chatham Hotel in New York one day. We agreed that the water snake from the Gulf of Mexico was about as deadly as they come, when the subject of cobras came up.

"How high can a cobra strike?" I asked. "I believe it's no farther than the height of his arc."

"You might be right," conceded Ditmars. "Let's find out."

A short time later we were at the Bronx Zoo. Ditmars started into the cobra enclosure. He was armed with nothing more than a broom; I with four martinis. I mumbled something about discretion being the safest part of valor.

"Nonsense," retorted the snake man, practically dragging me in with him. Three of the hooded devils were taking a siesta but Ditmars pushed them with his broom and started herding them into one corner. I was standing with my back to the door when the third cobra with a mind of his own started on an end sweep—in my direction.

"Ray," I wheezed. "You're a snake short." So saying, I backed out of that door so quickly I tripped and fell—outside the door. I never did get to measure the cobra's talents as a high jumper.

Another good friend was Emil Liers, whose school of trained otters played the comic leads in one of Walt Disney's recent technicolor triumphs, "Beaver Valley." Our *Sportlight* crew worked with Liers. We transported Liers and his otters from his farm at Homer, Minnesota, to Florida's Silver Springs nearly 20 years ago to film a one-reeler called, "Playmates of the Wild." Those otters, all clowns, had a houseparty.

Back in the middle 1940's a cloud no larger than a small man's hand suddenly appeared above the fields of sport. It was known as Television or TV. Within a few short years this cloud was a raging storm, spear-headed by a wrecking cyclone. It struck two of the country's most popular sports—baseball and football—with a devastating crash. In baseball it practically wrecked the minor leagues, or many of them; in the big leagues it cut attendance by nearly 500,000 a year. In football, only Notre Dame could sell out in the face of TV's power.

It was the old story of trying to sell something and give away the same product for nothing. You can't sell what you can get for nothing. As television sets increased, football and baseball attendances started dropping.

Back around 1949 I started keeping track of football's attendance figures at Yale, Pennsylvania, Michigan, Southern California and UCLA. I found attendance marks at each school dropping about 10,000 a year. Then the NCAA came into the picture. Nation wide television was partially abolished. Penn, Notre Dame and a few others protested vigorously.

Under the new NCAA agreement only one big college game each week could be televised. This meant about 26 teams could be shown, making it impossible to show *the* top game each Saturday, a factor which drove millions back to radio. College football faced an impossible job in trying to satisfy a sports public that looked on Notre Dame–Anybody, a Michigan–Ohio State; an Oklahoma–Texas, a Georgia Tech–Alabama televised contest as the game they wanted to see. All of which would kill the attendance at the local college contest level.

I can recall years when I had to work desperately to get a pair of tickets for such Ivy brawls as Harvard–Yale or Yale–Princeton—with sellouts the rule. Those games are gone, even without TV.

The fight is still going despite the fact that the average college certainly cannot buck the TV competition. In late seasons it has been discovered that, in baseball, even with the flag contenders, premium games have dropped off attendance-wise by as much as 40,000. The 80,000 paid for a Cleveland–Yankee night game is now closer to 50,000. Sellouts have become a thing of the past with the other 30,000 taking it by TV.

Yet TV was a boom for racing, where only one race was shown. To affect racing the TV people would have to supply book making or bet taking with each set. Racing is strictly a betting matter and in 1954 it reached the top in attendance popularity. But as 1954 passes out, big league and minor league baseball and TV are in a triple conflict. Meanwhile, due to the NCAA's stand, old-time standards in football, minus TV, were reached and held at Michigan, Ohio State, Illinois, Michigan State, Southern California, Oklahoma, Texas, Georgia Tech and other power plants who have no televised games except those "one time only" dictate of the NCAA.

Television has raised just as heavy havoc in the fight game. Here, the International Boxing Club raised a new type of boxing fan—the TV savant. The average fighter no longer needs to know the first principles of the left hook, the feint or the jab. Neither does the spectator, so they make a perfect combination.

These TV shows have practically killed the smaller clubs where boxing was taught. Madison Square Garden has felt its impact almost as severely. Fights that formerly lured from 15,000 to 18,000 now rate less than 5,000. The medium has wrecked boxing as a science and an art. It has reduced it to hill-billy entertainment, without the music.

Four major sports in the country are considered of national interest . . . baseball, football, boxing and racing. It is quite possible that basketball and bowling have many more entries. But of the above Big Four, racing is the lone flourisher. Instead of satiating the appetite it has whetted it.

In time all of the current problems will be solved and it will be found that television has done more good than harm but this is a story for future years.

CHAPTER TWENTY-TWO

Horses, Trainers and Jockeys

or

I Don't Care if My Horse Loses
IF the Price Is Right

Maxims from Methuselah

Take your pick from the tipsters, who give you the winning horse,
But kindly remember the answer in the heart of your black remorse,

Horse racing's an opium dream, beyond all dreams ever spun,
Where every sad bloke in the mob should have won every race that
was run.

Did you ever notice, my friend, in the race track's grotto of tears,
How many go to the seller's maw—how few to the lone cashier's?

Did you ever notice, old pal, in the race track's dizzy spin
There are ninety ways that a horse can lose—with only one way to
win?

I had my first mixup with race horses at an early date, 1901, and at an earlier hour, about dawn. I had just gone to work for the *Nashville News.* I soon found that my two bosses, managing editor Ed Martin and editor Buford Goodwin, were both interested in racing news as an important feature to the sporting page.

My regular job ran from 8:00 A.M. to 6:00 P.M. I was told to handle the clockings at Cumberland Park, Nashville's race track. That often pushed my starting hour ahead to 4:00 A.M. From my stand, Cumberland Park was much more important than any Louisville park. The Cumberland Derby was much more important than the Kentucky Derby. And there was much more blue grass in Tennessee than there was in Kentucky.

With a salary of five dollars a week I couldn't do any betting; but I discovered then that there's a slight element of chance in horse racing. I also learned that all tips from owners, trainers and jockeys in particular are worth practically nothing. It was a valuable lesson I discarded later on in life. No horse follower can discard any sort of tip. If you don't play a tip and it wins, you hate yourself. But beware of owners, trainers and jockeys. Most of them gab on about "breeding" but when I'm going to bet on a horse, I don't ask about his breeding. All I ask is about six inches of his nose in front of the wire.

Tennessee abandoned racing later and I took little interest in the track until Man o'War arrived. Man o'War was something different—something extra—as great a competitor as Ty Cobb, Jack Dempsey, Tommy Hitchcock, Ben Hogan, or anyone else. He struck me always as one who had a furious desire to win. He started running from the post and he was still giving his best at the wire—all the way with all he had.

I have been checking back on the great horses I have seen in action. They include Man o'War, Exterminator (Old Bones), Twenty Grand, Equipoise, Count Fleet, Sarazen, Johnstown,

Seabiscuit, Citation, Armed, Alsab, Stymie, Assault, Challedon, Noor, Whirlaway, War Admiral, Omaha, Native Dancer—and too many more to mention. In looking over this famous cast, the question comes back—who was the greatest?

As I have said, the most savage, furious competitor of the lot was Man o'War. For my money, because of his all-devouring urge to win he remains "the mostest horse"—as his faithful groom Will Harbut described him in darky superlative. That was during those lush years Big Red spent at stud and then in royal retirement at old Sam Riddle's Faraway Farms down in Lexington. Man o'War quit racing, I am sure against his will, as a three-year-old.

The first time I ever saw Man o'War was at Jamaica track in 1920 where he was entered in the Stuyvesant Handicap at one mile. I had taken along an old boy from Tennessee who knew nothing about the track. "Can you give me a winner?" he asked.

"Yes," I replied, "a thing called Man o'War in the fifth race."

"I had him," said my friend after the race. "He won but he didn't pay much."

"No," I replied, "but he won."

Man o'War was in all books at 1–100, or one penny on each dollar bet. My friend had played five dollars on his nose. His winnings didn't pay his carfare back to Tennessee.

I think the two fastest horses I ever saw were Johnstown and Count Fleet. I understand from authentic sources that Johnstown had a mile workout in 1.33⅘. But he had head trouble, breathing trouble, or some defect to which all thoroughbreds are heir. He was never quite dependable, although he won the '39 Kentucky Derby, defeating Challedon by about eight lengths. Over a fast track he was a streak of white lightning. So was Count Fleet. These two were speed masters. Count Fleet won a mile at Belmont in 1.34⅘. Hughie Keogh once wrote, "The race isn't to the swift, but that is where to look."

If you stop all careers at three years, I'd put Man o'War first —Citation a very close second, maybe a dead heat. But if there was an edge, it would go to Man o'War. And I might add that if Count Fleet were running at the same time—or Johnstown at his best—we might have got a mile in 1.34 on a standard track. I don't mean some of these dynamite western tracks. I would like to have seen a mile among Man o'War, Native Dancer, Citation, Count Fleet and Johnstown.

What about Tom Fool? Ben Jones, the well-known and successful trainer, one told me, "Tell Vanderbilt to keep his horse (Native Dancer) away from Tom Fool . . . if he don't want to get licked." You can't leave Tom Fool out.

A race horse must be judged in three directions—speed, stamina and time—the time he lasts. So while you might rate Man o'War or Citation as the greatest three-year-olds, neither should be classed as the greatest race horse. I think that distinction belongs to Exterminator, sometimes known as Old Bones. Exterminator ran his first race at Latonia, June 30, 1917. He ran his last race at Dorval Park, June 21, 1924. That makes a total of seven racing years, or more than twice what Man o'War faced. And in those seven years he was carrying high weight, from 135 to 140 pounds. Yet under this heavy burden he won 50 out of 100 races before he retired.

I once got into a rather brief but pleasant argument with my friend Ben Jones, "Plain Ben" of Calumet. Ben and his son Jimmy make a rare combination when it comes to getting a certain horse ready for a certain race at a certain time. I told Ben I had named Exterminator over Armed, another great horse.

"Just a moment," Ben said. "How many times did Exterminator carry a hundred and thirty pounds or higher?"

"Only thirty-four times," I said. "Most of these times he averaged around a hundred and thirty-five."

"I quit," Ben said. "Armed carried a lot of weight, but not that often."

In 1918 Willis Sharpe Kilmer was keen on racing Sun Briar in the Derby of that year. Sun Briar broke down and Kilmer, on the plea of Henry McDaniel, his trainer, reluctantly entered Exterminator. He won easily. That same year he won six firsts. In 1919, as a four-year-old, he won eight races, many of these stakes. As a five-year-old in 1920, he won ten races, getting better year by year. In 1922, as a seven-year-old, he won ten races again—six in a row—carrying from 135 to 140 pounds.

There was only one Exterminator. Talk with John Partridge, the veteran trainer, one of the best judges of horse flesh I ever saw. John has been looking at them run for over 60 years.

"I'd like to think what Exterminator would do with this modern bunch," he told me. "Six furlongs one day—three days later a mile and a quarter—then two miles, then six furlongs again. He didn't care."

If you care to rank them in set divisions, my pick would be:

No. 1—Exterminator: for speed, stamina, endurance, and most running.

No. 2—Man o'War: no faster than Citation but he had a furious desire to win. I doubt he could have been fenced in by a modern starting gate. He had more color than other horses.

No. 3—Citation: the solid horse—always dependable. His later defeats by Noor brought him down a bit.

No. 4—Count Fleet: Probably as good as the best. As fast as any. Didn't quite last out his three-year-old term, however.

There may be four finer horses than these that I can't recall. Tom Fool may be just as good—possibly better—but illness cut the Greentree star down to one big year. Native Dancer had a great two years and is an exceptional horse. I never saw unbeaten Colin, unbeaten in 15 starts with 12 victories at two and three more at three.

Great horses don't arrive in droves. Nearly 50 years ago we had Colin, Sysonby and Roseben. Later on Man o'War and Exterminator arrived. Then there was Citation. The last great one to arrive—owned by Alfred Vanderbilt, broken as a yearling by Ralph Kercheval, a Kentucky grid immortal and presently Vanderbilt's farm manager, trained by Bill Winfrey and ridden by Eric Guerin—was Native Dancer, the Gray Ghost of the track. This flying son of Polynesian, in the opinion of many, was even more popular than Man o'War. The reason for this is that Native Dancer not only had the same record, at four, that Man o'War had at two and three—20 of 21—but that he was a TV horse, seen and followed by millions. The Gray Ghost coming from behind or leading the pack became a national spectacle.

Tom Fool was equally great in his fourth year as a handicap star but sickness cut in on him as a three-year-old. Native Dancer was also waylaid twice by foot injuries, which seem to be the thoroughbred's heritage. Midway in 1954 he had another sore hoof that again checked his career in the handicap section. Dark Star who beat Native Dancer by a short neck in the 1953 Kentucky Derby bowed a tendon in the Preakness.

Discovery, the Iron Horse, who could win lugging a piano and piano player on his back, is the grandfather of Native Dancer on his mother's side but I never saw any such triumphant march as Ben Jones knew with Bull Lea at stud. The list included Whirlaway, Ponder, Citation, Coaltown, Armed, Pensive, Two Lea, Bewitch and many, many more including Hill Gail, Kentucky and Santa Anita Derby winner. C. V. Whitney, Greentree and Vanderbilt have known fine stables but nothing that could quite compare to the Jones Boys–Calumet span, where Bull Lea was in full charge.

What most people don't appreciate is the background that

such people as Sonny Whitney, Jock Whitney and George Widener furnish the game. They have no interest in the money-making side of racing. They are in the sport because they love it—not for anything they can make out of it. They and a few like them deserve the acclaim. Sport has no one to compare with this small but brilliant racing group. There are more that I could mention, including Harry Guggenheim, but such people as the Whitneys and Wideners are rare specimens in any game

During my time, I've witnessed perhaps a half dozen great "Match" races. In a pure sense, several of these weren't "match" (horse against horse) affairs, but for all purposes of description quickly developed into just that. The Man o'War–John P. Grier affair at Aqueduct in July 1920 was one. The duel between Equipoise and Twenty Grand, when both were two-year-olds was another. The Seabiscuit–War Admiral race at Pimlico, winner take all, was a third. And the knockdown series between Whirlaway and Alsab in 1942 left the customers hanging on the stretch fence like Monday's wash.

When Man o'War faced John P. Grier on a "weather clear, track fast" day at Aqueduct in the Dwyer Stakes at 1⅛ miles— they scared the rest of the field back to the barns. John P. was in with 108 pounds; Man o'War at 126, with Clarence Kummer in the irons. As these two magnificent thoroughbreds lined up at the barrier, the sky seemed alive with heat lightening—not generated by the heavens but by the flame-red chestnut who was raising his inordinate amount of hell, bounding and leaping about before Kummer could get him squared away on all four feet. (War Admiral was no picnic, but he couldn't hold a candle to his old man.) By contrast, John P. Grier, a smaller horse, was strictly Emily Post.

At the three-quarter pole, Man o'War was lapped on John P. by half a length . . . and that's how it was right through the quarter pole. Then John P. made a lung-cracking stretch

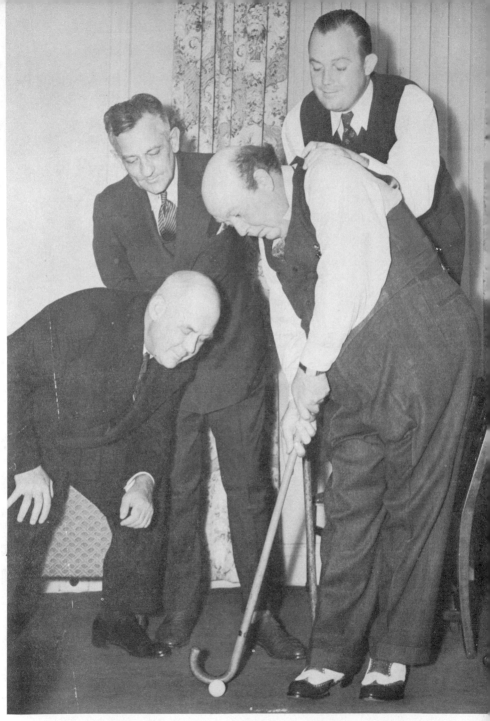

Gene Fowler and I instructing Guy Kibbee while the coy McLemore kibitzes—at the St. Francis Hotel, San Francisco around '38. Guy loved his golf.

At the height of his career in stud, "the mostest horse," Man
o'War, poses at Sam Riddle's Faraway Farms near Lexington, Ky.
Big Red's racing stride measured nearly 27 feet between leaps.

I don't recall just what this young lady told me about "fools and their money..."
but it didn't make her run any faster...or me any richer.

Man o'War and Will Harbut in a dress rehearsal for his final sweepstakes, "The Big Sky"...his ascent to heaven. Note in this Bert Clark Thayer study that the halter shank has parted as Will, with a tear in his eye, stands by as heaven opens up to claim his "baby." Postscript is the fact that Harbut died before his famed charge did. Man o'War...Babe Ruth...Jack Dempsey remain world-wide names.

Kay Smith

At Sunshine Park, Florida with (L to R) Frankie Graham and Red Smith, two of my closest pals down the homestretch.

Kay Smith

Touts and tout sheets are a failing of mine. After buying his sheet, this fellow said, "For $5 I can give you some *real* tips."

At Yale's Fence Club, in October '49, before Cornell game. Bernie Gimbel, Gene Tunney, Yale coach Herman Hickman and me. Only "pure" Bulldog in picture is fellow with highball.

With Steve Hannagan and Annie Sheridan at Yankee Stadium before Zale-Graziano fight in Sept. '46. Steve's untimely death in Africa in February of '53 was a shock.

Rex Beach congratulating me after an Artists & Writers match. Beach combined more brawn with better brains than perhaps anyone I've known.

With **Bill Dickey,** my all-time Yankee catcher, at **Bill's** home course at Little Rock, Ark. in '38.

To "Granny"
may I always
prove worthy of
your friendship.
your Sincerely
Lou Gehrig
(Christmas)
1940

No caption needed here. They'll come no finer than Lou, ever.

With golfers Lew Worsham, Jimmy Demaret and Jimmy Thomson, at LA Open in '51.

Following Ben Hogan's British Open victory luncheon at Shor's in August '53. I'm pointing out fact that Ben and Tunney (left) trained harder than any other champs I've known.

With three pals—(L to R) Bruce Barton, Frank Crowninshield and Rube Goldberg around 1932.

Look Magazine

Bud Kelland, Tunney, me, Hal Sims, Guy Kibbee, Frank Craven and Frank
Condon, at Lakeside, California, in 1936.

Acme

Sims cogitating...When he was 8
Hal learned cards from Senator
Bankhead—and never stopped.
recall Sims' great dane who landed
in jail for kissing the Mayor of As-
bury Park. Hal had a terrible time
getting him out.

My gal Babe, and the British Women's Amateur trophy she won in '47. Babe Didrikson Zaharias and Jim Thorpe were the greatest all-round athletes I've known.

Bill Mark

Toots Shor, flanked by Jimmy Demaret and me, indulging in one of our more "solemn" moments.

Pat O'Brien toes the mark at San Francisco's Press Club. I'd taken Kibbee, Fowler, O'Brien and McLemore along, hoping one would rock the crowd. Henry did.

Metropolitan

With Cobb at Augusta in '30 when
Jones won the Southeastern Open
by 13 shots and Ty cursed him for
not winning by more.

Tony Sheehan

Discussing his match with **Byron Nelson** at the **Goodall** Tourney at New
Rochelle, N. Y. in '39. I admired Nelson's terrific iron-play.

Sam Andre

Cutting up old touches with Episcopal Bishop F. A. Juhan at Jacksonville's Quarter-back Club in '51. Bishop Juhan was a star center at Sewanee around 1908. This was our first meeting in more than 40 years.

The Four Horsemen (L to R) Miller, Layden, Crowley and Stuhldreher applaud Notre Dame's John Lattner (center) at Heisman Award dinner in Dec. '53.

Alex J. Morrison

Enjoying our back porch at East Hampton with Jean McLemore around '38.

With daughter, Floncy, in California in 1950.

Christmas '52, at Floncy's home in Venice, California with "grandchildren" Czar, Ciota and Gay, three noble Siberians.

With Ed Furgol, '54 Open winner. Ed's pressure long shots were made with this No. 3 iron. Ed's steady play despite lame left arm was inspirational.

I tire easily these days. Sometimes, I think, perhaps, I've lugged too many typewriters to the top of too many stadiums.

challenge and was neck and neck with Man o'War as they thundered towards home. About a furlong from the wire the smaller horse seemed to go to pieces, Man o'War drawing away by perhaps two or three lengths for a new world record of 1:49⅕. Many claim Man o'War broke John P. Grier's heart in that struggle. Actually, Harry Payne Whitney's campaigner came back to win his share of stakes.

The duel at Churchill Downs in 1930 between Equipoise and Twenty Grand, running in the Kentucky Jockey Club Stakes, a fixture for two-year-olds, was another snorter. A large field was entered but this pair left the rest so far behind—all the way— that the race developed into a "match," with Twenty Grand winning by a flaring nostril.

The battle between Seabiscuit and War Admiral at Pimlico at 1³⁄₁₆ miles—winner take all—was a honey. I recall it was on my 58th birthday, November 1, 1938, and was the first of the Pimlico Specials. I rank it as perhaps the best race I've ever seen.

As they came on the track the odds were posted 1–4, War Admiral; 4–1, Seabiscuit. Much to everyone's surprise, Seabiscuit —with the late and great Georgie Woolf ("The Iceman") in the saddle—got the jump by two lengths. Then War Admiral, Man o'War's proudest son, flew at the Biscuit and down the backstretch they roared, paired as a team. You saw but one horse outlined against the outer rail. Then the Biscuit drew ahead a bit but the Admiral collared him at the home turn. As they stampeded the home stretch, Seabiscuit drew away, winning off by himself.

Whirlaway, Calumet's Mr. Longtail; and Alsab, the Cinderella horse, hooked up in some great showdowns during the '42 season. They first met at Narragansett (Rhode Island) at 1³⁄₁₆ miles. Whirlaway, the older horse, carried 126 pounds to Alsab's 119. As they thundered across the finish line, Ben Jones of Calumet stammered, "I'll settle for a dead heat." The judges posted Alsab first by a whisker. Never did two horses give more and never did a wartime crowd roar louder. That, ladies and gentlemen, was a horse race! Whirlaway won the Jockey Club Gold Cup at two miles that fall at Belmont. But in the New York Handicap at 2¼ miles and also at Belmont, Alsab won the rubber match with Obash, in with a feather, second and Whirlaway third.

A word here about Alsab, that powerful, short-bodied, Roman-nosed bay with black points, by Good Goods out of Winds Chant and bred by veteran bluegrass breeder Tom Piatt. Alsab was purchased for 700 dollars as a family present for Al Sabbath. As a two-year-old, he seldom stopped long enough to see where he'd been. Youngsters, as a rule, aren't hurried in training. But Alsab was rushed, going postward 22 times at two. Shipped directly to Florida before his plates had cooled, he was promptly embarked on his three-year campaign that saw him run 23 times! It was in Alsab's final start, at three, that he went lame —in the Victory Handicap in New York, which, incidentally, he won. Turned out for a spell, this unprepossessing looking horse got to the post but six times thereafter. In all, Alsab won 25 of 51 races, was second 11 times, third 5 times and was out of the money only ten times. He earned 350,015 dollars—not a bad return on a 700-dollar investment. He was like the high-headed Stymie; both worked their respective beats like two honest cops.

When all three were hot there was considerable clamor for a three-horse race with Stymie, Assault and Armed. Hirsch Jacobs and Ben Jones were willing, I believe, to enter Stymie and Armed respectively; but Max Hirsch, Assault's trainer, quickly withdrew the Kleberg colt from the picture. I questioned Max about it.

"Grant," he said, "I'll run against either of those horses but not both together. A come-from-behind horse will beat a sprinter every time. Why stick Assault in there to beat himself whipping a fast horse like Armed only to get nailed from behind by a plodder like Stymie?"

The race horse, or the thoroughbred, isn't the entire game as far as racing is concerned. There is the trainer . . . and there is also the jockey. There is something about a trainer that lures you. At least it does me. Ben and Jimmy Jones . . . Maxie Hirsch . . . Sunny Jim Fitzsimmons . . . John Partridge . . . Hirsch Jacobs . . . Bill Winfrey . . . John Gaver . . . these and many more I've pestered for the time of day concerning a certain horse in a certain race.

There is one detail I often marvel at. John Partridge and Sunny Jim Fitzsimmons are high in the 70's . . . maybe 77 . . . maybe 80. Yet they are up and around on winter mornings at daybreak. It's worthwhile listening to a yarn John Partridge tells of Ben Jones in those far gone years when Plain Ben was running his own horses against the Sioux and the Apaches . . . or was it the Comanches? John tells the bedtime story concerning one race that Ben ran against the Indians in which Ben's horse was leading by two lengths and suddenly disappeared! The Indians had dug an open gap, covering it with tree limbs and grass. "You could never beat an Indian," John reflected.

The first great jockey I saw was Earle Sande. The second was George Woolf, a diabetic, and the third was Eddie Arcaro. Those in close pursuit include John Longden, Ted Atkinson and Eric Guerin. And then there's a drip of ice cold water known as Willie Shoemaker.

I rate Sande, Woolf and Arcaro as standoffs. All three knew pace and how to handle a horse, were perfect judges of time to drive for an opening . . . or not to. Actually, in his one upset, as a two-year-old, by a horse called Upset, Man o'War was not turned around and completely left at the post as legend has it.

At least there were other horses behind him in that opening
scramble from the barrier. What did happen, however, was that
Man o'War was picketed during that drive for the wire . . .
and Johnny Loftus never drove him out or through it. And on
that particular day at Saratoga, my great little friend George
Ryall, who for so many years has written such beautiful stuff
about the track under the pen name of Audax Minor in *The New
Yorker,* had a bet, perhaps his last, on Upset.

"When it comes to busting for that opening," says Arcaro,
"it's all largely instinct. You've got a split second to decide. You
are right or you are wrong. You can't wait."

Tod Sloan was certainly one of the greatest, but I never saw
Sloan ride. They tell me he is the only jockey who could talk
to a horse. I've talked to thousands of horses—including Pound-
itout—but not in their tongue apparently.

Arcaro and Sande were on top until Willie Shoemaker, the
ice-cream cone, colder than the bottom of an iceberg, came
along. During the '53 season Shoemaker rode 485 winners, more
than any other rider in history over a one-year stretch. A young
Texan, Shoemaker gets the laurel from Arcaro.

"What's he got, Eddie?" I asked Arcaro.

"Only everything," Eddie, who is generous in his praise,
said. "He is missing nothing. He rides perfectly. He knows how
to sit in a saddle—not all good jocks do. He knows how to use his
hands. Ice water runs through his veins. He is never excited or
bothered. I came from behind and caught him once. It meant
absolutely nothing to him. He didn't care whether I was Arcaro
or Bill Smith."

It might be mentioned that Arcaro is a high-grade athlete.
"I know all about Eddie," John Partridge told me. "He is a fine
rider—best I ever saw. He is a fine golfer. He is a fine fisherman.
I went out with him once . . . fishing. He refused to fish. He
went away and took a two-day lesson in casting. He was the best

in the bunch. He would have made a fine boxer . . . a fine anything. When I was sick some time back, he came over and cooked my meals. They were perfect."

So when it comes to all around accomplishment—from jockey to housewife—I rate Arcaro Number 1.

I must admit, along about here, that one of my chief interests is the daily double. My partner in this soul-enriching enterprise remains Earle "Greasy" Neale, the famous college and professional football coach. Among other feats, Greasy hit .357 as an outfielder for the Cincinnati Reds in the 1919 World Series against the infamous Black Sox—and so will go to his grave claiming there was nothing fixed about those games. Being pigheaded never hurt in playing the ponies, but I can't prove, by Greasy's winnings, that it helps either.

My system is this: Take the first horse you like in the first race and hook him up with your three top choices in the second. Then hook your three top horses in the first with your three top choices in the second. Then wander around and take 20 more tips and finally wind up with some 40 daily doubles, or 80 dollars worth.

I honestly think I'm ahead in daily double bets. Not in racing bets.

I once discovered Neale with 1,000 dollars worth of daily doubles—and didn't speak to him for a week. Greasy, that year, won over 2,500 dollars on our System. Not on the other racing. You see, we've done very well on the "two for the price of one" side but lose it all back on the other bets. Nobody, not even Merlin the Wizard, can beat 16 per cent. The banks get along on two per cent . . . or perhaps three. Yes, there's a chance to beat the daily double game, but not the rest of it. At least not at a hostile 16 per cent. However, it still represents more fun than you can find in any afternoon if in trying to put over a sneaky longshot, you are willing to drift—and not plunge. But beware of those gratuitous tips. They can murder you. The most sensible tip I ever got, incidentally, was from George Ryall, whose reply to me one day was, "Who do I like in this race? I don't like anything—all season!"

As I've said, I like to move about in the paddock, in the clubhouse, in the field, in the bar and at five minutes before post-time of any given race I usually have the opinions of a hundred persons—from John Gaver, the Whitney trainer, down to Tony the bootblack from Grand Central Terminal, all relative to the merits of the eight horses in the upcoming race. The consensus, of course, would be that these eight horses must run a dead heat —for none could possibly lose.

Like the day Steve Owen, noblest Giant (ex) of them all, Pete Dolan and I were at Belmont. For five races we'd done pretty well. Having pre-empted some millionaire's box and having kept ahead to the extent of perhaps ten dollars each for the day, we were at least breathing. Pete, who likes to do his own handicapping, had come up with a horse called Sea Fare in the sixth. He pointed out that the horse was from an excellent stable, Ziegler's, that the distance was right, that he had been improving in his last two tests, that he was in light, that the *Morning Telegraph* figures had him second only to Tex Martin in a ten-horse field, and that Tex Martin, of late, had not been in form.

So Sea Fare it was and the board showed his number bouncing around at 40 to 1.

Owen went off to make his bet while Pete and I remained in our seats to work out a golf date for the following week. Meanwhile, an acquaintance of mine chanced by and casually dropped the word that John's Dear, at 15 to 1, seemed quite an overlay. We'd waited so long we were almost shut out from the windows before we could deposit a few tenners on John's Dear.

The race was at a mile and an eighth. As the horses rounded

the turn into the long home stretch, one was in the lead by nearly ten lengths. Stout Steve, all 300 pounds of him, jumped on the fragile wooden chair and started to boot home the leader.

Pete and I looked at him in amazement.

"What are you yelling about, Steve?" I shouted.

It was Owen's turn to be dumbfounded. "What am I yelling about?" he cried. "Why, didn't you tell me to bet on him? That's Sea Fare out there! I got ten across the board on him!"

Owen turned in his three bits of pasteboard for a neat profit of 650 dollars while Pete and I tore some other bits of pasteboard into very tiny pieces.

—That's what I mean about touts and touting.

Three major factors in a horse race are the horse, the jockey and the trainer. I once knew a handicapper for the old days of New York to Santa Anita and Hollywood who had 34 years of winning races against but one of losing. It was an incredible record. He was an incredible man. He went even further than I did. I mentioned the horse, jockey and trainer. This man, whose name I won't mention to prevent a flood of letters, adds these other factors: post position . . . condition of track . . . weights (very important!) . . . winning or losing stable. He figured every detail all the way through. He had a staff around him to keep tabs. Also, on any big bet, he'd fight to name the jockey for the horse! He couldn't do that today.

One day during the late 1920's I ran across Arnold Rothstein, the famous gambler, at the track. I knew he was a big winner so I asked him his system.

"I go to the leading trainers," he replied. 'Tell me if your horse is right,' I say. 'If he is, I'll bet one thousand or two thousand dollars for you. But don't double-cross me.' "

"In this way," continued Rothstein, "I get the best of the information. Information, sound information, is what you need at a race track."

I can't tell you how right he was. But try to get it. Rothstein told me that he averaged 100,000 dollars a year from the track. I think he did. He would bet 20,000 or 30,000 on what he considered good information quicker than many good betters would offer 500 dollars.

I knew Rothstein fairly well. He had a deep love for the race track and a deeper loathing for the stock market of years ago. Rothstein was right. The odds in those days were about 10 per cent at the track. They were 20 per cent against you in the market. I tried them both—no good as sound investments.

I seldom had better investments, however, than those tickets I purchased on a little thing named Nell K, owned by Jim Norris, trained by John Partridge—830 pounds of thoroughbred. When Jim retired her, in 1951 in her fifth year after placing in 21 of 33 starts, I saluted Nell K in verse. But being a horse and therefore smarter than many humans, she preferred carrots. You can't eat press clippings.

To Nell K

. . . and to Determine, the little gray horse I had in the '54 Derby Winter Book

No larger than a pony's mate,
I've watched you drive around the course,
The first time that I've ever seen
A heart much bigger than a horse.

Responding to the challenge still,
By neck and neck, by head and head,
I've cheered you to the winning wire,
Your heritage—a thoroughbred.

I only hope in pastures green
You find deep peace along the way.
And I may add, in parting words,
I owe you for a lot of hay.

CHAPTER TWENTY-THREE

Iron Men

There aren't any iron men left in sport today.

Perhaps, but yesterday there weren't any Roger Bannisters or John Landys either. The old time iron man has been replaced by the modern specialist . . . in business as well as sports. Platoon football was an example. Feeling that the game already is too complex, particularly in hunting All-America players, I remained lukewarm for the offensive and defensive hordes who shuttled between bench and playing field. I'm glad they've restored the old concept that a player must tackle as well as carry the ball. Football will again be represented by its iron men despite the cry that today's youngsters are losing the power of their legs to the era of the hot rod.

Lou Little, when he can't substitute freely, will go for the iron man . . . and he certainly had one at Columbia during the '53 season. I don't know of another major college player who stayed in there for every minute of nine consecutive games as the Lions' quarterback, Dick Carr, did.

But the age of the iron man was largely from another era. And I knew my share of them.

If Ty Cobb wasn't an iron man, who was? Ty traveled at top speed on a pair of fairly thin legs for 24 years. He hunted all winter and he played baseball all spring and summer. He played in more than 3,000 ball games and scored over 4,000 runs, always in rapid action.

If Cy Young wasn't an iron man, who was? Cy left a small farm in Ohio in 1890 for Cleveland, where he shut out the famous White Sox 3 to 0 in his first game. He won more games —511—than most pitchers ever pitched. He worked through more than 800 ball games in both leagues and finally retired when a kid named Grover Cleveland Alexander beat him 1 to 0 in 1911.

Bob Fitzsimmons had iron in his system. He was born at Cornwall, England, in 1862, 18 years before I arrived on this planet. Fitzsimmons was fighting bouts at 18 and didn't stop until he was 52, after a no decision affair of six rounds against K. O. Sweeney at Williamsport, Pennsylvania, in 1914. Ruby Robert was in the ring 34 years . . . and won the world's heavyweight title from James J. Corbett at Carson City, Nevada, when he was 35! He lost his title to Jim Jeffries at Coney Island two years later, in 1899. But he was still fighting—and winning—at 46. It took pneumonia to kill him, on October 23, 1917, in Chicago at the age of 55.

Bill Tilden certainly had an overdrive of iron to play the brand of tennis he featured for 30 years.

Another iron man, Jack Quinn, was in the majors from 1909 through 1933 and was pitching big-league ball at 47. His reason —"A wife and six kids."

Willie Hoppe, in championship billiards since 1908, is another amazing mixture of stamina and hairline skill. Having amassed 51 world titles, Willie recently estimated he'd spent more than 100,000 hours over the tables and had walked some 26,000 miles in 59 years of activity.

There were wrestlers and bicycle riders—Strangler Lewis and Frank Kramer—yes, and Reggie McNamara, who seemed to go on indefinitely. But there are two iron men who were especially close friends of mine. One was a baseball player, the other was a football player. Their names are Lou Gehrig and Pudge Heffelfinger.

Both were physical giants. Lou Gehrig was slightly over six feet and well over 200 pounds. He was perfectly built for power —"Bull throated, bare of arm," as Kipling once wrote of Hans, the blue-eyed Dane.

The first time I ever saw Lou Gehrig was on a Thanksgiving afternoon in 1922 at New York. Columbia was playing Colgate. I brought Dick Harlow, Colgate's famous coach, home with me after the game. Colgate, with Eddie Tryon at his best, had murdered the Lions. But there was a Columbia back who also impressed Dick. He was a young giant named Gehrig. About midway in the stampede, he broke his right collarbone. He finished the game. His right arm and shoulder were useless. But he stuck to his job.

When I saw Lou Gehrig again he was a ball player for the New York Yankees. Wally Pipp was hurt one day in 1925 and Gehrig moved into first. That was Wally's last appearance as a Yankee. When Gehrig finally retired after eight games in 1939, because of the sudden and slashing destruction to his body, he had played 2,130 consecutive games over a period of 15 years without missing his appointment at first base!

When I played golf with Babe Ruth years ago we often stopped by to pick up Gehrig. He followed us around the course but he wouldn't play. He had an idea that the baseball swing and the golf swing were too dissimilar, that golf was bad for baseball. One morning I dropped a ball and handed him Ruth's midiron. He took a smooth, easy swing and hit a perfect shot some 200 yards. I couldn't get him to hit another.

It was the same way with hunting. Lou enjoyed hiking along for company, but he wouldn't shoot anything. "I just can't kill," he said once. To Lou, a quail, a duck or a dove was a beautiful bird. That's the sort of fellow he was—tremendously powerful, but as gentle as a child.

If Gehrig hadn't been struck down when almost in his prime, he might have carried his mark to 3,000 consecutive contests, for he never cottoned to an injury or illness.

Bill Dickey and I called on Lou one night in St. Petersburg during the early spring of '39. I knew Lou was worried and brooding. In practice, the old Gehrig line drives had been reduced to pop flies but he kept working . . . trying to regain the old power. That night Lou tried to lift a large coffee pot with one hand—and failed.

One of the last pitchers to face Gehrig was Joe Krakauskas, a fast-balling young southpaw who worked for Washington. Gehrig, a left-handed hitter, used to plant himself squarely in the batter's box. Krakauskas pitched Lou close just once. Later, in the locker room, the big pitcher was shocked.

"They better get that Gehrig out of there before somebody kills him," said Krakauskas. "I pitched him inside, across the letters today—just once! If Gehrig saw that ball he couldn't move away from it. The ball went through his arms! . . . not over or under 'em but through his arms!"

Lou somehow struggled through eight games of the '39 season before he went to Joe McCarthy's hotel room in Detroit and quietly put down his glove. After 2,130 consecutive games, the Iron Horse at 36 years of age had completed its final run. Amyotrophic lateral sclerosis, insidious, cruel and deadly, was wasting Gehrig just as quickly and completely as cancer. For weeks,

Lou's pride forced him, as team captain, to insist on carrying the slip of paper to the home plate umpire before each game announcing the Yankee lineup. His balance all but gone, those walks must have seemed miles but Lou went it alone. On the trips from locker room to dugout however, other Yankees quickly fell into step with the shambling Lou to form an escort, and I'm not sure he ever actually realized this. In my book it is simply another unconscious mark of Yankee class, which Gehrig did so much to mold.

Two years later in early June of '41, Lou died. I have lost countless friends—so many of them very close—to such diseases as cancer. When the ticket comes up for me or a friend I'd rather it be in the form of an onrushing truck than any form of an incurable, wasting malady. In Gehrig's death, just as with Ruth with cancer seven years later, baseball and Grant Rice lost two irreplaceables.

The other iron man was a football player known as William W. "Pudge" Heffelfinger. Pudge was on Walter Camp's All-America teams of 1889, '90 and '91. He was another giant, better than six feet and about 190 pounds. But he was faster than most halfbacks. Some 25 years later, Pudge told me that after practice one day Walter Camp had called him to one side. "The trouble with you, Heff, is that you play guard only one way," said Yale's coach. "You are a fine guard; but remember, there are at least two ways to play your position."

"I began to study things and practice on students in the dormitory," related Pudge. "They soon began to run when they saw me. But ten days later I told Camp I had followed his advice and I now had six different ways to play guard." Pudge was undoubtedly the first guard to leave his position and run interference for the ball carrier. He was a terrific blocker.

Heffelfinger first played football at the age of 16. He played

his last game at the age of 65, with a pro outfit in a charity game
at Minneapolis against a team of college all-stars. That's practically 50 years of playing time.

When Pudge was 40 or more he played some football with
Colonel John J. McEwan—the old Minnesota center who was
later Army's center and Army's head coach. "He was a star
then," McEwan said.

When he was 43 or 44 he came back to New Haven when
Tad Jones was in charge. Pudge lined up with the scrubs, much
against Tad's wishes. He was afraid a man of 44 might be hurt.
That was an historic afternoon for Pudge. When the scrubs got
the ball, Heffelfinger said to Jess Spalding, second team halfback, "Jess, follow me."

"I followed him," related Jess. "I also ran fifty-five yards for
a touchdown with at least four tacklers sprawled out on the field.
Every man Pudge hit was flattened."

"They say," Pudge told me later, "I broke a couple of Kew-
pie Black's ribs. I didn't. I happened to bump into Baldridge and
I drove him into Kewp. Baldridge did it—after I bumped him."
The collision occurred just a week before the Princeton game
and two weeks prior to Harvard. It marked the last time Heffelfinger was allowed on Yale Field in a football suit.

"Back in my day," reflected Pudge, "Princeton was Yale's
climax opponent—the season's big objective. I vividly recall my
last game against the Tigers on Thanksgiving Day at the old
Polo Grounds, One Hundred and Tenth Street near Broadway.
It was 1891. We used to play sixteen games each season but our
schedule had since been shortened to include only thirteen
games.

"Yale headquarters in New York City was the Fifth Avenue
Hotel at Twenty-Third Street—a landmark I missed on later
trips East after retiring. I never used to pass it without thinking
of the hero-worshippers in the lobby on the day of the game and

the tallyho draped with Yale blue bunting and drawn by six horses. We used to ride up Fifth Avenue in style, the route taking us on up through Central Park to the football grounds. We all sat on top of the stage and waved at the pretty girls who flirted with us, or jeered at the Princeton rooters when they gave us the Bronx cheer.

"And I sure recall that ride in 1888—my freshman year. The horses got away from the driver in Central Park and we smashed into a hansom cab.

"'Hey youse guys!' bellowed the disgusted cabbie. 'Ain't you got enough trouble today with Princeton without looking for more?' We won it ten to nothing."

Pudge always said he would have liked to take the Yales of his day and stack them up against the more modern powerhouses.

"We'd hold our own," he'd snort, "though we'd be outweighed from ten to fifteen pounds per man. Those old Yale Lines were faster than today's barriers. In my day every lineman was also a ball carrier. Foster Sanford, Yale's 1896 center, won the Booth Hall Plate in England as a sprinter. He could do the hundred in ten flat. Wally Winter, Stan Morison and I frequently carried the ball from our line positions. We were speedy enough to weave through a broken field. The average lineman today would be lost if you asked him to lug the ball."

Back in 1906, Brick Owens, a hard-bitten baseball umpire, found himself surrounded by a vicious mob of hoodlums in Minneapolis. Armed with sticks, stones and bottles, they closed in on Owens whose decisions had infuriated them. Two of Brick's assailants drew guns. He feared no foe in a rough and tumble scrap but this mob meant business.

"Things looked grim," Owens told me years later when we were discussing Heffelfinger. "Suddenly a tall, rawboned, bareheaded giant of a fellow burst through the crowd and took his place beside me. Snatching up a bat, this big fellow shouted,

'Nobody is going to lay a hand on this man! You folks know me
. . . open up there and let us through!' "

Mobs yield to the will of a determined, fearless leader. And
this mob knew Pudge Heffelfinger.

"That mob opened up for us," said Owens. "Heffelfinger
conveyed me to a waiting bus, with the hoodlums yelping at
our heels and throwing stones from a safe distance."

When he was 53, Pudge played in a professional charity
game at Columbus, Ohio. Bo McMillin was a quarterback. Before the game started Pudge somehow dislocated his shoulder.
"I twisted and jerked it until the shoulder snapped back in
place," he said. "They didn't think I could last five minutes. I
played fifty-four minutes of that game."

"He was always riding me to speed up," Bo said later. "Him
fifty-three and me twenty-two. He played one of the best games
at guard I ever saw."

Heffelfinger could never understand how the "mousetrap"
play worked. "I know," he said, "they are supposed to let you
come through the line and then sideswipe you. What's wrong
with breaking through the line and knocking them down? A
fellow that's on the ground isn't going to spring any foolish
mousetrap!"

To give 50 years to playing football in fast, rugged company
should win Pudge some sort of Oscar for an iron-man role. Both
Gehrig and Heffelfinger were complete gentlemen—on the
quiet, gentle side. But both had iron in their systems.

Perhaps a citation for stamina should also go to a few others.

Adrian Constantine (Cap) Anson, legendary figure of baseball's Pliocene age, from 1871 through 1897, played all nine
positions before settling down on first base in 1886. Cap put 26
seasons under his belt, five more than Babe Ruth. Incidentally,
it was during the 1934 season, his last with the Yankees, that
Ruth made a significant remark. We were sitting in the dugout

watching batting practice. It was August. Babe had taken his cuts, sending a few practice pitches out of the park, and was mopping his face with a bath towel.

"Grant, a ball player should quit when it starts to feel as if all the baselines run uphill. I'm thirty-nine and that's how they're beginning to look." It was the next year, 1935, that Ruth finished out his string in Boston.

Mel Hein, all-time center for Washington State and the New York Giants, played big league college and professional ball for something like 20 years. Ken Strong, Chick Meehan's marvel at New York University in the middle 1920's, remained a fine kicker in the pro game at 40, his last year with the Giants, in 1947. Sammy Baugh was brilliant for 16 years after graduating from Texas Christian.

They were all marvels and merit admiration. But they won't be playing at 53 or 65 as big Heff was. Shortly before his death, April 2, 1954 at Blessing, Texas, Pudge was in New York for a Touchdown Club dinner where they gave him an award of some kind. "It's fun to look back on a half century of football playing," he said, "but I'm reconciled to a seat in the stadium now—even if it's not on the 50-yard line. I know folks say I never outgrew a 'campus hero complex' but at least they know I never rested on my oars. Granny, I stood up to 'em all for three generations."

> As we look them over in the big corral
> As the years march by—as they rise and fall,
> Here's to Big Pudge—my pick and my pal,
> The greatest Roman of them all.

Right up to the end, Pudge Heffelfinger carried into life's battle all the enthusiasm of a rookie.

CHAPTER TWENTY-FOUR

McGraw, Mack, McCarthy
and Others

Of all the big league baseball managers I have known most intimately, perhaps John McGraw of the Giants, Connie Mack of the Athletics, and Joe McCarthy of the Yankees lead the list. They won a total of 27 pennants: McGraw—10; Mack—9; and McCarthy—8.

The first manager I ever knew was Newt Fisher, owner and manager of Nashville's Southern League team. In 1901 he offered me 250 dollars a month to play shortstop for Nashville when the best job, outside of this, was five dollars a week. I had to pass up the juicy offer because I had broken my right shoulder blade and right collarbone playing football. The throwing arm was gone.

McGraw, Mack and McCarthy were totally unlike in every way. I met McGraw and Mack in the same year—1905—when I came up from Atlanta to cover the World Series in which Christy Mathewson pitched three shutouts in six days.

McGraw, a bantam rooster, a fiery leader, was always in active charge, on the field and off. He was the umpire's foe and the foe of every team he played. He courted dislike in various cities, for he was shrewd enough to realize that additional fans would come out to see the "hated Giants" beaten. He would get all the dope and gossip about umpires and then spill it on the field in the arguments that always arose.

It was on my first trip with the Giants, in 1911, after I had moved to New York. We were traveling on an off day. I was trying to figure out a piece to write for the *Mail*. I was in a Pullman seat pecking away when to my surprise McGraw moved in with me. "What are you writing about today?" he asked.

I told him I hadn't yet stumbled on anything worth wiring the paper.

"I've got a story for you," he said. Together we worked out a good yarn. After that we were always good friends although he used to get a bit peeved at me for lugging off Mathewson, Merkle and Donlin to play golf. Especially one Sunday in Pittsburgh. Matty seldom pitched on Sunday. It was a hot day and Matty insisted on playing 36 holes. We both staggered in, exhausted. Matty had won 11 straight games at that time. But McGraw pitched him Monday and he was knocked out of the box in the fourth inning. I hid out from McGraw for four days. Matty and I were both in the doghouse. McGraw never liked golf—that is, during the baseball season.

One night when the Giants were going badly, McGraw invited me to his room. Other writers were present and also five players who had gone sour. McGraw served a dinner that included champagne. The players became mellow, if not downright stiff. The tension was over. Next day they hammered the hide off the ball. Their slump was finished.

Connie Mack was quite different. Even Rube Waddell rarely upset Connie, a quiet man who was rarely excited. He would turn over many problems to the team. If a player was loafing, drinking or cutting up, Mack would let his players handle the culprit. Headed by Eddie Collins, they quickly realigned him or had him fired. Nobody could handle Waddell. He would take a few days off and tend bar. Or he would go fishing for three or four days. Once the Rube bought a mocking bird that had lived by a peanut vendor's loud whistle. All the bird would imitate was this whistle. The team got little sleep until someone strangled the feathered "Johnny One Note."

Rube had the greatest combination of speed and a deep, fast-breaking curve I ever saw," Connie said. "He almost had Johnson's speed, but Johnson hasn't his curve. Nor has anyone else."

I recall a game in Cleveland when Waddell was pitching. He came to the park with a well-painted lady of the town on each arm and planted them in a box back of home plate near the press box. Waddell had the game in hand, 1 to 0 in the ninth, when Cleveland filled the bases with none out. Lajoie, Flick and Bradley, three great hitters, were coming up. Waddell walked in from the pitcher's box to the box containing his lady friends. Connie looked on in astonishment. Lifting his cap and making a deep bow, the Rube said, "Ladies, I'll be with you in just a minute." In that minute, or nearly so, he struck out Lajoie, Flick and Bradley on nine pitched balls.

Joe McCarthy, like Mack and McGraw, had one striking feature—he had the deepest respect of his players. One day at St. Petersburg I was playing golf with Bill Dickey, Joe Gordon and "King Kong" Charley Keller. We had a tough, close match. We came to the 16th tee practically even. Somebody asked the time. "It's twelve forty," I remarked.

Gordon said, "The battle is over. McCarthy told us to meet him at one twenty today."

"What's the trouble?" I asked. "A few minutes won't make a big difference."

"It does with McCarthy," Dickey said. "One minute makes a big difference."

Winner of eight pennants, McCarthy was a quiet, dignified man who rarely got into an argument. He never liked ball players cutting capers around the hotel lobby or in any public place. "You are a Yankee now," he would say. He was on the inconspicuous side himself and he wanted his Yankees to be the same way. "Remember, you're a Yankee" had a sobering, soothing influence on his band.

One day I asked Bill Dickey, an old and close friend, about McCarthy's ability. "He is one of the best, Grant," Bill said. "He knows his job from every angle. He's the boss and we know it. His judgment in handling pitchers is exceptional. There's nothing phony about Joe. He runs this club from top to bottom. No favorites. They talk about a push-button manager—that's crazy. He's a great manager. He doesn't like show-offs or pop-offs."

I recall one star ballplayer McCarthy had who was getting out of hand. He was hitting .350 and, in addition, was a brilliant fielder. He felt fixed, no matter what he did. McCarthy gave him an order one day which the player disregarded. McCarthy called him to his office after the game.

"You're a great ballplayer," he said quietly. "You are young and fast and you can hit. I'll miss you on this club. For you are leaving us tonight. Report tomorrow to so-and-so."

The star was dazed. McCarthy stuck out his hand. "Goodbye and good luck, kid," Joe said. "And for God's sake, take a tumble to yourself. Don't be quite so smart."

McGraw, Mack and McCarthy—they loved the old game with the deepest devotion. They wanted it played to the hilt. They got results in different ways, but they got results. The answer is 27 pennants.

It was not until 1949 that Casey Stengel returned to the vicinity of New York. I had known Casey when he played with the Giants and when he managed the Dodgers and Braves—but only casually. When he finally landed at the head of the Yankees he came with a rush and a roar, something like a continued explosion. He won five successive pennants and five World Series —an all-time big-league record for pennants and World Series.

I rode west with him just after he had signed his first Yankee contract in December, 1948. His previous managerial experience had been slightly on the melancholy side. "I wonder how things will be next season?" he said . . . "Where I'll be a year from now."

A remarkable person, Casey is a close student of psychology. In the spring of 1953 at St. Petersburg, I was standing with him during practice. He happened to look around and spotted six or seven forlorn rookies sitting together.

"Come along," he said, grabbing my arm. He walked over to the rookies, kids from 19 to 21, and told them he wanted to see them inside the clubhouse. We all went along. Casey had Cokes served them. He told several stories. There wasn't a point to any story he told—all were gibberish. But those kids began laughing. Fifteen or twenty minutes later we started back to the field. "These kids were just homesick," said Case. "They're all right now."

Casey will protest violently and bitterly at times, but not too often. He never took on the field the vitriolic quality that stamped McGraw and typifies Leo Durocher who, in my opinion, is a shrewd, able field leader.

I've known and admired Lou Boudreau; Frank Chance of the Cubs; Bill McKechnie of many teams, a great fellow and an able team director; Bucky Harris; Bill Carrigan; and George Stallings of the 1914 Braves, a forceful, fiery manager. Frankie Frisch, one of the great second basemen, is another top man.

The game has known only one Frisch. Years ago, when Charlie Dryden, the famous baseball writer, was introduced to Frisch, Dryden remarked, "Sounds like something frying." Frankie always was sizzling for battle.

Miller Huggins who won six pennants, had a tough crew to handle, headed by a young Babe Ruth when he was just emerging as a star. In Ruth, Miller had two tigers by their tails, for Babe would accept a 5,000-dollar fine and a long suspension with a grin.

CHAPTER TWENTY-FIVE

Bantam Ben Hogan

I was watching the World's Four Ball Championship at the Miami Biltmore course in 1941 in which Ben Hogan, a comparative newcomer who had taken a long time coming, was paired with Gene Sarazen, an old-timer who has taken a long time going. At the eighth hole, Gene stepped over and said, "Know something? I've just found the game's toughest golfer. I thought Bob Jones, Hagen and myself belonged in that class. We don't. I'm playing with him today." Gene pointed at Hogan coming up on the green.

"Just what do you mean?" I asked.

"I'll tell you," replied Gene, a top star for 32 years. "We have just finished seven holes . . . and we've won six of 'em! Hogan comes over to me on the last tee and says, 'Wake up, Gene. We are loafing. Let's get to work.'

" 'We've won six of the last seven, haven't we?' I said.

" 'Yes,' Ben said. 'But we halved the other. We can't throw holes away like that!'

"I looked at him to make sure he wasn't kidding. He was as grim as a rattlesnake."

Sarazen and Hogan won that tournament, defeating Sam Snead and Ralph Guldahl, 4 and 3 in the final.

I knew something of Hogan. In 1940, at the North and South Open at Pinehurst, North Carolina, I had watched Hogan head for the 18th tee in the final round. The last four years had been very rough on Ben and his bride Valerie. As Ben walked by, Valerie, tears streaming down her cheeks, slipped over to him. "Don't break your leg, honey . . . just don't break your leg!" she said. These two kids had known the pitfalls, ulcers and poverty that stalk the circuit swinging pro. If Ben could just stumble through that 18th hole, he'd still win, with shots to spare. Starting at Pinehurst that year, Hogan, within two weeks, won the North and South, the Greensboro and Asheville Opens, shooting 216 holes in 34 strokes under par!

I had seen Hogan climb from privation to plush before Sarazen got a load of him in that Miami Four Ball a year later. Ben has never forgotten the "poor years."

Another example of Hogan, the gamecock, came at Chicago several years later. Ben was paired with Bob Jones. Bob quit the grind in 1930, but used to enjoy playing an occasional tournament. I was in the sheep herd following the pair.

"I thought I was a hard fighter," said Jones. "I thought Hagen and Sarazen both were. We're not in a class with this fellow, Hogan. When he has a ninety-yard shot to play, he expects to hole it. He's sore as a pup if his pitch is more than a foot away. If he has a Number three iron shot from a hundred and ninety yards out, he expects to lay it stone dead. He's fighting for every inch, foot and yard on a golf course."

"Will he become one of the greats?" I asked.

"He can't miss," replied Jones. "He has the shots sure; so do a lot of the others. But Hogan's attitude is better. He's willing to absorb that mental punch."

That was Hogan; that is Hogan; that will always be Hogan. The greatest of all "concentrators," he plays with more lasting determination than anyone. Concentration and determination—unbroken. That means Ben Hogan.

The first time I saw Hogan, around 1937, he was practicing a wedge shot some 90 yards from the pin. He had been there an hour. He stayed much longer, placing the ball in good lies and bad. He hit many close to the cup—inches away. "What I want to do," he said, "is to make a habit of hitting them *all* close to the cup. Golf, or winning golf, should be the habit of hitting every ball well. There is no reason to miss a shot."

After he once hit his stride just before his accident, and on through to the present moment, Hogan has, I believe, hit fewer bad shots over a period of years than any other golfer. He is practically always putting for a par or a birdie, more often for a birdie. This didn't help Ben too much when he wasn't putting too well. So he started to work on his putting, and you'd find him at it hour after hour, month after month.

It was evident sometime back that it was not genius but hard work that carried Ben to the top. For example, Gene Sarazen and Francis Ouimet won the U.S. Open at 20—Bobby Jones at 21—Hagen at 22. Sammy Snead passed 40 without winning a U.S. Title. And it was not until 1948 that Ben, at 36, finally crashed through at Riviera in Los Angeles.

I saw him one day when his left hand was creased, cut and split from constant swinging of a golf club.

"I don't like a glove," he said.

"But you can't play with that hand," I said.

Ben grinned. "I've practiced with it two hours this morning and I'm going back this afternoon for two or three hours more."

There was a time around 1946, when I thought Ben was verging on serious trouble, the kind that could become a habit. It was the missed short putt. In April of 1946 Hogan came to the last hole at the Augusta National with a 4 to tie the leader for the title in the Masters. He hit a magnificent drive. His iron also hit the pin and stopped just 12 feet beyond the cup. He rimmed the cup to win with a 3 but the ball drifted 18 inches below. Then he missed this one for his 4.

About two months later at Canterbury the same thing happened. Again he needed a 4 to tie for the U.S. Open. Again a great drive—a great iron second—another 12 feet for a 3 to win. Once again the ball drifted by—18 inches. Once again he missed coming back. Here were two three-putt greens on final holes that cost him his big chance in two major tournaments— the Masters and the U.S. Open. Two experiences of that nature might have wrecked many golfers, since bad mistakes repeated are likely to come back and haunt you. They didn't haunt Hogan. He merely brushed them aside, although they cost him two tournaments or the chance for two tournaments he would rather have won than any others in golf.

Don Marquis once said—"Mind is superior to matter when there's nothing the matter."

There was a lot the matter with Hogan in his earlier days. However, Fred Corcoran tells a story on Hogan which shows that he works just as hard when there is nothing the matter. In 1945, Hogan had won the Portland Open with a 261—19 strokes under par. That, I think, was a record.

"It was an incredible, an unbelievable performance," Corcoran told me. "It broke many records for seventy-two holes. Yet the next morning Hogan was out practicing. And I think he had some pro he liked watching his swing and correcting any mistake he might make."

I am not going as far back as Ben Hogan's beginning be-

cause I saw nothing of it. All that I know is that a remarkable
flock of young golfers suddenly broke loose in Texas. Why? I
don't know. There were Byron Nelson, Jimmy Demaret, Ben
Hogan, Ralph Guldahl, winner of two U. S. Opens, Lloyd
Mangrum, and "Babe" Zaharias, along with Jackie Burke and
Tommy Bolt of the younger crowd. This was the greatest out-
burst of playing talent any state has ever known. These players
have won eight U.S. Open championships and a team of them
could murder the best four any state has known. Their play, particularly their long irons, has been tremendous. Perhaps the fact
that they feature low soaring, quail-high shots is due in part to
their having played the ball off concrete-hard Texas fairways
during their formative years.

Texas is the kingdom of golf and has been for fifteen years.
It seems odd that this rugged state is now "in charge" of golf—
world golf—and is winning most of the major titles. When golf
first came to this country, from Scotland and England, it came
to Newport and the other social centers of the east. It was
played largely at Newport, Bar Harbor and around the secluded
habitations of the wealthy in New York. That was from 1896
to around 1905. The amateur championships were being won by
Charles Blair MacDonald, "Jim" Whigham, Walter Travis,
Chandler Egan, Findlay Douglas—the Opens by transplanted
Scots or by foreign pros.

I was at the Los Angeles Open in 1950 and heard Hogan
had just arrived, but I had no idea he would play. As I understood things, he was still a cripple. I saw him in the clubhouse and went over to speak to him. Barely able to stand up,
he was still smiling.

"What are you doing here?" I asked.

"Playing a little golf," he said.

"In the tournament?" I asked.

"Sure," he said. "Why not?"

I ran into Cary Middlecoff. "Is this right?" I asked. "Can he do anything?"

"Sure he can," Middlecoff said. "Watch him. If he can last he'll win it."

Hogan played brilliantly although his leg veins were still sutured and tied up with various knots. Photographers swarmed all over him and he protested bitterly. They finally reached an agreement. Late on the last day of the tournament I sat with his wife Valerie for a while and then with Ben. He seemed completely safe. He was four strokes ahead of Sammy Snead with only four holes left for the lean Virginian. Sammy spoiled it by finishing with four birdies, and winning the subsequent playoff.

At the 1950 Open Championship, held at Merion just outside Philadelphia, I ran into Hogan two days before the championship.

"How are things?" I asked. I knew his legs were not too good. I knew he wasn't back in shape. I knew he was worried about that 36-hole finish.

"This is a tough course," Ben said. "It can't be attacked. You must play defensive golf here."

"What do you mean?" I asked.

"The greens are fast and hard. You can't make a ball bite. The pins are placed in front of traps—or just back of traps. I won't play for any pin here. I'll play for the middle of the green —or away from all traps—and then depend on two putts to get down."

In his final round Ben was near collapse at the 14th hole. He had to play 36 holes that final Saturday. After his legs refused to carry him any farther, his mind "walked" him home. He barely finished, winding up in a triple tie with Mangrum and George Fazio. Valerie and the doctor worked on his crippled legs until 4:00 A.M. But he had enough left to win the next day, the most remarkable finish I've seen in golf.

But Hogan's third stand at Oakland Hills, Detroit, in June '51 in the Open, with no physical handicap to consider, was just as fine a deed as even Hogan has yet brought about. For his final round was a magical matter of concentration and determination that has never been equalled before in golf.

In this last round Hogan proved again the tremendous hold he has upon head, heart, nerves and physical structure.

He had started badly in his first round over a course that had them all in a daze. He hadn't been much better his second round. In his third round he practically had the tournament won after the first 12 holes. He was then 3 under par at which spot he suddenly blew wide open and finished 4 over par on the last six holes. So there was the job to be done all over once more.

Knowing the length and killing penalties at Oakland Hills it seemed impossible that under such a severe strain and such a killing test anyone could possibly, in Hogan's place, have fired a par-equalling 70. A 70 wouldn't have done Hogan any good. He would have lost his title by a stroke to Clayton Haefner.

Here was a golf course where one was dead sure that par might not be equalled in any round—that par would never be broken. But in this final and deciding fourth round, with the pressure at its roughest, Hogan not only shot a 67, but finished his last nine in 32 strokes.

His 32 on the final nine at Oakland Hills, ending with a birdie three on the 459-yard last hole, was certainly the most spectacular final nine holes any golf championship has ever known. He carved out that course with his mind, not his body.

Recently I was discussing Hogan with Craig Wood, one of the game's finest.

"Hogan really started upward around 1936," Craig said. "He came close often. What I admired about him was this—he was no longer getting any younger, but he was fighting harder than ever."

"Bobby Jones tells me that golf—championship golf—is about seventy-five per cent mental and twenty-five per cent physical," I said.

Craig paused a moment. "I think Bob is right," he said. "Except in Hogan's case. Hogan has a fine swing. So has Snead—perhaps a better one. So has Mangrum—as did Hagen, Jones, Armour, Barnes, Mac Smith—many others. But the main problem in golf is this: what do you do with your swing? Not part of the time, but all of the time."

"This," said Craig, "is the main answer. Hogan knows what he is doing all the time. He concentrates better than anyone I ever saw. Concentration means thinking of the one thing—the important thing—with everything else blotted out."

Hogan spent nearly three years in Service during World War II, but when he came out in the fall of '45 he exited with a rush. Since 1946, the little man with the ice-green eyes has won nine major titles including two PGA championships, four Opens, two Masters and the British Open at Carnoustie, Scotland, in the summer of 1953. Six of these (he won his first Open in '48 and his two professional titles in '46 and '48) have been won since the slim Indian-Irish ex-caddie from Fort Worth was all but crushed to death in that accident. While stalking these and so many other titles, Hogan has "murdered" par in relentless fashion. Ben's score of 61 at Seminole, Palm Beach, in March 1954 over a course that measures more than 7,000 yards may be his all-time "best" single round of golf. However, Hogan's shot making in the Masters tournament of 1953, in which his total of 274 for 72 holes was five strokes off the 279 record of Claude Harmon in '48 and Ralph Guldahl in '39, stands as his greatest single tournament.

Hogan's toughest scrambles have been in play-offs. He was hooked up in four of these, winning but one. Ben was beaten by Snead at Riviera, Los Angeles, and in the 1954 Masters at Augusta. He was beaten by Byron Nelson after coming from a long way back to tie. But he won the big one at Merion in 1951. Against Nelson and Snead at Augusta Hogan broke par both times but caught them on fast days.

His last battle with Sam Snead, a brilliant but unlucky golfer when in the Open, was spectacular. Hogan played almost perfect golf with one exception. With a 10- or 12-foot to win the short 16th, he stubbed (hit behind the ball) his putt, finished two feet short and then blew the two-footer. This incident would happen to Hogan once in 10,000 times. In losing twice to Snead he lost to perhaps the greatest "swinger" of all time.

A 3-putt green, plus the pressure-cooking play of Snead spiked Ben's guns in the Masters' play-off . . . and, several months later, in the '54 Open at Baltusrol, one poor round knocked Hogan into a fifth place tie with Patton, the amateur. A dark horse, Ed Furgol, believer in the old adage, "If at first you don't succeed, keep on shooting," won the Big one.

I've seen Furgol in tournaments around the map since 1945, the year he hit the circuit. I couldn't take in the '54 Open . . . except by television. I'd worked the Marciano–Charles fight the night before the Open started. After writing my overnight and extricating myself from the mob I was pretty tired. However, Ed met me at the Park Lane Hotel in New York the following Monday. Heading for a plane to St. Louis, he "made" time to meet and tell me about his victory.

For nearly eight years of tournament play—going into the Open—Ed had averaged competitive scoring rounds of between 70 and 71. That's sound golf. But in all that time the Utica, New York swinger who learned his game in public course play, had earned less than $15,000 in his biggest year—1947.

"I decided the Furgol family needed more security . . . and less rainbow chasing," he said. "I decided to try teaching . . . but with this cock-eyed left arm, well, I wasn't sure how my pupils, if any, would react. The answer came from the Westwood

Country Club, at Clayton, Missouri—near St. Louis. I've been out there for more than a year . . . and I've got almost more pupils than I can handle.

"I've worked hard with them," Ed continued. "From the start I've *HAD* to go with the, 'Do as I say, not as I do,' school. No, I haven't forgotten how important a straight left arm is for a player, if he has a good left arm. But I've worked more with the hand action which is even more important to a good swing . . . more important to a good hit.

"Baltusrol measured seven thousand and fifty yards—longest layout ever for an Open," he continued. "Also, the ground was moist which meant the course played even longer than its distance. It demanded bold hitting . . . all the way. You had to attack, attack . . . you couldn't finesse a shot—ever. I knew I was in good physical shape but I never realized how much the hours I spent teaching—eight and nine hours a day—had helped my condition. I was strong all the way . . . and I'm pushing thirty-eight."

Eight holes at Baltusrol measured 450 yards or more—long par 4's on anybody's course. Ed relied heavily on his set Number 3 iron for those long carries to the green. The key to Furgol's victory, in my mind, was that in 72 holes of shooting, he never blew to a 6 . . . where many headliners scattered to 7's.

Did Ed run into the jitters anywhere along the line?

"Not until the last day, Granny," he grinned. "I was clicking along fine until the seventh hole. There, I three-putted. Then on the eighth, another three-putt green! Walking to the ninth tee I was steaming, 'Oh, my God, is this the end? . . . Rounds of seventy-one, seventy, seventy-one to lead the field and now this!'

"I hit a good Number three iron on the ninth that slipped over the green a bit but I got down in three. Then I had nine consecutive pars for the last nine holes for a seventy-two . . . and jackpot."

Furgol's battle to reach the top is one of the most inspiring stories along the way of the ancient green. It was a long, drawn out fight in which full faith in himself finally carried Ed to the top. Ed, you're a living lesson in the many ways that can be used successfully by those who have gotten the tougher breaks from fate.

Hogan's place in the parade no longer has to be proved. With four U.S. Opens under his belt, there isn't much one could add. He happens to be starring in one of the most uncertain games as far as unbroken form is concerned. Hughie Keogh once wrote that "Form is the brief interval between getting ready and going stale." The answer is that in all the Masters tournaments held since 1934, no player has repeated.

Ben has won most of his tournaments with his head. I understand he is writing a golf book for Lowell Pratt along the line of "mental" golf. Such great golfers as Jones, Hagen and Sarazen will tell you that golf is 75 per cent mental—25 per cent physical. Hundreds can swing a golf club almost 100 per cent correctly. But only the few ever master the mental side: Hogan, Jones, Hagen, Sarazen perhaps—not many more. But Hogan is certainly the top thinker—shot by shot. He rarely guesses wrong or makes the slightest mistake. One reason is that he rarely has to guess. He knows!

Looking back over the golf parade, I find unnumbered memories. The brilliant Tommy Armour—and his massive hands —his amazing iron play . . . Gene Sarazen and his 30-odd years of championship or close to championship golf . . . Long Jim Barnes, triple champion, with the cloverleaf over one ear . . . the famous Jock Hutchison . . . the stately Craig Wood, one of the game's best . . . Alex Smith, three-time Open champion, whose motto was "Miss 'em quick" . . . Jerry Travers, one of the greatest putters that ever waved a blade . . . Jones and his Grand Slam . . . Hagen and his competitive fire . . . Bobby

Cruickshank . . . the many Turnesas . . . Johnny Farrell . . .

Great iron shots for birdies that won a title—short putts that missed by a hair and cost a title . . . I can still see most of them. But through these memories shines a light like no other I've seen while swinging along through a half century of golf —Ladies and gentlemen, Ben Hogan. Through his complete dedication to his sport, Hogan has built in himself that "more of everything"—particularly brains—it takes to win than any golfer I ever saw.

CHAPTER TWENTY-SIX

The Arthritis and Neuritis Set

During the mid-1920's *The American Golfer*, edited by our former amateur champion, Walter J. Travis, had been moving along under a conservative head of steam when it was purchased by new owners. They offered me the job of editor but I wasn't much interested until I was told that fresh capital, 200,000 dollars of it, was behind the book. That and the fact that I would be given a free rein with the make-up of the book induced me to give it a whirl. I immediately went after Innis Brown, of the *New York Sun*, for my managing editor. Monthly contributions came from such writers and golf enthusiasts as Ring Lardner, George Ade, Rex Beach and others. The editorial side of *The American Golfer* seemed to be solid enough; the business or advertising side of the book was less sensational. Then, in 1929, Condé Nast bought the magazine for his stable, which included *Vogue, Vanity Fair* and *House & Garden*. I lined up such "good-willers" as Tommy Armour, Walter Hagen, Mac Smith and other professionals to push the book. Our circulation had reached 70,000—very good—when the '29 crash hit and 20 pages of automobile advertising immediately fell out—kerplunk! That was the death rattle for *The American Golfer.*

My association with the depression may be summed up by the fact that I watched Goldman Sachs, a stock I was particularly heavy in, plummet from 121 to 3 before I sold! I fared about as well with several other securities. There is one blessing that I realized from the big crash. Had it not occurred, I'd have long since been a dead millionaire. Without further incentive to earn money . . . something I've had to do since the age of twelve, I might have drunk myself to death.

The Artists and Writers—or, as Monty Flagg rechristened us, "The Arthritis and Neuritis"—was born prior to the depression, around 1925. I think the inception of this bunch is interesting. Ray McCarthy, a golf writer on the *Herald Tribune* from 1920–24, had started his own publicity office. One of his accounts was the Florida East Coast Hotel and Railway Company, one branch of the sprawling Flagler interests.

Ray asked George Ade and Charley Williams, the illustrator, to go along on one of his advertising promotional safaris to St. Augustine, Florida. It must have been a good blowout. As Ray, Williams and Ade were leaving, Williams commented, "We ought to have an association like this for artists and writers." McCarthy didn't let the idea die.

The following spring, at a luncheon at the Algonquin Hotel in New York, a group of professional men gathered to discuss the matter. Rex Beach was there. So were Rube Goldberg, Ade, Clare Briggs, Bud Kelland, Fontaine Fox, Arthur Somers Roche, George Abbott, Ray and Clair Maxwell, Billy deBeck, Doc Newman, Frank Willard, Arthur William Brown, H. T. Webster, Frank Crowninshield, John Golden, Jeff Machamer, McCarthy, some others and me. The idea of a "fun" association appealed. "We'll go for the association . . . but no work," seemed the

tempo of business. I was tossed in as president. McCarthy, a
digger, was made executive secretary and Briggs was record-
ing secretary—Clare wasn't exactly the parliamentary type.
Goldberg was treasurer and Beach was vice-president. Golf and
stag conviviality were the bywords which, come to think of it,
might not be a bad credo for all world organizations.

Each winter for years I would head, usually from Los
Angeles, towards Palm Beach. The trip was tougher than crossing the Hump. Four or five days of bad connections . . . it
seemed an endless trek. But at the end there was the bunch
—one of the greatest.

I won our first tournament. Rex Beach won the second . . .
and after that we alternated most of the time until Hal Sims at
last reported with a better game. It was at Palm Beach that I
first got to know Rex Beach, in some ways the most amazing
person I've known. He was 6 feet 2 and weighed 220 pounds.
He had been an Olympic swimming ace. He had played professional football with the Chicago Cherry Circle (Chicago
Athletic Club) team. At that time, around 1900, he was rated
the best tackle in the country. Rex was a fine boxer and puncher.
Many thought that, had he turned pro, he might have beaten
Jim Jeffries. He boxed often with Fred Stone, who had gone
six rounds with Jim Corbett without being hit once. One night
in Rector's, the famed New York restaurant, Beach collided
with a 230-pound Princeton tackle. In the ensuing scuffle, which
lasted 27 seconds, Rex put the ex-Tiger into a hospital bed for
two weeks.

With all these physical assets Beach was the gentlest of men
—until aroused. I had read most of his books—*The Spoilers, The
Silver Horde, The Barrier, Going Some, The Iron Trail* and many
more . . . most of them about Alaska and the frozen North.
A wonderful skier and fine shot, Beach hunted Kodiak bears
without a dog. There was no limit to this 220-pound giant who

could move like a halfback. Rex was three years older than I. He had migrated from his home at Atwood, Michigan, to Winter Park, Florida. There, from 1891 to 1896, he attended Rollins College. Later he followed up with various law schools in and around Chicago. He quit law for the Yukon Trail . . . and writing.

As a golfer, Rex's main trouble was, "worry." A powerful hitter, from 260 to 270 yards off the tee, he would qualify with a 70 or 71 . . . which should have been his game. I don't know how I ever managed to beat him. However, I think what favored me most was that I seldom worried in any match, particularly against Beach, because I knew he was a better golfer. He worried—I didn't, and we broke about even. (I've played my best golf when I didn't care. The more I *tried*, however, the worse I became.)

My reward for these trips to Palm Beach was nearly 30 years of close communion with Beach, Bud Kelland, Rube Goldberg and their like—sociable friendship, the richest reward known to man. In our various meetings that wonderful bunch contributed a large share of whatever deep pleasure I've found along the endless, winding road.

For such a gifted crew of professional men, their homely attitude towards golf was priceless. I recall the day I was playing in a foursome that included John Golden and Billy deBeck, Barney Google's creator. Following what Billy assumed had been a wicked hook, he disappeared into the tall underbrush. A few moments later I heard him call, "Never mind looking for the ball, caddie. Find me!"

"Here it is, Mr. Golden," one of the caddies said, "out on the fairway."

"You're a liar," Golden retorted, hammering in the brush. "I've never been on the fairway in my life."

There was the time when, following a bad round, Rube

Goldberg came over to a bunch of us and asked, "Is there any way you can play golf except right or left handed?" I have given this much thought.

More than 60 per cent of that old mob has gone. After Don Marquis died in '38, I wrote a bit of verse for one of our dinners.

Via Charon, The Ancient Boatman

(To Frank Condon, Ring Lardner, Don Marquis, Odd McIntyre, George Daley, Bill McGeehan, Bill Macbeth, Eddie Neil, Bill McNutt and others of the old guard who recently have beaten us to the border)

> There are too many gaps in the ranks I knew
> When the ranks I knew were young.
> When the roll is called, there are still a few
> Who answer, "Here!" when the call is due—
> There are too many songs unsung.
> But Charon's boat is a busy barque—
> And the dock gets closer as dusk grows dark.
>
> Pilot who looks to your river trade
> Where the shadowy Styx rolls by
> You've taken your pick of the mystic glade,
> Lardner, McGeehan—and Hammond's shade
> Drift through a starless sky—
> And somewhere—deep in the reedy tarn—
> Boze Bulger is spinning another yarn.
>
> Charon—answer me this today—
> From all of the world's corrals,
> Why do you always look *my* way?
> I'm not worried about *your* play
> But why do you pick my pals?
> From the Inn we knew where the flagons foam,
> One by one you have called them home.

One by one, on a mist-blown eve
Wearing your ghostly hood,
I've seen you plucking them by the sleeve,
Telling them each it was time to leave,
Just as the show gets good.
With a lifted glass, as I looked about,
I've seen them leave as the tide rolled out.

Charon—I'm sorry I failed the test—
You're not the one to blame—
You picked the brightest—you picked the best—
You carried them off to a dreamless rest
That towers above all fame.
Don—Odd—Percy—and Bill and Ring—
No wonder the angels soar and sing!

Listen, Pilot, the last of all
Who knows where the journey ends—
When you have come to the final call
Where the candle flutters against the wall,
Kindly forget my friends.
For friends are all that a little earth
Has yet to give that has any worth.

Fame and Gold? They are less than dust—
Less than an April song—
They are less than weeds in the earth's dull crust
When a friendly hand in your own is thrust
And an old mate comes along.
But dock lights flame with a sudden flare—
And Charon beckons—and who is there?

The Flame of the Inn is dim tonight—
Too many vacant chairs—
The sun has lost too much of its light—
Too many songs have taken flight—
Too many ghosts on the stairs—
Charon—here's to you—as man against man—
I wish I could pick 'em the way you can.

CHAPTER TWENTY-SEVEN

Writers and Pals

I believe that I came along in gayer, happier times for both newspaper readers and writers. Somewhere in the late 1920's, there was a sudden change. In those earlier days columnists wrote verse and paragraphs. There was Franklin P. Adams of the *Mail* and *Herald Tribune*, whose two columns—"Always in Good Humor" and "The Conning Tower"—were magnificent. Bert Leston Taylor (B.L.T.), who conducted "The Line-A-Type-or-Two," in the *Chicago Tribune*, was equally wonderful. These were the two stars, but there were many others who were excellent.

Frank L. Stanton, the serious poet in the *Atlanta Constitution,* was in front of them all. Others were: Judd Mortimer Lewis in the *Houston Post;* John D. Wells in the *Buffalo News;* Don Marquis of the old *Sun,* whose "archie, the cockroach" and other superb verse held high attention; Eddie Guest; and Henry Sydnor Harrison from Virginia.

These and some others ruled those days of column readers.

They suddenly gave way to Westbrook Pegler, Heywood Broun, Alexander Woollcott, Ralph McGill, Walter Lippmann, Frank Kent, E. V. Durling, John O'Donnell, Bob Considine, and many more. Certainly Frank Adams, Bert Taylor and Don Marquis had an appeal that could equal that of any columnist of the present era with, perhaps, the exception of Westbrook Pegler. Pegler's fiery diatribes which keep you wondering what he will say or whose scalp he will lift.

Nevertheless, I got a far greater thrill in reading Adams, Taylor or Marquis in other years than I have got since. Maybe it was because I was a graduate of the verse and paragraph school from the days of the *Nashville Tennessean.*

Frank Adams was the best light-verse writer I ever read, in this country or Europe. He translated the Odes of Horace into modern verse. Here's just one sample of his intricate rhyming.

To Be Quite Frank

Uxor Pauperis Ibyci
Horace Ode 15, Book 3

Your conduct naughty Chloris is
Not just exactly Horace's
Ideal of a lady
At the shady
Time of life.
You mustn't throw your soul away
On foolishness, like Pholoë
Her days are folly laden—
She's a maiden—
You're a wife.

Your daughter, with propriety,
May look for male society,
Do one thing and another
In which mother
Shouldn't mix.

But revels Bacchanalian
Are—or should be—quite alien
To you, a married person
Something worse'n
Forty six!

Yes, Chloris, you cut up too much,
You love the dance and cup too much,
Your years are quickly flitting,
To your knitting
Right about.
Forget the incidental things,
That keep you from parental things,
The World, the Flesh, the Devil,
On the level,
Cut 'em out.

It was Frank Adams who wrote one of baseball's few immortal lyrics—

These are the saddest of possible words—
Tinker and Evers and Chance.
Pricking forever our gonfalon bubble,
Causing a Giant to hit into a double,
Words that are heavy with nothing but trouble,
Tinker to Evers to Chance.

I was at the *Evening Mail* in 1912 when Mr. Miles, the managing editor, called me to his office. He showed me the verse Adams had just turned in. "Frank may write a better piece of verse than this," Niles said, "but this is one he will be remembered by." He was right.

One of the finest columnists I ever read was Hugh E. Keogh, who conducted a sporting page composium in verse and paragraphs. Keogh had but a short burst. He began his column in 1905 and died in 1911. A master, a fine verse writer and a brilliant paragrapher, Hughey had the most interesting sporting column

I ever read. Here are a few examples of his one line master-pieces.

"The race is not to the swift—but that is where to look."

"The art of self defense—100 yards in 10 seconds."

"Throw your bread upon the waters and a carp will beat you to it."

"You can't pay off people in the square set with technicalities."

"The rules of sport arc all founded upon fair play."

Whatever happened, the Peglers and the Winchells, the Brouns and the Ed Sullivans drove off the rhymers and para-graphers from most newspapers to the sorrow of many, many readers.

I think one reason the papers switched from verse to prose is this—good poets suddenly disappeared and readers for some reason lost the old poetic zest. I know that I started keeping a poetry scrapbook around 1905. I kept this up for 25 years. I have many rare things in it. Suddenly, around 1930, I quit col-lecting. The reason—I found little worth pasting in my treasured book.

This is a much more serious age than the old days ever were. There was a lightheartedness that the world knew before the first World War that has never been worn since. Thank God for H. I. Phillips! There has been war or the shadow of war for the past 40 years and the dark shadow hasn't ever been absent from the scene in that time. Most of the true singers have had little heart with which to sing.

❊   ❊   ❊

No newspaper man hits the road more often than the writer assigned to a major-league baseball team—or the one who en-joys syndication and can hunt at large in search of game. Sports

writers, as a group, tend to be nomads, gypsies. If they weren't
of that basic cut, they wouldn't be in that field.

It was in Bill Corum's drawing room aboard the train returning to New York from Cincinnati following the Detroit-
Cincinnati World Series in 1940, that I heard a wise sum-up of a
sports writer's approach to his job. Joe Williams was there and
so were Tom Meany, Garry Schumacher, and Tommy Laird, the
sage of San Francisco. The talk—over juleps—got around to
jobs. Laird mentioned that Lefty O'Doul, as manager of the
San Francisco Seals, was happier than he had ever been in the
majors.

We were all sounding off on what we'd do if given another
whirl at fate's old wheel.

"As for me," said Corum, "I don't want to be a millionaire;
I just want to live like one . . . or a sports writer."

Toots Shor put it another way. Watching a group of baseball writers carving their initials in his bar at 3 A.M. after a
Baseball Writers' party, Toots said, "Grant, there's not a millionaire in that bunch. They just live like 'em!"

While stopping over for a brief stand, "We who are travelers
for the night at this old wayside inn called Earth," we meet
many people—few of them alike and Toots Shor, a fellow who
runs a great restaurant, is strictly himself. There hasn't been and
there won't be anybody like him. He is the only world-wide man
I know. I was sitting with Toots recently at lunch when he lifted
the phone and called Ben Hogan at Fort Worth to cheer Ben
up after he'd been beaten by Sammy Snead in the '54 Masters.
Ten minutes later he called up Ford Frick, the Baseball Commis-
sioner to discuss some knotty problem that had come up in
baseball. Five minutes later he was on the line to two close
friends, Ernest and Mary Hemingway in South Africa. He found
that Hemingway had been much more severely injured in that

plane wreck than he had let anyone know. Then Toots called
Gene Fowler in Los Angeles to see how Gene felt. "Heard he
wasn't so good," Toots said.

Jimmy Cannon tells a true story from Louisville at the '53
Derby—when Dark Star upset Native Dancer's applecart. Before a certain race Toots told his bunch he would get the right
tip from his old friend Horatio Luro, the Argentine pill muncher
and horse trainer. Toots left, got the tip, and the horse was out
of the money.

"Can you imagine an old friend double crossing you like
that?" Toots howled.

"Is Luro a close friend of yours?" Cannon asked.

"I met him yesterday," replied Toots.

Shor is a friend of the world at large, barring all communists
and hypocrites. In turn he is respected and loved by those that
know him. A close friend of the athlete, sports writer and
columnist, Toots and "Baby" his bride are tops in my little old
book.

Certainly my most exciting days—and nights—have been
spent on the road. There is a fresh outlook when you move out
on the trail that takes you around the map—Los Angeles, Chicago, Miami, New Orleans, Louisville, Dallas, St. Louis, Atlanta,
Philadelphia, Boston, Shelby, St. Petersburg, wherever there's
a big sports story, that's where the compass points.

Since 1901, years of work and travel, I've enjoyed meeting
and knowing so many stars and champions. But I don't think
this feeling quite reaches the deeper glow that has come from
my more affectionate connections with the writers and friends
I've made along this almost endless trail.

In the earlier days a lot of us were often broke or next to
it. But one thing about The Greatest Profession, a little thing like
money or the lack of it never gave us much concern. I remember

it was the night before the Willard-Dempsey fight in Toledo. There was a big party in the outskirts. It was on the house and nearly all the writers covering the show went. A good looking girl was checking them in. "Ring Lardner," "Damon Runyon," "H. C. Witwer," "Gene Fowler," "Heywood Broun," "Percy Hammond," "Rube Goldberg," great trade names were given, one by one. The hostess, thinking it was all a fake, was getting sore. Finally another came up to sign in. She hardly looked at him but blurted, "And you, you big bum . . . I suppose you are Irvin Cobb." It was.

One of the livelier additions down the long journey has been Tom Meany, a fine writer, a keen story teller and a high-grade wit. One night after a World Series game in New York, Meany was the victim of a fellow who meant well but bored deep. Tom couldn't get rid of him. He wasn't a bad fellow but you know the type. He hung on like a leech. Finally Tom decided to leave the party.

His loquacious friend said, "I'll drive you home, Tom."

"You already have," replied Meany.

Writer-pals I've known go back to Bozemen Bulger of the *Birmingham Age-Herald* and Ren Mulford, Jr. of the *Cincinnati Enquirer* in 1901. That first wave consisted also of Hugh Fullerton, Sr. and Hugh E. Keogh (HEK) of the *Chicago Tribune;* Sid Mercer of St. Louis and the *New York Globe;* Ed Camp of the *Atlanta Journal;* Don Marquis and Frank L. Stanton of Atlanta; Charley Dryden of the *Philadelphia North American;* and Bob Edgren of the old *New York World.*

The second wave, starting around 1910, would include such writers as Ring Lardner of Chicago, Francis Albertanti and F. P. Adams of the old *Evening Mail,* Harry Salsinger (*Detroit News*), Bill Hanna (*N.Y. Tribune*), Bill Phelon (*Cincinnati Times Star*), lovable O. B. Keeler (*Atlanta Journal*), and Clyde McBride (*Kansas City Star*).

And coming strong in the third wave would be: Damon Runyon (*N.Y. American*), Heywood Broun (*N.Y. Tribune* and *Telegram*), Westbrook Pegler (*Chicago Tribune, N.Y. Post, World-Telegram, Journal American*), W. O. McGeehan (*Herald Tribune*), Harry Cross (*N.Y. Times, Herald Tribune*), Gene Fowler and Bill Corum (*N.Y. American*), Bob Kelley and John Kieran (*N.Y. Times*), Frank Graham (*N.Y. Sun, Journal American*), Fred Digby and Bill Keefe of New Orleans, Braven Dyer (*Los Angeles Times*), Bill Cunningham (*Boston Herald*), Dan Parker (*New York Mirror*), Stanley Woodward and Red Smith (*N.Y. Herald Tribune*), Freddie Russell (*Nashville Banner*), Roy Johnson (*Nashville Tennessean*), Joe Williams (*N.Y. World Telegram*), Henry McLemore (U.P., McAdams Syndicate), Harry Grayson (N.E.A.), Jimmy Cannon (*N.Y. Post*), and such comparative moderns as Tim Cohane and Vincent X. Flaherty.

Perhaps the finest group to grace American journalism flourished from 1910 to 1925. This list included Runyon, Lardner, Broun, Fowler, McGeehan, Pegler, Salsinger, McBride, Danforth and some others. With that pack sweeping down the field, how could this era miss?

Writing men necessarily are creative men and, as such, run to no set formula. There were odd varieties among the tops. As odd as a Chinese puzzle was Bill Phelon, the Cincinnati sage who could write, and well, about anything. He would write you 5,000 words for ten dollars and not junk. He neither smoked nor drank. It was different with women, art and other details. Built and clothed like great shaggy dogs, Phelon and Heywood Broun were as rare as pair of clothes horses as ever condescended to wear shoe leather.

Bill was an animal collector of sorts. One day in the Polo Grounds press box I was sitting with Phelon and Harry Salsinger. There was a white cigar box in front of me—punctured with many holes. I was leaning on it.

"By the way," Phelon said, "I was down at the wharf this morning and I bought a young fer-de-lance. Most poisonous snake in South America—a slender snake who strikes quick. I got him cheap."

"Where is he?" I asked.

"In that box you are leaning on," Bill said. I covered 20 yards in a second. Salsinger beat that. The openings in the cigar box were bigger than the fer-de-lance.

In the Cincinnati press box another day Bill asked me if I would like to make 250 dollars.

"For that amount," I said, "I would rob a bank. What's the idea?"

"Well, it's this way," Phelon said. "I have a six-foot alligator living in my apartment." (He also had, I knew, a Gila monster, a squirrel, and a rattlesnake sharing the room.) "Now there's a Dutchman down the block who has a big bulldog. He wants to bet me five hundred bucks his bulldog can lick my alligator."

"What makes you think the bulldog can't win?" I asked.

"I know he can't win," he said. "I'll tell you why. I got a pit and I matched my alligator against three bulldogs at different times. He sheared the legs off all three dogs."

I bowed out. And yet, as I said, Phelon was a brilliant writer on almost any subject. Like Julius Caesar, he could talk to you on some outside subject and write a forceful story at the same time about the game.

William B. Hanna was one of my closest friends. He wrote perfect English and was an expert on football and baseball reporting. He was with the old *New York Sun* first, then the *Herald Tribune.* When you read one of Bill's stories, you knew that's the way it happened. He was a brilliant writer and a perfect reporter. A small fellow, he seemed a trifle shrivelled.

Hanna was an eccentric. He would never stop above the fifth floor of a hotel. Twice on the same night he had been caught in hotel fires. Also, he hated number 13. One day, in making a reservation in Florida, I got the top floor for Hanna and myself.

Hanna almost fainted. "No higher than the fifth," he shouted at me.

I got another room. Bill had another fit. "You got fifty-eight," he called.

"That's the fifth floor," I said.

"But five and eight adds up to thirteen!" he said.

One afternoon, Phelon passed Hanna headed down Broadway in New York. "Hello, Bill," he said.

"Hello, Phelon," Bill responded.

A practical joker who knew Bill's eccentricities, Phelon hopped a southbound cab, got out a block below the oncoming Hanna and greeted him again with "Hello, Bill!"

A surprised Hanna returned the greeting. Phelon did this three or four more times. At the fourth "Hello, Bill!" Hanna started for the river and was barely prevented from diving in.

But for all his strange and at times brooding characteristics, Bill was a lovable fellow with a wonderfully keen, direct mind.

In the earlier years of my wandering about in the sporting domain, Westbrook Pegler was one of my closest companions. Later, Peg left our field flat to shoot at bigger game, in politics. He was a fine sports columnist, usually working in the role of offering bitter protests against various people and conditions. In his social connections, however, Peg could lay aside his protesting role and have more fun than most.

One summer at East Hampton we attended a big fancy dress party. The ladies took charge of Pegler and dressed him up as Sadie Thompson, the famous heroine of *Rain*. Sadie was the hit of the evening. But, as a rule, Peg remains a serious and, in some ways, the most fearless writer I have known. Nothing can keep him off the critical course when he feels criticism is in order. He was the same in writing about sport as he is in writing of

politics and politicians, including union labor leaders. He usually
has a hot target and rarely misses his aim. Such outspoken critics
as Westbrook Pegler and Dan Parker, for two examples, are
badly needed.

To Peg, "The Golden Age of Sport" was "The Era of Wonderful Nonsense." Some years ago when he was covering both
politics and a World Series in New York, the game was post-
poned on account of rain. We came back to my apartment. Peg
was restless. He couldn't see any "off day" baseball story. So he
began scanning the library ranged around the room. He got
up from his chair and finally picked out a book.

"How big is a giant panda?" Pegler asked. He was scanning
a book written by General Theodore Roosevelt about his year's
search for the beast and how he had brought one home.

"He is about as big as a collie dog, although he weighs
more," I said.

"Is he ferocious?" Peg asked.

"I don't think so," I said.

No more was said on the subject as Peg went back to work.

Next day there appeared a terrific blast at Teddy, Jr. for
capturing what was believed to be a dangerous animal that,
in reality, was as docile as a kitten or a puppy. A good friend of
Peg's, Roosevelt took the column as a joke.

For 40 years and more, Frank L. Stanton turned out a
column of verse and paragraphs for the *Atlanta Constitution*. By
all odds the finest poet I ever met, he was like a mocking bird
singing in a Georgia oak which happened to be flooded with
moonlight.

Don Marquis, a far better judge of poetry than I, rated
James Whitcomb Riley first and Stanton second among American poets. "Mighty Lak A Rose," "Just a Wearyin' for You," and
hundreds of other remembered songs in his more than 40 years
of service are pure Stanton.

One year, 1903, Marquis and I lived at the Aragon Hotel in Atlanta. Stanton liked a nightcap or two before the bar closed at 10:00 P.M. So did Don and I. Stanton had to escape to make port and he was frequently late. I remember the bartender one night saying, "Sorry, but time's up, Mr. Stanton."

"I will write thee a verse for a drink," Stanton said. He immediately dashed off a verse beginning "Time's up for love and laughter." It was a beautiful thing and later on it appeared in *Judge* or *Puck*. The bartender received 25 dollars for sending it along.

Another night, with Don and me peering over his shoulder, Frank wrote the following lines on a piece of wrapping paper:

Hasten not, O traveler, to yonder distant town,
Where shadows shut the stars out and the dead leaves tumble down.
Tarry at life's tavern—one more cup they'll fill,
They'll light no lamps to guide you to that distant town and still.

But there is one who dwells there, in the night's embrace,
Love in life's sweet morning dreamed in her dear face,
The lilies are her altars where the winds kneel down to pray,
But all the violets loved her so they hid her face away.

I brought on Frank's deep displeasure once—a peeve that lasted several weeks. He had written a short piece of verse that went—

This old world we're living in
Is mighty hard to beat.
We find a thorn with every rose
But ain't the roses sweet.

This verse was widely quoted at the time. I was with Marquis one day when we ran across Mr. Stanton.

"I have just written a verse," I told him. "I think you'll like it. It goes—

"This old world we're living in
I think is on the blink.
You find a thorn with every rose
And don't the roses stink."

We barely escaped with our lives.

Many good writers have tried to put together a book about Ring Lardner but none has as yet succeeded. To contain Ring would be like wrapping up a wraith. I lived side by side or house by house with him for many years and yet I never quite knew that I knew him.

Ring was closer to being a genius than anyone I've known. He had a sense of humor that was at times beyond this world. He was tall, dark and slender and was never what you'd call loquacious.

Charley Van Loan was appointed by George Horace Lorimer to go to Chicago and get Ring to write for the *Saturday Evening Post*. Van could get nothing from Ring, not a word, as he marched from saloon to saloon. Van Loan himself was on the wagon.

Finally, about two in the morning, Van Loan said, "Say, I can't walk all night on water."

"Christ did!" retorted Ring.

I was with him one Mardi Gras night in New Orleans. We were surrounding a bar when an 80-year-old Southerner stepped up to Ring.

"You probably don't know who I am," he drawled. "My grandfather was General so-and-so on Napoleon's staff. My father was Count so-and-so of France. I was a general in the Confederate Army and, suh, I wear the Legion of Honor."

Ring spoke. "I was born in Niles, Michigan, of colored parents," he said. The general fled into the night.

Ring was a fine baseball writer and equally good at football. He was a magnificent comedy writer but the savage bitterness of his best work was his main feature. I never knew anyone who hated a phony more than Ring.

I took him to Washington with me for a golf match with President Harding. Harding said at the meeting—"Rice is here to get a story. Why did you come?"

"I had a good reason," Ring said. "I want to be appointed Ambassador to Greece."

"Why?" Harding asked.

"My wife doesn't like Great Neck," Lardner said.

"That's a better reason than most of these people have," replied Harding.

Following a luncheon of highballs and sandwiches, Harding told the secret service men assigned to him to take the day off and we went out to Burning Tree.

Harding had a way of driving and then walking from the tee, on ahead. Ring followed him on one drive and called "Fore" about three times. Harding had walked about 40 yards and was now under an apple tree. Ring drove, hitting a lusty ball with a slight slice. The ball struck a thick branch just over Harding's head. The branch fell on Harding's shoulder. He was startled and waited for Ring to come up and apologize.

"I did all I could to make Coolidge president," was all Ring said. Harding dropped his club and roared with laughter.

Harding was a poor president but he was quite a fellow and, I think, an honest man.

After Harding's death I decided to go back to Washington when Mr. Coolidge was in the White House to dig up another Presidential story. The President was making a talk that day before a press gathering. When he was through, I was introduced to him. The party was very short.

"The last time I was in Washington," I said to President Coolidge, "I played golf with President Harding. Do you happen to play golf or tennis?" I asked him.

"No," he said, "but I have my game."

"What is it?" I questioned.

"Walking," he said.

"I couldn't write much about that," I said.

"No," he answered.

I found later that he had two other sports. One was fishing with worms. The other was wild turkey shooting.

Mr. Coolidge went turkey hunting with a South Carolina guide. He was hidden away under thick cover. The guide said to him, "When I nudge you, shoot."

The guide called the turkey up to about 20 yards. He nudged. The President shook his head. He tried again when the gobbler stopped about six yards away. This time the President let him have both barrels. The turkey disappeared. It was a massacre. But there was no turkey left.

Mr. Coolidge practically took no chances on anything.

My earlier traveling mates inside the profession were Westbrook Pegler, Ring Lardner and Bill McGeehan. They made any trip worth while, although it usually took some time to wipe out their initial annoyance with me. This trio had the habit of making a train by an hour. I had the habit of just making a train—several times after it had started moving. This habit—also shared by Babe Ruth—annoyed my traveling mates.

I soon discovered, however, that Peg, Ring and Bill were seldom covering the same event. So I sought other mates. I soon settled on three men willing to leave home and roam, now and then. They were Clarence Budington Kelland, the late Frank Craven, and Bruce Barton. In different fashions, all were ideal company.

Top man, perhaps because he "suffered" more, was Bud Kelland, noted novelist, short-story writer, elder statesman, after-dinner speaker, famous wit—with at times the tongue of a cobra. Kelland, who always took time off from some 80 or perhaps 90 novels to get away, required advance notice—from two hours to one week. I could count on Bud to be at Grand Central or at Pennsylvania Station at 7:00 P.M. on any given date. Bud never seemed to care where we went or what sport we were covering. At least he never cared to be bothered with these unessential details. He always knew there was some adventure waiting.

There was the week end we traveled to Columbus, Ohio, to see Jock Sutherland's Pittsburgh Panthers meet Ohio State. At the press gate I presented our two tickets.

"No good," the ticket taker said.

"What's the matter with them?" I asked.

"Look," he said, handing them back. They happened to be for the International Polo Matches at Meadowbrook. Fortunately, at that moment I spotted Sutherland and his team entering another gate. I rushed over.

"Jock," I said, "today I am your assistant coach and Mr. Kelland is assistant team doctor." That's how we covered the game.

One morning at breakfast in Philadelphia, Bud looked terrible. He began cursing me. I discovered that around midnight I had ordered up two ice cold watermelons and had inadvertently left half a watermelon in Bud's bed. He hadn't closed an eye, with first his right foot then his left entangled with the iced melon. His genius, however, hadn't prompted Bud to remove the foot warmer.

One night I heard a soliloquy delivered by Mr. Kelland, who thought no one was listening.

"Why do I do it? Why am I here? I didn't have to come. Nothing but drunks and bums. I don't drink, but I rarely see a glass of water. No sleep—no nothing that makes any sense. Never again."

The reason Bud kept taking these trips for 25 or 30 years was his love for sport—also, he loved meeting people. He became a friend of every coach we ever met. They all wanted him around, especially Sutherland.

Down the trail of many years, and up to the Open Golf Tournament at Merion in 1951, Bud covered the map—golf tournaments, fights, football games. He didn't care so long as he heard the tocsin sounding from the tower. From New York to Los Angeles—from Minneapolis to St. Pete, we hit all stops.

Occasionally, I was prodded into getting Bud to say a few words at some dinner or function. Usually, it was a sad mistake. Annoyed at something that had happened or by someone present, Bud would take the toastmaster, club president, mayor or whatever, completely apart with a devastating attack that was totally unexpected. His rancor was and remains no light matter, and at times it's easily aroused. Yes, with Bud everything took place except the peace and quiet and orderly action which Kelland thought he sought.

Trips without Bud, who has retired from expeditions and safaris after a long and tumultuous experience, never have seemed quite the same.

Frank Craven, the superb actor who died in 1945, was another grand trouper. A keen fan, Frank knew all sports, especially baseball, football and golf. He was one of the most entertaining men I ever knew. He also had a keen sense of humor and a ready Irish wit.

Once, on a visit to London, he was stopped by some butler while trying to visit an English friend.

"Step aside," Frank ordered. "I've played a thousand of you."

In addition to being a great actor, he was a fine playwright. *The First Year* was one of his contributions. Frank and

John Golden, one of the great men of the theater, worked together for many seasons.

In golf, Craven rarely varied from an 80 score. At Lakeside, in California, he played many rounds with Henry McLemore, winning almost every match. Finally McLemore had to go away for a week. When he returned, Frank sent him a bill for 45 dollars.

"What's this for?" Henry asked.

"For the money I would have won if you had not left," Frank said.

"That's right," Henry replied as he shelled out 45 dollars. "You couldn't have missed."

Since Craven died I have missed him heavily many times. No one could take his place on the golf course, on a trip, or standing bravely in front of a dry martini. He was one of the immortals—beyond all price.

Bruce Barton showed better judgment than Kelland or Craven. He suddenly realized he didn't have to take such beatings, like grabbing my typewriter and dashing for trains. However, during the few short years that Bruce accompanied me, he was a valuable blocking back. He swung a wicked portable through crowds, clearing the way like an icebreaker. A bristling conversationalist, decisive in action, he was a remarkable companion. The combinations of Kelland, Craven, Barton, Pegler, McGeehan, Lardner, Frankie Graham and Red Smith have been vital factors in holding the road.

Graham and Smith—both lovable guys—came along as a star team when most of the others had died or quit. Both are superb columnists—for the *New York Journal American* and *New York Herald Tribune,* respectively. Marvelous companions in every detail, they are also experts whose opinions have been useful on many occasions. I hope they will be around at the last march.

There is another I always hope to see. His name is Gene Fowler. He writes movies for money, and books for his soul. He is the only one I know who would greet me now and then with a special column.

"I know you're tired after the trip," he would say. "This might help."

It happens that Gene, meanwhile, was probably the busiest of all the writers. He sent me the first hilarious story ever written on the highly-scented Gorgeous George, the marcelled wrestler, which started George towards considerable notoriety and cash.

For some reason, there are only two men in history I think of in terms of the world "gallant." They are the Gallant Fowler and the Gallant Stuart, meaning Jeb. Gene Fowler is certainly worth traveling across country to California for—even for a brief hello.

One night in the late 1930's I ran into two of my all-time favorites—both Army men. Their names were Rosie O'Donnell and Blondie Saunders, two of West Point's immortals. Saunders, a fine Army tackle in '28, became a one-star general in the Air Force and lost a leg in the Far East during World War II. Rosie was in a class alone. Among his minor acts he flew over Tokyo dropping bombs as he went.

But this is a different story. That night I ran into Rosie and Blondie and we took in New York. We called on Bob Neyland as well as the night spots. I arrived home about 7 A.M. Naturally Kit wanted to know a few details of this all-night pilgrimage. I had only one answer.

"Everything's all right," I muttered sleepily. "I've had a great time. Been out with Rosie and Blondie."

It took me a week to square myself . . . before I could

explain that Rosie and Blondie in my book are two of the finest fighting men who ever lived.

Sporting writers have their particular idols—some whom they cherished from boyhood, others whom they helped create in the headlines. San Francisco's Tommy Laird, archon of the Coast writing fraternity for so many years, chronicled most of Stanley Ketchel's bouts when Ketchel ruled the middleweights in 1908 and 1909. In Tommy's world, Ketchel was the greatest, period.

It was in 1939 that I decided to make my young confrere, Henry McLemore, aware of the facts of life, at least concerning Laird. We were covering a golf tournament in San Francisco. Gene Fowler, who had hung the questionable halo of "Dean" on my snow-flaked brow, an appellation he still uses, had mentioned that we ought to be on the lookout for a "Junior Dean." Perhaps McLemore, then writing for the United Press, might be our man. An indefatigable person, the Georgia-born McLemore is a hard man to down, either with refreshing drink or at charades. His mind has been known to fire as rapidly as a string of Chinese firecrackers. Fowler appraised Henry of our plans for him but informed him that he would be judged for his role through "a series of tests." Henry did not flinch.

This particular night, I was having dinner at the St. Francis Hotel with Laird and McLemore. Things were unusually sedate. I quietly suggested to Henry that he tell Laird that Stanley Ketchel was no good. Grabbing the bait like a tiger shark, Henry leaned across my bows and facing Laird, crackled, "Ketchel was a lousy bum."

That did it. Turning a horrible crimson, Laird screamed, "What!" . . . grabbed the completely baffled McLemore by the shirt collar and whacked him. As he was trying to escape from the ruckus with his life, Henry's head was bashed by a woman swinging a loaded handbag.

I had to flunk McLemore on this, his opening test, but gave
him an "A" shortly after. The San Francisco Press Club, which
owns its own building just a few blocks from the St. Francis, is
well known for its annual dinners, at which all comments by
the speakers are "behind the cat" or off the record. Arriving with
Pat O'Brien, Guy Kibbee, Fowler and McLemore, I was worried
over their condition to render a fit talk on anything to a gathering of perhaps 500.

I had to literally drag Henry from the washroom and sit
him down. Following the introduction, Henry rose from his
seat—in stocking feet—stepped upon the table, and strode
through the asparagus to the microphone.

"Ladies and gentlemen," he intoned. "I would like to give
you my recipe for apple butter. . . ."

He did, too, in one of the most lucid, most pristine, informa-
tive and certainly the most humorous of speeches I ever heard.

McLemore was just about "in" as Junior Dean when we
arrived at Detroit the following September to cover the Joe
Louis–Bob Pastor fight. We were staying at the Detroit Athletic
Club. Our suite became a crossroads. In our corner was Hunk
Anderson, Rockne's all-time guard and, I repeat, pound-for-
pound the roughest human being, when aroused, I've ever
known. At one time or another during the evening prior to the
fight it seemed we had everybody including Louis and Pastor in
our rooms and Hunk was prepared to engage them all—singly
or in pairs.

"This should be a good test for you, Henry," I said. "Why
not say a few words to Hunk?" Game to the core, Henry mentioned something about Hunk's bark being worse than his bite.
The next thing I knew my little friend was being bounced on the
floor as if he were a tennis ball. That night Henry resigned as
Junior Dean.

There's another night I won't forget, the eve of the World

Series between the Tigers and the Cubs in '45. Charley Hughes, manager of the Detroit A.C., decided to toss a quiet little party for me. "Bring four or five," he said. I may have told a half dozen but between 40 and 50 showed up. It was a lovely dinner. Over the brandy, Harry Grayson asked McLemore to say a few words. Still in uniform following three solid years in Service, including a long hitch in the Pacific, Henry was happy to oblige. He told us of his early Georgia upbringing: how he was the son of a Methodist minister, who, when Henry went North to write, said, "Henry, when you're up there, beware of The Killer."

In the course of time, Henry said he met The Killer. He then ran through a list of writers who had died during the past 20 years. It was a very long list of people like Lardner, McGeehan, MacBeth, Broun, and so many others.

"The Killer's intended victim, before me," continued Henry, "was Clarence Budington Kelland. Kelland, thank God, succeeded in breaking away from him just in time. For nearly five years now he's been in Arizona trying to regain a semblance of his health. It took a near physical breakdown to save Kelland. It took a second World War to save me! Gentlemen, I give you Grantland Rice."

Next to Brutus', that was the most unkindest cut.

CHAPTER TWENTY-EIGHT

Icing on the Cake

Down the years we had rented summer homes at a variety of places not too far from New York. We summered at Plandome and Port Washington, Long Island, and then moved some 70 miles down the island to Bellport.

We spent another summer at Greenwich, Connecticut, up near the Round Hill Country Club. Then, in 1928, Ring Lardner and I bought a four-acre tract of sand and sod facing the Atlantic Ocean at East Hampton, Long Island. We purchased the land from the late Jim Strong, whose son Dick now runs the real estate office down there.

The late Edward Gay, who erected the majority of East Hampton beach homes, handled the construction, and the summer of '29 was indeed lovely. Perched on our porch on our dune, we could stare straight out and into the bull rings of Lisbon . . . or perhaps it was the clearness of the gin cocktails. At any rate, nothing but gulls, whales and water separated us from Portugal and Spain.

During the first week of March 1931, Kit and I had arrived in Florida to cover the baseball camps when we learned that high seas around East Hampton with waves 30 feet high had done damage estimated at nearly 200,000 dollars. We then learned that, "the Rice and Lardner homes are taking the brunt of it . . . have been already undermined ten feet below their foundations, and are now hanging to the banks by a thread." Bulkheads were somehow being built despite the loss of a piledriver and other heavy apparatus to the storm. Several days later, on March 8, another northeastern hit, doing a million dollars worth of damage from Fire Island to Montauk Point. Those bulkheads had saved what remained of our homes. On March 11, Joe Miller, the house-moving man, came in, threw out his anchor and didn't halt work until both homes had been relocated some 200 feet behind the dunes where, praise be, they still stand. The reason I recall these details so clearly is that that storm damage loomed large in my tax returns for '31 . . . to the tune of nearly 26,000 dollars. I also recall that Edith Gould Wainwright's massive home was saved by one yard of turf. The seas swept up to within that brief distance that stood between her home and destruction. Lardner and I, it seems, got 90 per cent of both barrels.

It was rumored that Lardner's garage, separate from the main house, went out to sea. It happened to stand steady as a rock. But it came as straight news to Bugs Baer, who cracked, "I've heard of a captain going down with his ship, but this is the first time I ever heard of a chauffeur going down with his garage."

Chauffeurs brings to mind the man who has been working at this job for me for more than 30 years. His name is Charles Goering, the perfect operator. Charles was a gunner with the 18th Machine Gun Battalion of the 6th Division in the 1st World War, and since our paths crossed he has never been a minute late nor has he had an accident of any kind. He is also a fine mechanic, important for one who can't drive nor spot the difference between a wheel lug and a carburetor. Charles knows all the sporting writers as well as I do. He can also remember their names better. Car and household duties were simple for the Rices for at the same time Mrs. Rice had Helga Christenson for some 30 years as her maid and all-around household director.

When the big "move" at East Hampton had been completed I found that the good Lord had left the Rice family with an acre of turf, minus sand and sea grass, upon which we decided to build an all-around sporting club. During many wonderful summers we had a number of interesting guests and neighbors, ready for membership at no cost to anyone. Along with the Lardners there were the Irvin Cobbs, the Percy Hammonds, the James Prestons, the Arthur William Browns, the P. Hal Simses, the Merlyn (Deke) Aylesworths, the John Goldens, the Henry McLemores, the Jesse Sweetsers, the Bud Kellands, the Jack Wheelers, the Gene Tunneys, the Reed Kilpatricks, the Harold Rosses and many others. In our limited space, the members had their choice of five sports. There was a nine hole chip and putt course . . . a croquet layout . . . a horseshoe pitching setup . . . an archery lane and swimming in the ocean only a few rods away. Plus beverages. As a result, each Sunday afternoon we could count on from 30 to 50 people who engaged in these weekly frolics.

The sport was very pleasant, but to me the various contests were not to be matched with the conversation that crackled over the sea grass on those occasions.

Lardner, the tall and silent one, had more to say in fewer words than anyone I ever knew. I remember one day introducing Cobb to John Lardner, Ring's oldest son, then about 16. John has since developed into one of our finer writers, a worthy son of a brilliant father. Cobb spoke to John, who had nothing to say.

"Oh," said Cobb, "another one of these garrulous Lardners."

Lardner, Cobb, Hammond—where can you find three more brilliant minds?

It so happened that it was my wife who arranged anything that had to be arranged and was the central figure of each Sunday gathering. I don't know who her favorites were; but I have an idea they were Ring Lardner, Frank Condon, Frank Crowninshield, and Percy Hammond. As a Big Four I would say they stood unequalled. I always thought of Frank Crowninshield as the Last of the Gentlemen. He fitted in every known way. The Prestons, May and Jimmy, were famous artists. May Preston was the star artist for the *Saturday Evening Post* for many, many years. Jimmy's paintings are now in many homes. Henry and Jean McLemore were two active lives in any party from start to finish. I don't believe anyone could locate as many brilliant minds as we used to assemble for golf, archery and other sports.

One of the best all-around guests was Hal Sims. A star at bridge and golf and a keen gambler, Hal was hard to take on any bet.

You could sit down and write a long book about such people as Lardner, Crowninshield, Hammond, Ross, Cobb, and others with whom we spent so many never-to-be-forgotten afternoons in other days and other years. They live with me today as they did years ago. From the old bunch, Lardner, Cobb, Hammond, Crowninshield, Condon, Harold Ross and Hal Sims have crossed the border. It would be a wonderful thing to reassemble that crowd again. In my opinion it had more class than any group I ever knew.

There have been many other friends, but these have contributed more to the happiness of my wife and me over past years than perhaps any others. For they came to us when the sun was just above the meridian, before sunset was due.

It was late September, 1933. I had come up to New York

to pack a bag for Philadelphia where I was to cover the Jack Sharkey–Tommy Loughran fight on the night of the 27th, when the phone rang. It was midnight and Kit was at the other end.

"Granny," she said quietly, "Ring died a little while ago. Young Ring came over to tell me. I've been with Ellis (Mrs. Lardner) and I've just this minute returned."

The news didn't come as a shock . . . rather as a heavy wrench. Ring's death had been expected for some weeks. The combination of a bad heart—weakened perhaps through an early bout with tuberculosis, had finally drawn the curtain. Ring had simply worn himself out and so there was nothing left I sat down and wrote the following for the next day's paper.

RING LARDNER

Charon—God guide your boat—
On to the journey's end.
Keep it safe and afloat—
For it carries a friend.
One who has given the world
Drama and wit and mirth—
One who has kept unfurled
The flag of a cleaner earth.

Charon—the night is dark—
Watch for a port ahead—
Stick to the wheel of your barque—
Charon—a friend is dead;
The friend of a shattered age,
Standing upon Time's brink—
The friend of the printed page,
For those who could read—and think.

Here is one you can say
No one can fill his gap—
Left in a morbid day—
Left on a yellow map—

One where the bright sword gleams,
Set for the cutting blow—
One who has followed dreams
Greater than men might know.

Charon—here is a mate
Where mystic shadows lie—
Ready to face all Fate,
When fading dock lights die;
Drama—or wit—or sport—
What we may have on earth—
Bring him safely to port—
The gods should find his worth.

Charon—I speak for a friend—
Wherever the reefs may form,
On to the journey's end,
Keep him away from the storm;
Where the last candle's burned,
Out where the dark is deep—
Give, give him the rest he has earned—
Bring him a dreamless sleep.

I wish you could know his worth,
Out in the realm of ghosts—
What he has meant to the earth,
What he has meant to the hosts
Of those who can understand
The message of brain and heart,
Flashed upon sea or land
With only the master's art.

Clean as the west wind's sweep—
Strong as the northern gale—
Charon—a friend's asleep—
Give him your stoutest sail—
Out through the mystic gate,
Over the ghostly foam,
Let all your half gods wait
Till he is safe at home.

Out of this drab corral,
Drama—or life—or sport—
What can you say when a pal
Sails for an unknown port?
When the last candle's burned—
When the last sunset gleams—
Here's all the luck you've earned—
Luck—to the end of dreams.

East Hampton, without Ring, has somehow never seemed quite the same. If it hadn't been for Kit I don't think I would have held on to our home at the beach.

One of the features of East Hampton is the Maidstone Golf Links—a links and not a course in that it is entirely surrounded by water, ocean or bay. One of the finest layouts I have seen, I have played there for years.

John Kieran, a golfing compatriot before he gave up the game, once told me that he never would have quit golf if he had been playing at Maidstone. Why? The sandpipers and other marsh birds intrigued him and Johnny has a deeper yearning for birds than for birdies despite the fact that he was a first-class golfer, a crack shortstop at Fordham and a good hockey player. One of the best of the sporting writers until he heard the call of the wild, Kieran was at Merion with me in 1916 when Bobby Jones played in his first Amateur.

Johnny and I were standing near the ninth tee waiting for Bob to come up. Suddenly there was a clear, keen and most unusual birdlike call from the thick woods near us. Kieran froze. The bird call came again.

"My God," Johnny almost shouted. "A yellow-breasted snook!"

He was off through the woods, gone over two hours. He had found the bird and followed him practically to downtown Philadelphia.

"You will only be a golf writer, Johnny," I said, "on a western desert where there is not a tree nor a bird." I know he never would have seen the finish of a football game or a World Series if a green-breasted woodpecker or a purple-tinted grouse had only given him the call.

One night I was with him and Roy Chapman Andrews, the famed explorer who always had a hankering to hatch dinosaur eggs. Johnny, who had been listening to woodcocks chirp at night, heard Roy mention something about woodcock hunting. I barely averted a murder. Killing a woodcock was as bad, to Kieran, as shooting mockingbirds or nightingales.

I believe that next to golf, a game I've been able to play and follow for nearly a half century, hunting takes second place in my affection for the outdoors. This, despite the fact that every place I hunted I established as a sanctuary. There always seemed to be more birds there when I left than when I came. Golf, hunting, yes and fishing, carry about all the entertainment or fun that one can take along the road.

Fishing off East Hampton and Montauk was fine sport. I roamed the seas in that vicinity in the boats of Buddy Arndt and Fritz Ryan. Our favorite target was bluefish—a game, hard fighting fish ranging from two to ten pounds. I went for swordfish several times, but only had one good break under the direction of the late Dr. John Erdman, the surgeon. We got two that day by harpooning, 350- and 450-pounders. A swordfish was ordinarily much too strong and big to monkey with in any direction, by harpoon or by rod and line.

Of course, as a "pure" fisherman, I am something less than Izaak Walton. As a rule I'm perfectly willing to allow all the game fish of creation—from rainbows to the giant tarpon—to go their own finny way without any hook of mine gaffing their jaws.

One summer a good many years ago I fished in Canada with a group including Max Foster, then famous as one of the *Satur-*

day Evening Post's stable of top authors. We had fished the Miramichi River for salmon—caught few—and on the return trip stopped over at Montreal. Foster's reputation as a fishing authority rated one-two with his selection of equipment and conversation thereof. One of the Montreal papers sent a young writer around to interview Foster. Max was out. Answering the phone, I told the boy to come up and I posed as Foster. When he asked about the fishing, I replied it was pretty good but that we had had a hell of a time getting enough worms (Foster naturally would never have been so plebeian as to use worms for bait). I also talked about poles instead of rods, rubber boots instead of waders and so on. When the interview appeared in the paper as attributed to him, Max wanted to kill me.

Hunting, with me, always had to be divided three ways— quail, duck and wild turkey. Quail shooting offers the most dependable diet but when it comes to the big thrill, the wild turkey takes over. I have followed this great bird—from 16 to 25 pounders—in many states from Maryland to Georgia. For me, however, the gobbler's most fascinating habitat was at Bob Woodruff's place at Ichauway, Georgia. This is a spot of some 50,000 or more acres, thick with quail, dove and turkey. Down there I used to ride the only living birddog mule "Edna Ferber" —who, in one day's hunt, pointed two quail coveys.

The turkey is the most elusive of all birds—also the hardest to see. I've had them light in a pine or oak 20 feet away and then lose them completely. Due to their blending markings of black, gray, gold, crimson and green, they become invisible phantoms. A wild gobbler can hear you breaking a match 400 yards away. He has remarkable sight and can fly or run like a thief.

On this particular hunt at Ichauway my guide, Roy Carter, and I had hidden in a deep swamp near a turkey feeding ground. We were there at 3:30 A.M. in the pitch dark, and 15 minutes later it began to pour. The only noise you could hear was the far

off, dismal call of the mourning dove. We waited two hours or
more for dawn, hardly breathing. It was around 6:00 when the
turkeys came in. My target glided in to perhaps 20 yards from
me. I blasted "neck high" at him. He went up in the air like a rodeo bronc. Then with a great thrashing he was gone. I foundered
in to catch sight of his tail feathers disappearing behind another
clump. I dived. It was like jumping into a threshing machine.
He all but beat me to death with his wings. At this point it
was either the turkey or me. I used my shotgun stock like a bat.
Finally, as I came out of there dragging my prize by his well-
wrung neck, I felt like Dempsey after he had finished off Firpo. I
must add that Carter was a valuable "second" in this particular
struggle. The bird, a 22-pounder mounted, strides rampant today
over the fireplace in Woodruff's hunting lodge.

Bagging your bird this way seemed hard work. I was looking for an easier way. Once I was riding with Carter along a
red clay road which always seems more like home to me than
any city street. Suddenly we saw five or six big turkeys in a
group.

"There's one strange thing about a wild turkey," said Roy.
"If he sees you standing or walking he's off like a shot. But he
won't get up and fly if he sees you in a car. Let's try to land
one from the car." This may not have been quite ethical, but
at that moment it seemed a good idea.

We started for the birds through a pine woods. They ran
like a set of Man o'Wars. Those woods were full of pine stumps,
big pine limbs, heavy rocks and every obstacle known to the
roughest course. There were numberless gobblers half buried
in trees along the way. We were traveling at about 40 miles an
hour and barely gaining on the turkeys. As I'd get set to shoot
through the car window, my head would hit the top of the roof
or I'd be crashed against the floor. Twice when we drew alongside I was thrown against the front seat and half stunned. I
finally knocked a turkey over and Ray rounded him up. But I

was a wreck for a week. Both shoulders were bent, I had knots
all over my head, my shins were badly skinned and I had a
sprained wrist. I finally decided there was no easy way to find
or kill a wild turkey. They are as different from the tame variety
as a tiger is from an Angora cat.

Bob Woodruff is an ideal host; his invitations to the nation's leaders always carry an appeal. I recall one morning before daybreak I came out the front door, starting on a turkey
hunt. A huge form rose up in the darkness and started my
way. I didn't feel any too happy until he sat down before me
and extended his right paw in welcome. It happened to be a
Labrador Retriever, king sized. He had the old Woodruff spirit.

The rural life of Georgia can be magnificent and varied. In
addition to Ichauway, I have often dropped in to see an old
friend, Cason Callaway at Hamilton in the central-western part
of the state. Son of the late Fuller E. Callaway Sr. who organized
the now sprawling Callaway Mills, Cason after running the
textile side of the family interests for years, has more recently
devoted his energies to farming his vast acreage near Hamilton.
He set out to prove on a vast-scaled farm that cotton wasn't all
that Georgia could raise—and he proved it both with cattle as
well as food stuffs. More than 5,000 tame turkeys and over 10,000
mallards are full citizens. Then he threw in one of the most attractive golf courses I've seen—plus a few covered barges or
boats for his lake that is swarming with fish. Then he invited the
public to come in and enjoy it. Cason and Virginia, his very good
looking wife, think nothing of having 400 or 500 guests on stated
occasions.

It was in December 1950 that Red Smith and I hunted the
wild gobbler on the King Ranch in South Texas, ancestral home
of Assault and Stymie and the spawning ground for the King
Ranch thoroughbreds, with Bob Kleberg at the helm and his
trainer, Maxie Hirsch, in charge. The King Ranch turkeys seem

to arrive in droves or herds—like bleacher fans at the World Series—and push you aside to drink out of the swimming pool. These birds indulge in traffic jams of 40,000 birds in one flock! But the rules down there were different. You had to use a .22 calibre rifle and shoot only at the head. As I wasn't any too good with a shotgun at ten paces, this put a definite kink into my act. I might add that this wrinkle didn't help establish Red Smith as a pioneer gunman either. However, Red did land a big brute of a gobbler by creasing him across the sacroiliac. This particular safari seemed to have most everything that Hemingway ever found in Africa except a couple of plane crashes. At the end Red was concentrating on armadillos and peccaries, wild pigs with the toughest hide, the fiercest snout and the meanest disposition imaginable.

We hunted those "dead end" porkers from a hunting car. The first time we got close enough to shoot, Hirsch, a comedian when he's not gunning for a stake race, invited me to shoot. I bracketed the porker. However, when I found that a peccary invariably charges back at you, I had no further interest in him.

We also encountered a swarm of deer, all beauties. One great white-tail with a tremendous rack of horns invited me to shoot him. I raised my gun, but couldn't squeeze the trigger. They called me a sissy.

"It's not that, exactly," I said. "It's just that I never shoot a deer until he pulls a knife on me first."

While caroming around that King Ranch I often dreamed my old dream—the one I shared with Frank Buck and Martin Johnson. There's a lot of country down there. What a place to relive my dream of loosing pairs of jungle beasts . . . lions, tigers, elephants, gibbon apes—the works. But I realized what a hardship it might work on my host, Bob Kleberg, and his St. Gertrudis cattle. So I said nothing and let the dream pass.

CHAPTER TWENTY-NINE

Through the Mists

These Are My Dreams

My dreams are not tomorrow—nor yesterday.
For yesterday is gone, and on its way.
And by tomorrow it may be much too late
To find my way through darkness and through fate.

When you have reached a certain span in life,
Today is all that counts, for fun or strife.
The past is blurred with fogs and mists and myth.
The future is too brief to bother with.

I dream today with no vain, vague regrets
For yesterday—and all its unpaid debts,
With no fear of the future's fading sun,
Since it may end before this rhyme is done.

I dream of romance and a song that rings
Above the duller, elemental things,
Not caring what may happen to skies dark or blue,
If I can know that just one dream comes true.

Having spent 64 of 74 years in the maelstrom of sport, I seem to have spent the vital segment of my life in crowds of 50,000 and 100,000 people. As I look back, the picture is a vast canvas of tumult and shouting, where, on many occasions, I was seeking a "solitude I could call peace."

It's been an endless highway of thrills. I look back on countless examples of gameness, smartness, stamina, uphill struggles—and with them all the varying tides of luck that test human character.

> I see them walk by in a dream—Dempsey and Cobb and Ruth,
> Tunney and Sande and Jones—Johnson and Matty and Young—
> Alex and Tilden and Thorpe—was there a flash of youth
> That gave us a list like this, when our first tributes were sung?

> Man O'War waits for the break—Shoeless Joe Jackson's at bat.
> John McGraw barks from the line—Hagen is taking his swing.
> Gehrig is watching the pitch—Greb is outclawing a cat—
> Milburn and Hitchcock rise up—taking the ball on the wing.

> Where the old dreams move along—shadows that drift to and fro—
> Moving on back through the years—I've seen a pretty good show.

And what does it all mean? It means that sport—games, hard competition played under the rules, is the greatest thing a country can know. Sport offers the greatest fund of national entertainment. It offers relief from the drabness and dullness of making a living. It is a cure for lonesomeness, the dark spectre so many people face. Because it builds character, sport can also help in curbing the current curse of juvenile delinquency. About adult delinquency, I'm not so sure.

Most of the headliners in sport that I've known have been decent humans. Exceedingly few have been dull or stupid. They have all had the proper rhythm, the right angles. What are the

most important qualities that should belong to a champion? In
no particular order, I've found them to be:

Confidence
Co-ordination
Concentration
Condition
Courage—at impact
Fortitude—stick-to-it-iveness
Determination
Stamina
Quickness
Speed

To a degree, these ingredients belong to any topflight business man, doctor or lawyer just as they belonged to a Dempsey,
Jones, Cobb or a Ruth. There is also the highly important factor
of innate Ability. Yes, and Luck, too, is worth cultivating.

Dame Fortune is a cockeyed wench, as someone's said before,
And yet the old Dame plays her part in any winning score.
Take all the credit you deserve, heads-up in winning pride,
But don't forget that Lady Luck was riding at your side.

Two other qualities often identified with a leader—intelligence and education, are missing from this list. Neither, I've
found, is necessary for a champion. Intelligence usually denotes
imagination which can be a positive deterrent, especially in
heavy contact sports . . . or golf. However, awareness, a form
of intelligence, is something I've found in most champions. I
mention intelligence and education together because the two are
often confused. There may be a yawning gap between an intelligent person and one who happens to be educated.

In all these years I have run across only two big scandals

in sport—the World Series corruption of 1919 and the far deeper basketball scandal of recent years. There have been minor incidents that were little more than some deflection from the code.

The West Point sacking was not, in my opinion, a matter of cheating in any game and was badly handled at the Point. The scandal was as much with the higher-ups at the Academy as it was with the football squad.

There is little chance for any big scandal, outside of boxing, with the alertness shown by most of those in control plus the public sense of moral indignation that is unusually strong.

Over the same span of years I have seen politics with far more than its share of crookedness including governors and others high in the affairs of state. The statesman is different. But there are so few statesmen. Politics, unhappily, is loaded with crooks and cheats a hundred to one over those honest servants of the public's welfare.

Sport today is, however, much more commercial and much more stereotyped than in my heyday. I doubt if we will ever again have the devil-may-care attitude and spirit of the Golden Twenties, a period of boom, screwballs and screwball antics. The almighty dollar, or what's left of it, hangs high. The magnificent screwballs have been crowded to the wall. The fleet Washington outfielder who, when asked to race Mickey Mantle against time before a recent Yankee–Senators night game, replied, "I'll do it . . . for five hundred dollars" is testimony to the times.

While I saluted the golden days of the amateur in sport, I've watched the professional take over almost completely. I have a keen sympathy and understanding for those sportsmen whose game must lay midway between the pro and amateur label. It is the rare bird who can hustle a living in today's going and still find time to excel as an amateur. That's why I thrilled with the rest of America when amateur Billy Joe Patton shot everything from an ace to a 7 in the 1954 Masters golf tourney, and finished just a shot off the collective heels of Ben Hogan and Sam Snead. The fact that Patton played every shot for 72 holes stiff to the pin and let the devil do his worrying was a tonic today's cash register game needs desperately.

While sport has been a big part of my life, I must admit that verse has meant even more. Frank Stanton, in his tribute to poetry, gave the answer:

> "Had it not been for thee,
>   Life had been drear to me
>   And all its flowered ways untraveled and alone—
>   No song in any stream,
>   No daisy in a dream,
>   And all that makes life beautiful, unknown."

Verse and sport together make up the menu perfectly. Nothing else is needed where brain and brawn, heart and ligament are concerned. Rhythm, the main factor in both, is one of the main factors in life itself. For without rhythm, there is a sudden snarl or tangle.

It has long been my belief that each of us needs a certain philosophy of life. As for me, I was around 12 when I first discovered Shakespeare. Two years later I found the brilliantly lighted domains of Keats, Shelley and Carlyle. I was about 20 when I had full contact with Homer and Rudyard Kipling.

While in my 'teens I ran across two proverbs or injunctions which have traveled with me ever since. One is from the Bible: "Judge not, that ye be not judged." The other is from the Koran, "Know thyself." Just why they should have had such an appeal at such an age I'll never know. The first one changed slightly to, "Judge not too swiftly that ye be not judged too swiftly in turn." This Biblical injunction has served me often down the years. It was an order not to be in too big a hurry to condemn.

I discovered also that "Know thyself" carried a decisive

message. Why spend all your time studying the faults and virtues of others while learning little of what you actually are? "Know thyself," meant the destruction of self-pity, the end of alibis and excuses, the placing of the blame where it belonged. I learned that good rarely comes from kidding yourself.

Another part of my philosophy stems from Ralph Waldo Emerson's "Self-Reliance" and "Compensation." There I learned that often when things are at their worst, brighter days are just beyond. Conversely, when skies are bluest, then is the time to look out for black clouds. It was a check either way—not to become too optimistic when everything looked good—not to get too low and depressed when everything seemed black.

There's an old song entitled, "The Life That Loves the Valleys Is Lonely on the Hills." I would certainly be lonely on the hills. And I would always feel at home in the valleys. I'd rather look up to some peak than to be on some peak looking down on those who need help. Of course, those on the peak sometimes need help too. Often they, in their loneliness, are the more bewildered. They expect a way of life they can't have—or a happiness that an unsound philosophy has made impossible.

I recall so well the time I read Keats' "Endymion" and saw this line: "Time, that ancient nurse, rocked me to patience." I thought then, here is *all* the philosophy of life.

Because so much of my life has been wrapped up in sports in which victory is the most important thing, I have come to applaud success . . . but without losing regard for the vanquished. Many coaches miss the philosophy of Hughie Keogh who had this to say: "The rules of sport are all founded upon fair play. . . . You can't pay off people in the square set with technicalities." "Square" in Keogh's day meant decent, solid— not today's bebop "square" meaning "not with it."

Human nature is often perverse—which is one reason why it remains so interesting. When arguments develop between

square shooters and the chiselers, much of the public drifts to
support the chiseler. Winning is important. But to win at any
cost, through any form of trickery one can devise, is never worth
while.

While watching every type of record smashed, with more
to follow in the briefer time left, I've found that all records were
made to be broken. Previous marks have fallen with a crash on
land, on water, and in the air. Year by year, each record has only
been the incentive for another. Today when anyone sets a new
mark, he puts up a sign which reads, "There's Your New Target."

If this happens to marks that can be measured or timed,
doesn't it apply to the individuals—to ball players, football players, fighters, golfers and tennis stars? It must. The old-timer looks
back on the stars of his youth as much faster, stronger and better
than those of today. I don't agree.

There have been ball players in recent years to match all
but the great exceptions of Ty Cobb, Babe Ruth and Honus
Wagner. The Dodgers and Yankees of 1953 and 1954 were full
of players better than most of the names who played for the
1906 Cubs or the 1910 Athletics.

In the New York area alone, the '54 season saw two, perhaps three present day stars who may take their place with the
immortals. I mean Duke Snider, Willie Mays and Mickey Mantle. With Brooklyn's Snider climbing the center-field walls to
haul in certain home runs . . . and breaking these same fences
with his bat; with Mays contributing glittering heroics each day
(I write this in late June '54 with the Giants bidding fair to
make a shambles of the National League) with his basket
catches, his rubber arm, booming bat, and, most important, his
contagious, irrepressible zest; with Mantle commencing to play
the ball George Weiss and Stengel *hoped* he'd play as DiMaggio's replacement in the Yankee's center field—well, how good
can you get? All three boys, incidentally, are the direct results

of growing up with a bat, glove and a ball, practically from the cradle. All three stem from fathers who didn't or couldn't make the big step themselves but who saw in their sons the potential realization of their own dreams. I don't know of a country in the world—or another field—where this type of thing could happen, except right here in a democratic, sports loving America.

The best doesn't belong to the past. It is with us now. And even better athletes will be with us on ahead. When we arrive at the top athlete, the Jim Thorpe of the Year 2,000, we should really have something. But by that year I will have slight interest in what the field has to show.

The Long Road

Here is my traveler's cloak, dusty and torn.
For half a century it has known the road.
Once it was clean and new, now it is frayed and worn.
The end is near, beneath a heavy load,
But from the valley to the topmost hill,
The sky is blue, the birds are singing still.

Yes, I have seen my share along the way,
Ruth, Jones, and Tilden, and the mighty Cobb,
The fists of Dempsey with their deadly sway,
The speed of Owens on the record job,
And coming on still driving like the surf,
Milburn and Hitchcock ripping up the turf.

I've seen my share upon a busy trip,
I've looked at Johnson's fast ball outspeed time.
I've seen Pete Alexander's deadly whip,
And I've seen Matty in his golden prime.
And there was Grange, the ghost, of super rank
The Four Horsemen—and Nagurski moving like a tank.

One by one I watch them march on by,
From vanished years they move across the field,
Sarazen, Hagen, Pudge and Thorpe and Cy,

Louis and Paddock decked with sword and shield,
The mighty thousands who have done the same,
To leave this epitaph—He Played the Game.

The long line forms through life's remembered years,
The flaming heart—cold brain and firm command
Of nerve and sinew, blotting out all fears,
The will to win beyond the final stand,
These are the factors in each hour of need
That mark the pathway of the Winning Breed.

But there is more than winning to this game,
Where I've seen countless thousands give their best,
Give all they had to find the road to fame,
And barely fail against the closing test.
Their names are lost now with the swift and strong,
Yet in the final rating they belong.

For there are some who never reached the top,
Who in my rating hold a higher place
Than many wearing crowns against the drop
Of life's last curtain in the bitter race.
Who stand and fight amid a bitter brood,
Knowing the matchless gift of fortitude.

Far off I hear the rolling, roaring cheers.
They come to me from many yesterdays,
From record deeds that cross the fading years,
And light the landscape with their brilliant plays,
Great stars that knew their days in fame's bright sun.
I hear them tramping to oblivion.

Index